INTERPRETING
APOCALYPTIC
LITERATURE

HANDBOOKS FOR OLD TESTAMENT EXEGESIS

INTERPRETING APOCALYPTIC LITERATURE

An Exegetical Handbook

Richard A. Taylor

David M. Howard Jr.
SERIES EDITOR

Interpreting Apocalyptic Literature: An Exegetical Handbook
© 2016 by Richard A. Taylor

Published by Kregel Publications, a division of Kregel, Inc., 2450 Oak Industrial Dr NE, Grand Rapids, MI 49505-6020.

The Greek font GraecaU and the Hebrew font New JerusalemU are from www.linguistsoftware.com/lgku.htm, +1-425-775-1130.

ISBN 978-0-8254-2761-9

Printed in the United States of America
16 17 18 19 20 / 5 4 3 2 1

To
Diane
with love and appreciation

CONTENTS IN BRIEF

CONTENTS

SERIES PREFACE

AN APPRECIATION FOR THE RICH DIVERSITY of literary genres in Scripture is one of the positive features of evangelical scholarship in recent decades. No longer are the same principles or methods of interpretation applied across the board to every text without regard for differences in genre. Such an approach can lead to confusion, misunderstanding, and even wrong interpretations or applications. Careful attention to differences in genre is a critical component of a correct understanding of God's Word.

The Handbooks for Old Testament Exegesis series (HOTE) offers students basic skills for exegeting and proclaiming the different genres of the Old Testament. Because there is no one-size-fits-all approach to interpreting Scripture, this series features six volumes covering the major genres in the Old Testament: narrative, law, poetry, wisdom, prophecy, and apocalyptic. The volumes are written by seasoned scholar-teachers who possess extensive knowledge of their disciplines, lucid writing abilities, and the conviction that the church and the world today desperately need to hear the message of the Old Testament. These handbooks are designed to serve a twofold purpose: to present the reader with a better understanding of the different Old Testament genres (principles), and to provide strategies for preaching and teaching these genres (methods).

These volumes are primarily intended to serve as textbooks for graduate-level exegesis courses that assume a basic knowledge of Hebrew. There is no substitute for encountering God's Word in its original languages, even as we acknowledge the limitations of language in plumbing the depths of who God is. However, the series is also accessible to those without a working knowledge of Hebrew, in that an English translation is always given whenever Hebrew is used. Thus, seminary-trained pastors for whom Hebrew is a distant memory, upper-level college students, and even well-motivated laypeople should all find this series useful.

Each volume is built around the same six-chapter structure, as follows:

1. The Nature of the Genres
2. Viewing the Whole: Major Themes
3. Preparing for Interpretation
4. Interpreting the Text
5. Proclaiming the Text
6. Putting It All Together: From Text to Sermon

Authors are given freedom in how they title these six chapters and in how best to approach the material in each. But the familiar pattern in every volume will serve students well, allowing them to move easily from one volume to another to locate specific information. The first chapter in each handbook introduces the genre(s) covered in the volume. The second chapter covers the purpose, message, and primary themes in the individual books and canonical sections under consideration. The third chapter includes such diverse matters as historical and cultural backgrounds, critical questions, textual matters, and a brief annotated bibliography of helpful works. The fourth chapter sets forth guidelines for interpreting texts of the genre(s) under consideration. The fifth chapter details strategies for proclaiming such texts. The final chapter gives one or two hands-on examples of how to move through different stages of the interpretive process, in order to demonstrate how the principles discussed previously work out in practice. Each volume also includes a glossary of specialized terms; these terms are boldfaced at their first occurrence in each chapter.

The Scriptures themselves remind us in many ways about the importance of proper interpretation of God's words. Paul encouraged Timothy, "Do your best to present yourself to God as one approved by him, a worker who has no need to be ashamed, rightly explaining the word of truth" (2 Tim. 2:15 NRSV). In an earlier day, Ezra the scribe, along with the Levites, taught God's Word to the postexilic community: "So they read from the book, from the law of God, with interpretation. They gave the sense, so that the people understood the reading" (Neh. 8:8 NRSV). It is my prayer, and that of the authors and publisher, that these handbooks will help a new generation of God's people to do the same.

Soli Deo Gloria.

—DAVID M. HOWARD JR.
Series Editor

PREFACE

OVER THE PAST HALF-CENTURY OR SO, APOCALYPTIC LITERATURE has moved from the shadows of biblical scholarship to the forefront of research. The result is a large and ever-growing bibliography of secondary literature dealing with the topic of Old Testament apocalypticism. Only a small portion of that literature can be represented in this work. At the publisher's request, only English-language sources are included.

However, those who wish to pursue research in the area of Jewish apocalyptic literature will not lack for material to read. In my personal database for apocalyptic literature, I have collected more than one thousand items that deal with this topic in fairly general terms and which are relevant for Old Testament study. This database does not include specialized works devoted more narrowly to particular ancient texts, such as the book of Enoch. To include those items would add considerably to the size of the bibliography. There is also a substantial corpus of published research dealing specifically with the book of Daniel. Much of this material is relevant not only for the study of Daniel in particular, but also for the study of apocalyptic literature in general. My database for the book of Daniel approaches four thousand items. Other Old Testament books relevant to the study of apocalyptic literature, such as Zechariah, also have significant bibliographies.

I take this opportunity to express my thanks to some of those who have contributed in one way or another to the completion of this volume. I am grateful to Jim Weaver, formerly editor for academic acquisitions at Kregel. Jim first suggested that I contribute this volume to the Kregel series and then encouraged me along the way. By the time Fred Mabie joined the Kregel editorial staff, this project was more or less complete. But Fred was able to move things forward, and I appreciate his advice and counsel. I am also grateful to David M. Howard Jr., editor of the series Handbooks for Old Testament Exegesis. David has provided helpful editorial supervision and suggestions for improvement of this volume.

I am especially grateful to my wife Diane for her encouragement and patience throughout the process of research and writing of this volume. It was during this time that we first learned of her cancer and began a long journey of chemotherapy, radiation, and surgery. She has been an unfailing example of courage, perseverance, and optimism in the midst of circumstances that were at times discouraging and disappointing. We are thankful for renewed strength and improved health. I lovingly dedicate this volume to her.

—RICHARD A. TAYLOR

For in them is
the spring of understanding,
the fountain of wisdom,
and the river of knowledge.
—*4 Ezra* 14:47

ABBREVIATIONS

1QDan^a	a fragment of Daniel discovered at Qumran cave 1
1QDan^b	a fragment of Daniel discovered at Qumran cave 1
4QDan^a	a fragment of Daniel discovered at Qumran cave 4
4QDan^b	a fragment of Daniel discovered at Qumran cave 4
4QDan^c	a fragment of Daniel discovered at Qumran cave 4
4QDan^d	a fragment of Daniel discovered at Qumran cave 4
4QDan^e	a fragment of Daniel discovered at Qumran cave 4
pap6QDan	a papyrus fragment of Daniel discovered at Qumran cave 6
1QM	*Milḥamah* or *War Scroll* discovered at Qumran cave 1
1QS	*Serek Hayaḥad* or *Rule of the Community* discovered at Qumran cave 1
5Q15	*New Jerusalem* Aramaic discovered at Qumran cave 5
Ant.	Josephus, *Jewish Antiquities*
Apoc. Ab.	*Apocalypse of Abraham*
Apoc. Zeph.	*Apocalypse of Zephaniah*
2 Bar.	*2 Baruch*
BDB	Brown, F., S. R. Driver, and C. A. Briggs. *A Hebrew and English Lexicon of the Old Testament.* Oxford, 1907.
BHQ	*Biblia Hebraica Quinta.* Edited by A. Schenker et al. Stuttgart, 2004–.
BHS	*Biblia Hebraica Stuttgartensia.* Edited by K. Elliger and W. Rudolph. Stuttgart, 1983.
DCH	Clines, David J. A., ed. *The Dictionary of Classical Hebrew.* 8 vols. Sheffield: Sheffield Academic Press, 1993–2012.
1 En.	*1 Enoch*
2 En.	*2 Enoch*

Ep. Barnabas   *Epistle of Barnabas*
HALOT   Koehler, L., W. Baumgartner, and J. J. Stamm. *The*
                 Hebrew and Aramaic Lexicon of the Old Testament. Translated
                 and edited under the supervision of M. E. J. Richardson.
                 5 vols. 1994–2000.
Jub.   *Jubilees*
T. Ab.   *Testament of Abraham*
T. Levi   *Testament of Levi*
T. Mos.   *Testament of Moses*

1

WHAT IS APOCALYPTIC LITERATURE?

IN MODERN LIFE, WE ARE OFTEN CONFRONTED with various types of literature. We read newspapers, novels, and academic textbooks; we read wedding invitations, birth announcements, and obituaries; we read summaries of sporting events, magazines, and collections of poetry—and much more. In spite of their many similarities, these means of communication have striking literary differences as well. Perhaps without even realizing it, we understand that different types of literature, each with their own distinctive styles and sometimes stereotypical forms, may impose very different requirements on their reader. We do not read poetry in quite the same way we read the sports page or a comic strip; we do not read a novel in quite the same way we read a calculus textbook or a Hebrew grammar. We instinctively know that such **genres** are distinct, that they may require differing levels of concentration and effort, that some may be less demanding and more enjoyable than others, and that their language does not always work in exactly the same way. By experience we gain the necessary skills that enable us successfully to navigate our way through these various forms of literature.

The literature of the Old Testament also has its distinctive genres, some of which differ appreciably from others. While much of the Hebrew Bible is historical in nature, consisting of narrative accounts of specific events and human dialogue, one also finds in the Old Testament a great deal of hymnic poetry, wisdom literature, prophetic utterances, and legal literature, to mention just a few of these forms. Each of these genres requires special attention from the interpreter in order to ensure that proper conclusions are drawn from the text. Otherwise, one runs the risk of bringing incorrect assumptions or faulty expectations to the text. This can distort the intended meaning and lead to flawed understanding.

Genres vary considerably in the way they use language to communicate meaning. Some genres, for example, make abundant use of figurative language and complex symbolism. If taken in an overly literal fashion, such language could lead one to misconstrue the message of the author or even to miss the point altogether. Some genres use language in a highly allusive—perhaps even elusive—way that differs considerably from the normally straightforward style of a narrative text. Some genres make extensive use of strange and even bizarre symbols, the meaning of which may not be immediately clear or obvious to the reader. Good readers develop an awareness of these features and approach such literature in light of the expectations signaled in part by the genre. They resist the temptation to impose on such texts expectations that are contrary to those intended by their author. A proper understanding of genre is therefore an important key to valid interpretation of a text. In this work we will focus on a particular genre of Old Testament literature, one that differs in important ways from other genres found in the Old Testament. We will focus on **apocalyptic literature.**

The purpose of this volume is fourfold. First, it presents a summary of the main features, themes, origins, development, and purpose of Jewish apocalyptic literature of the **Second Temple period**. Such an overview will contribute to a better understanding of what sets apocalyptic literature apart from other types of literature. Second, it situates Old Testament apocalyptic literature within the broader context of ancient apocalyptic thought by analyzing its relationship to similar extrabiblical writings. This analysis provides insight into the history of this literature, as well as its relevance and appeal for its original audience. Third, it offers some guidelines that should inform interpretation of apocalyptic literature. These general interpretive principles provide guidance for reaching sound conclusions regarding the interpretation of Old Testament apocalyptic literature. Fourth, it provides a sample treatment of two Old Testament apocalyptic texts. These samples illustrate some of the principles and suggestions presented in the earlier portions of the book.

Our discussion of apocalyptic literature begins by considering a number of preliminary matters related to this unique genre. This initial chapter seeks answers to such questions as the following: What makes apocalyptic literature so different from other forms of literature? Why is there, at present, a revival of scholarly interest in this material? What exactly is meant by the term *apocalyptic*? By what means can this genre be identified as a distinct category of literature? The answers to these questions will provide direction and clarity for topics to be considered in the following chapters.

DISTINCTIVENESS OF APOCALYPTIC LITERATURE

When compared to the bulk of writings found in the Bible, apocalyptic literature is a very distinctive form of literature. For that reason, it requires special attention and effort in order to grasp accurately its message. When Bible students first approach the book of Daniel in the Old Testament or the book of Revelation in the New Testament, they immediately realize that things are very different from what one finds in most other portions of the Bible.[1] Here the reader has entered a different world, one in which the sights and sounds described therein may bear little resemblance to what one finds in the rest of Scripture. The terrain seems unfamiliar. The scenes portrayed by **visions** and dreams are not immediately clear or understandable. Instead, these writings are characterized at times by seemingly impenetrable mysteries, puzzling symbolism, startling predictions, and foreboding announcements. What do these strange things mean? It is as though a mysterious veil rests over the language. Such is the world of apocalyptic literature.

The children's film *The Wizard of Oz* provides an analogy to this befuddlement. Young Dorothy awakens after a fierce tornado, only to find herself no longer at home in Kansas but transported instead to the dazzling and magical land of Oz. With amazement she exclaims to her pet dog, "Toto, I have a feeling we're not in Kansas any more!" The familiar scenes of inviting farmland and welcome faces of family and friends were only distant memories. They had been replaced by scenes of an amazing new world full of both pleasant surprises and foreboding dangers. Dorothy was not sure what to make of it all.

In a similar way, those who visit for the first time the world of apocalyptic literature may find themselves struck by the realization that they too have entered an unusual and unfamiliar realm—one that leaves the reader both with a sense of amazement and with a sense of disorientation. Kansas (i.e., most of biblical literature) and the land of Oz (i.e., apocalyptic literature) are two very different worlds indeed!

---

1. D. S. Russell, a well-known specialist in Jewish apocalyptic literature, recalls his initial impressions when he began his study of apocalyptic texts as a student: "I found myself in a weird and wonderful world of fantasy and dreams—beasts with sprouting horns, dragons spouting fire, falling stars, mysterious horsemen, mystical mountains, sacred rivers, devastating earthquakes, fearsome giants, demon progeny, monstrous births, portents in heaven, portents on earth. Its often frenzied and frenetic descriptions of coming woes sounded like the product of over-heated minds." Russell's initial impressions of apocalyptic literature are probably not that different from those of many readers who encounter such texts for the first time. See D. S. Russell, *Apocalyptic: Ancient and Modern* (Philadelphia: Fortress, 1978), 1.

RENEWED INTEREST IN APOCALYPTIC LITERATURE

Investigation into apocalyptic literature as a distinct genre is largely a development of the past two centuries or so. Scholarly research on apocalyptic literature seems to pick up steam in the first half of the nineteenth century with the work of the German scholar Friedrich Lücke.[2] Lücke's investigations focused on the book of Revelation, which led him to consider the broader field of apocalyptic literature as well. He is sometimes regarded as the founder of modern study of apocalyptic literature.[3]

The study of apocalyptic literature in modern biblical scholarship has had a checkered history. Scholarly attitudes toward this literature range from serious interest to benign neglect to complete rejection. Prior to about the mid-twentieth century there was a tendency for biblical scholars and theologians alike not only to neglect apocalyptic literature, but in some instances to treat it with a certain dislike or even disdain.[4] The world of apocalyptic literature was one with which many scholars were relatively unfamiliar, and with which they felt uncomfortable. Some were more at home with the cadences of Hebrew poetry and prophecy, or the practicality of the Jewish **wisdom literature**, or the ethical teachings of Jesus and the apostles. To them, apocalyptic literature may have seemed like a foreign land that spoke an unfamiliar language—a strange country whose inhabitants had odd ways of thinking and peculiar forms of expression. Although there were exceptions to this general tendency, many biblical scholars took an unsympathetic stance with regard to this genre of literature.[5] Some simply avoided it. Like an unwanted and rejected Cinderella, apocalyptic literature became a stepchild in the family of biblical scholarship.

---

2. Friedrich Lücke, *Versuch einer vollständigen Einleitung in die Offenbarung des Johannes, oder allgemeine Untersuchungen über die apokalyptische Litteratur überhaupt und die Apokalypse des Johannes insbesondere*, 2d ed. (Bonn: E. Weber, 1852). [English: "Attempt at a comprehensive introduction to the Revelation of John, or general investigations into apocalyptic literature in general and the Apocalypse of John in particular."]

3. So, for example, Ulrich H. J. Körtner, *The End of the World: A Theological Interpretation*, trans. Douglas W. Stott (Louisville: Westminster John Knox, 1995), 23.

4. As Tupper says, "Apocalypticism is mostly an embarrassment to modern theology. Apocalyptic evokes images of the weird and menacing, the fantastic and grotesque, the ridiculous and the absurd. The label 'apocalyptic' has become a catchword for everything eschatologically illegitimate." See E. Frank Tupper, "The Revival of Apocalyptic in Biblical and Theological Studies," *Review and Expositor* 72 (1975): 280.

5. Wellhausen, for example, stressed the importance of the classical Israelite prophets of the eighth and seventh centuries B.C. In his view they represented a high point in the development of Old Testament religion. Wellhausen attached less significance to the later apocalyptic writings, since according to him these later writings by comparison represented a decline in the vitality of Israel's religion. See Julius Wellhausen, *Prolegomena to the History of Israel*, Scholars Press Reprints and Translations Series (Atlanta: Scholars Press, 1994).

Nonetheless, about a half-century ago the world of academic biblical scholarship began to experience a renewal of interest in apocalyptic literature. A turning point in German scholarship came around 1960, due in part to the publications of theologian Wolfhart Pannenberg and New Testament scholar Ernst Käsemann.[6] Käsemann embraced apocalyptic literature in a way that most scholars of the day had not done. He considered the message of Jesus to be apocalyptic at its core. His approach is summarized by his memorable yet surprising claim that apocalyptic "was the mother of all Christian theology."[7] Käsemann's thesis assigned unprecedented importance to the role of apocalyptic thinking in the preaching of Jesus and the early church. In his view, the message of Jesus was in large measure an apocalyptic message. This approach stood in stark contrast to that of most interpreters of his day, who tended to downplay and minimize the significance and relevance of apocalyptic literature. The result was a growing acknowledgment that, while Käsemann might not be correct in all the details of his thesis, his position merited serious consideration.[8]

Käsemann's understanding of the significance of apocalyptic literature sparked a renewal of interest in the role that **apocalypticism** played in the development of biblical theology. That interest has remained a force in biblical studies over the past four or five decades.[9]

---

6. For a summary of Pannenberg's understanding of apocalyptic theology see Hans Dieter Betz, "The Concept of Apocalyptic in the Theology of the Pannenberg Group," in *Apocalypticism*, ed. Robert W. Funk, Journal for Theology and the Church, vol. 6 (Tübingen and New York: J. C. B. Mohr [Paul Siebeck] and Herder and Herder, 1969), 192–207.

7. See Ernst Käsemann, "The Beginnings of Christian Theology," in *New Testament Questions of Today*, trans. W. J. Montague, New Testament Library (London: SCM, 1969), 102. See also Ernst Käsemann, "The Beginnings of Christian Theology," *Apocalypticism*, 40. See also the following responses to Käsemann: I. Howard Marshall, "Is Apocalyptic the Mother of Christian Theology?," in *Tradition and Interpretation in the New Testament*, ed. Gerald F. Hawthorne (Grand Rapids/Tübingen: Eerdmans/Mohr, 1987); Gerhard Ebeling, "The Ground of Christian Theology," *Apocalypticism*, 47–68; Ernst Fuchs, "On the Task of a Christian Theology," *Apocalypticism*, 69–98.

8. Tupper seems to speak in exaggerated terms when he claims that "Käsemann rescued apocalyptic from peripheral obscurity and thrust it into the center of theological debate with his essay on 'The Beginnings of Christian Theology.'" Käsemann clearly played a pivotal role in the revival of interest in apocalypticism during this time, but that should not obscure the fact that there were others who assisted in the rescue operation that Tupper describes. See Tupper, "The Revival of Apocalyptic in Biblical and Theological Studies," 279–303, especially 279.

9. In addition to the numerous published books and essays written on this topic, at least nine academic journals or series have devoted an entire issue to apocalyptic literature over the past several decades. See *Journal for Theology and Church* 6 (1969); *Interpretation* 25 (1971); *Review and Expositor* 72 (1975); *Explor* 4 (1978); *Semeia* 14 (1979); *Die Ou-Testamentiese Werkgemeenskap in Suid-Afrika* 25–26 (1982–1983); *Ex auditu* 6 (1990); *Journal for Near Eastern Studies* 49 (1990); *Calvin Theological Journal* 44 (2006).

During this period, modern scholarship has rediscovered apocalyptic literature and embraced it with fresh enthusiasm.[10]

A CONTEXT FOR APOCALYPTIC LITERATURE

This discussion will focus primarily on apocalyptic literature as found in the Old Testament. However, it will be helpful in this process to consider apocalyptic literature within a broader setting of the history and use of this genre in extrabiblical literature as well. In this way it is possible to avoid an atomistic approach that divorces biblical texts from their original religious and historical settings or from their subsequent use by later communities of faith. Although (for reasons that will be discussed later) it had its beginnings to a large extent in Old Testament prophecy, Jewish apocalyptic literature subsequently flourished during the intertestamental period, reaching its zenith in the second century B.C. It continued its trajectory into the early Christian period, during which time it morphed into a popular vehicle for the expression of Christian **eschatology**. Jewish apocalyptic writings that were produced and circulated from the third century B.C. to the first century A.D. were often intended for a community of faith that was undergoing intense persecution and suffering. These writings offered hope to such communities by emphasizing imminent divine intervention into human events so as to bring deliverance to the righteous and judgment to the wicked.

The writing of Christian apocalyptic literature continued well into the first millennium A.D. There are more than fifty postbiblical apocryphal works based to one degree or another on the book of Daniel.[11] The apocalyptic genre flourished, as certain Christian writers reshaped and imaginatively reused Danielic material.[12]

---

10. I have borrowed the language of rediscovery from the English title of Koch's important work on apocalyptic literature. See Klaus Koch, *The Rediscovery of Apocalyptic: A Polemical Work on a Neglected Area of Biblical Studies and Its Damaging Effects on Theology and Philosophy*, trans. Margaret Kohl, Studies in Biblical Theology, 2d series, ed. Peter Ackroyd, James Barr, et al., vol. 22 (Naperville, IL: Alec R. Allenson, [1970]). The word *Ratlos* (i.e., "puzzlement" or "perplexity" of apocalyptic) in the German title of Koch's work reflects a less positive assessment of apocalyptic literature than the word "rediscovery" that appears in the English title.

11. See Lorenzo DiTommaso, "The Early Christian Daniel Apocalyptica," in *Apocalyptic Thought in Early Christianity*, ed. Robert J. Daly, Holy Cross Studies in Patristic Theology and History (Grand Rapids: Baker, 2009), 227.

12. For a helpful discussion of genre issues, with regard to apocalyptic writings of the historical sort dating to the fourth century A.D. and later, see Lorenzo DiTommaso, "Biblical Form, Function, and Genre in the Post-Biblical Historical Apocalyptica," in *The Reception and Interpretation of the Bible in Late Antiquity: Proceedings of the Montréal Colloquium in Honour of Charles Kannengiesser, 11–13 October 2006*, ed. Lorenzo DiTommaso and Lucian Turcescu, 145–61, Bible in Ancient Christianity, ed. D. Jeffrey Bingham, vol. 6 (Leiden: Brill, 2008).

Some Jewish apocalyptic writings became influential to an extraordinary degree. Even New Testament writers made use of them on occasion. The epistle of Jude, for example, is familiar with the so-called *Book of Enoch*, citing a prophecy of Enoch not found in the Genesis account of Enoch's life. Jude also seems to allude to the *Assumption of Moses*, describing an encounter between Michael the archangel and the devil over the body of Moses. Jude draws these details not from the Old Testament but from familiar apocalyptic writings of the intertestamental period. This says something about the influence and importance of these works during the first century.

Non-biblical apocalyptic writings have much in common with their biblical counterparts in terms of interests, concerns, style, themes, and purpose. Those who are primarily interested in apocalyptic writings such as the book of Daniel should not neglect these extrabiblical apocalyptic writings. They provide a useful context for thinking about how apocalyptic language works and how this genre is to be understood. By situating the biblical writings within such a framework it will be possible to draw conclusions regarding similarities and differences between these two groups of writings.

PROBLEM OF DEFINITION

Of all the literary genres employed in the Bible, none is more difficult to define than the apocalyptic genre. Scholars have not found it easy to reach a consensus on what exactly is meant by the word *apocalyptic*. Does this term refer primarily to a particular genre of literature? Or does it refer to a concentration of particular themes, such as final judgment, angelic mediation, and vindication of the righteous? Or does it refer to a particular style of writing, one characterized by strange symbolism and obscure numerology? Or does it refer to a particular form of eschatology, one characterized by imminent divine intervention into human activities? Or does it refer to something entirely different? As Morris remarks, "it is not easy to define what we mean by apocalyptic literature."[13] As a result of this difficulty, there has been a certain amount of imprecision in the way many biblical scholars use the term.[14] A number of factors contribute to this problem of definition.

---

13.   Leon Morris, *Apocalyptic* (Grand Rapids: Eerdmans, 1972), 20.

14.   The situation, however, is not quite as bleak as that described by Kaufman, who seems to exaggerate the problem. He says, "Unfortunately, there are probably as many different definitions of apocalyptic and lists of works to be included under that rubric as there are writers on Biblical literature." See Stephen A. Kaufman, "Prediction, Prophecy, and Apocalypse in the Light of New Akkadian Texts," in *Proceedings of the Sixth World Congress of Jewish Studies, 13–19 August 1973*, ed. Avigdor Shinan, vol. 1 (Jerusalem: World Union of Jewish Studies, 1977), 225.

First, apocalyptic elements are sometimes embedded in writings that are not otherwise apocalyptic in nature. Certain parts of the Old Testament that are not distinctly apocalyptic contain blocks of material with strong apocalyptic elements. The so-called Little Apocalypse (or Isaiah Apocalypse) found in Isaiah 24–27, for example, is a unit of apocalyptic material situated within a much larger corpus of prophetic writing that is not apocalyptic in terms of genre. The book of Joel has certain apocalyptic elements, even though that book as a whole is not what one would call apocalyptic literature. One finds in the books of Ezekiel and Zechariah material that has much in common with apocalyptic literature, although these prophetic books are not entirely apocalyptic. Even in the book of Daniel, which is the most obvious example of apocalyptic literature in the Old Testament, roughly half the book is not apocalyptic, consisting instead of stories related to the life of Daniel. This mixture of genre makes it difficult to define precisely what is meant by the term *apocalyptic* and to delimit properly its literary boundaries.

Second, ancient texts vary a great deal in the degree to which they use features commonly associated with apocalyptic literature. Some works contain stronger concentrations of apocalyptic features than certain other works that should nonetheless be classified as apocalyptic literature. This variety leads to a question more easily asked than answered: How many features or characteristics of apocalyptic literature must be present in a given writing before we allow that the label *apocalyptic* is appropriate in that case?[15] The more numerous or pronounced such features become in a particular text, the more comfortable we are likely to be in assigning the label *apocalyptic* to that text. But there is a grey area here as well. A text may be apocalyptic in terms of its use of symbolism and **determinism**, for example, while other important apocalyptic themes are less emphasized or perhaps even absent altogether. For this reason it may be helpful to think of apocalyptic literature as a continuum, with some texts further along in their utilization of apocalyptic features than other works that may still warrant the label *apocalyptic*. Such variation contributes to the difficulty in defining what is meant by the term *apocalyptic*.

Third, there has been a tendency in biblical scholarship to use the term *apocalyptic* very loosely, without giving adequate attention to what is meant by this word. The word *apocalyptic* was apparently first used in

---

15. Vawter frames the question this way: "But it is unreasonable to demand that a text must exhibit every statistical note of apocalyptic before it can be considered apocalyptic, especially such notes as were incidentally acquired by apocalyptic in its process of development; and it is unreasonable to demand that an early apocalypse should read exactly like a later one, and that anything short of this must not be called apocalyptic." See Bruce Vawter, "Apocalyptic: Its Relation to Prophecy," *Catholic Biblical Quarterly* 22 (1960): 42.

biblical studies by K. I. Nitzsch in the eighteenth century to refer to works at least vaguely similar to the book of Revelation, which identifies itself as an **apocalypse** (Rev. 1:1).[16] However, the details of the proposed similarity are rather subjective and perhaps even amorphous at times. Consequently, according to some scholars the term *apocalyptic* has become in biblical studies a slippery word, resisting demands for precision and accuracy in terms of proper use.[17]

Fourth, use of the term *apocalyptic* as a noun is especially beset with difficulties. Without an accompanying word to clarify its meaning, the term can be ambiguous and unclear. As a noun, does *apocalyptic* refer to a genre of literature, or to a community, or to a way of thinking? In light of the resulting confusion, some scholars prefer to jettison altogether use of the term as a noun, retaining its use only as an adjective.[18] Others retain both the adjectival and the substantival uses, regarding *apocalyptic* when used as a noun to be equivalent to the term *apocalypticism*.[19] Still others have questioned the usefulness of the term *apocalyptic* even as an adjective.[20] Since usage varies so much from one writer to

---

16. See Margaret Barker, "Slippery Words: III. Apocalyptic," *Expository Times* 89 (1977–1978): 324.

17. See, for example, Margaret Barker, "Slippery Words: III. Apocalyptic," *Expository Times* 89 (1977–1978): 324–29; Robert Webb, "'Apocalyptic': Observations on a Slippery Term," *Journal of Near Eastern Studies* 49 (1990): 115–26; Richard E. Sturm, "Defining the Word 'Apocalyptic': A Problem in Biblical Criticism," in *Apocalyptic and the New Testament. Essays in Honor of J. Louis Martyn*, ed. J. Marcus and M. L. Soards, 17–48, Journal for the Study of the New Testament: Supplement Series, vol. 24 (Sheffield: JSOT Press, 1989).

18. So, for example, T. Francis Glasson, "What Is Apocalyptic?," *New Testament Studies* 27 (1981): 98–105. Glasson says, "I would advocate the abandonment of the word Apocalyptic. I know what an apocalypse is, and I see there is a place for the adjective 'apocalyptic' to denote matters relating to this type of literature. But, as we have seen, Apocalyptic has no agreed and recognizable meaning." His subsequent description of the noun *apocalyptic* suggests a certain amount of frustration on his part: "This is a useless word which no one can define and which produces nothing but confusion and acres of verbiage" (105). Webb concurs: "The word 'apocalyptic' must be limited to adjectival use and its use as a noun abandoned." See Robert L. Webb, "'Apocalyptic': Observations on a Slippery Term," *Journal of Near Eastern Studies* 49 (1990): 126.

19. So, for example, Grabbe. See Lester L. Grabbe, "Introduction and Overview," in *Knowing the End from the Beginning: The Prophetic, the Apocalyptic and Their Relationships*, eds. Lester L. Grabbe and Robert D. Haak, Journal for the Study of the Pseudepigrapha: Supplement Series, eds. Lester L. Grabbe and James H. Charlesworth, vol. 46 (London and New York: T. & T. Clark, 2003), 3. Elsewhere Grabbe suggests that objections to use of the term *apocalyptic* as a noun may for the most part be a North American phenomenon. He remarks that "some North American scholars object to 'apocalyptic' as a noun, but it has a long and respectable history of such usage and is still so used on the European side of the Atlantic." See Lester L. Grabbe, *Judaic Religion in the Second Temple Period: Belief and Practice from the Exile to Yavneh* (London and New York: Routledge, 2000), 9.

20. Newsom, for example, admits that "To be honest, I have some reservations about the usefulness of the adjective 'apocalyptic'. There are serious questions whether it refers to a perspective with enough specificity and coherence to be useful in identifying the common

another, care must be taken to understand how the term *apocalyptic* is used by a particular author. In order to avoid confusion, in this work *apocalyptic* will normally be used not as a noun but as an adjective, along with an accompanying word to clarify what the adjective modifies.

The terminological problem that plagued this discipline in the past was due partly to a failure to distinguish sufficiently between two separate categories. On the one hand, there is the cultural and religious mindset that underlies interest in this way of thinking. On the other hand, there is the literary product that this mindset often produces. It is possible to have the former (i.e., the mindset) without necessarily having the latter (i.e., the written document). There is also a problem of ambiguity with regard to precisely what features in an ancient text—and just how many of them—are necessary in order to justify the label *apocalyptic*. What is the minimum requirement for classifying a document as apocalyptic in nature? There is considerable disagreement on this matter.

The terminological problem of the past continues to be an issue in discussions of apocalyptic literature. It is not possible to answer adequately questions related to this literature unless one first knows what exactly is meant by the terms that are employed. [21] We will therefore distinguish between the following terms that are frequently encountered in the secondary literature dealing with this topic: *apocalypse*, *apocalypticism*, *apocalyptic literature*, **apocalyptic eschatology**, **apocalyptic discourse**, and **proto-apocalyptic**. [22] Clarity with regard to the terminological issues relevant to this topic will add clarity to the overall discussion that follows.

---

element in a very diverse body of texts. Still, it remains unavoidable, even if it sometimes seems to be little more than a scholarly grunt and gesture toward something that we recognize but cannot quite articulate." See Carol A. Newsom, "Apocalyptic and the Discourse of the Qumran Community," *Journal of Near Eastern Studies* 49 (1990): 135.

21. I am indebted to Hanson's attempts to clarify the definitional issues. See, for example, Paul D. Hanson, *The Dawn of Apocalyptic* (Philadelphia: Fortress, 1975), 11–12. However, Hanson's suggestions have not remained unchallenged. Grabbe in particular has been critical of certain aspects of Hanson's proposals regarding definitions in this area, although Grabbe does not offer any new definitions to resolve the problems he finds. See Lester L. Grabbe, "Prophetic and Apocalyptic: Time for New Definitions—and New Thinking," in *Knowing the End from the Beginning: The Prophetic, the Apocalyptic and Their Relationships*, ed. Lester L. Grabbe and Robert D. Haak, Journal for the Study of the Pseudepigrapha: Supplement Series, ed. Lester L. Grabbe and James H. Charlesworth, vol. 46 (London and New York: T&T Clark, 2003), 107–33.

22. Although Cook questions how helpful these distinctions in terminology actually are, his own categories do not seem to offer much of an improvement. He distinguishes between apocalypticism as a literary phenomenon, as a type of religious thinking (or *Weltanschauung*), and as a social phenomenon. The issues remain about the same. See Stephen L. Cook, *Prophecy and Apocalypticism: The Postexilic Social Setting* (Minneapolis: Augsburg Fortress, 1995), 21.

Apocalypse

Various ancient works, including the one found at the conclusion of the New Testament canon, describe themselves as apocalypses. But what exactly is an apocalypse? The word derives from the Greek noun ἀποκάλυψις, which refers to an "unveiling" or "**revelation**" of some sort. In early Jewish and Christian literature such revelation typically had to do with specific and detailed disclosures of allegedly future events that were thought to lie outside the grasp of unaided human intellect. This information, however, was assumed to be knowable through divine disclosure to a faithful remnant that was often thought to be living in a time of eschatological crisis. An apocalypse sets forth such information. The disclosure of this information usually takes place through an angelic mediator, often to a famous hero of the community's past. The author of the New Testament apocalypse (i.e., the book of Revelation) introduces his book this way:

> The revelation of Jesus Christ, which God gave him to show his servants what must soon take place. He made it known by sending his angel to his servant John, who testifies to everything he saw—that is, the word of God and the testimony of Jesus Christ. Blessed is the one who reads the words of this prophecy, and blessed are those who hear it and take to heart what is written in it, because the time is near (Rev. 1:1–3).

The author of this apocalypse describes it as a divinely imparted revelation of future events whose fulfillment is imminent. The revelation was conveyed through angelic mediation to a human recipient, who testified to others concerning the revelation he had received. A special blessing is promised to those who read this apocalypse, to those who hear it, and to those who take it to heart. For this biblical writer, these are features that help define what an apocalypse is.

Recent discussions of apocalyptic literature often begin with a definition of the term *apocalypse* that was first formulated several decades ago by a group of scholars working under the aegis of the Apocalypse Group of the Society of Biblical Literature Genres Project. Their definition is based on an analysis of all extant examples of such literature during the period 250 B.C. to A.D. 250. According to this definition,

> "Apocalypse" is a genre of revelatory literature with a narrative framework, in which a revelation is mediated by an otherworldly being to a human recipient, disclosing a **transcendent** reality which is both temporal, in-

sofar as it envisages eschatological salvation, and spatial,
insofar as it involves another, supernatural world.[23]

This definition summarizes well the form and content of an apocalypse.
Missing from this definition, however, is anything that clarifies the
purpose of such writings. The definition was subsequently amended to
include the following clarification regarding purpose.

> [An apocalypse is] intended to interpret present, earth-
> ly circumstances in light of the supernatural world and
> of the future, and to influence both the understanding
> and the behavior of the audience by means of divine
> authority.[24]

Taking the two parts together, this definition helpfully articulates the
essential features of what can properly be called an apocalypse, whether
biblical or extrabiblical. Several features of the definition are especially
important. First, apocalypse is a literary genre. Its content is revelatory
in nature, disclosing information inaccessible apart from divine disclosure. Its literary form is that of narrative literature. The narrative describes the reception of this information from a spiritual intermediary.
Second, an apocalypse highlights the role of an angelic messenger. This
messenger is sent by God to interact with and communicate to a divinely chosen human being. Third, the revelation conveyed by the angelic
mediator has both temporal and spatial dimensions. On the one hand,
its salvific significance has to do with final events of the **eschaton**; on
the other hand, its message brings the unseen spiritual realm into direct
contact with the natural world. Fourth, the purpose of an apocalypse is
to shed light on present events by appealing to eschatological events. Its
purpose is not only to inform the intellect but also to alter the lifestyle

---

23. See John J. Collins, *Apocalypse: The Morphology of a Genre*, Semeia, vol. 14 (Atlanta: Scholars
Press, 1979), 9. About a decade following the publication of this volume, Collins reflected
on how his thinking on the definition of apocalypse had changed in certain ways since the
publication of the Semeia volume. See his preface to the following work: John J. Collins,
"Genre, Ideology and Social Movements in Jewish Apocalypticism (Appendix: A New
Proposal on Apocalyptic Origins)," in *Mysteries and Revelations: Apocalyptic Studies since the
Uppsala Colloquium*, ed. John J. Collins and James H. Charlesworth, Journal for the Study
of the Pseudepigrapha: Supplement Series, ed. James H. Charlesworth, vol. 9 (Sheffield:
Sheffield Academic Press, 1991), 13–14.

24. Adela Yarbro Collins, "Introduction," in *Early Christian Apocalypticism: Genre, Social Setting*,
ed. Adela Yarbro Collins, Semeia, vol. 36 (Decatur, GA: Scholars Press, 1986), 6. The
clarification cited above regarding the purpose of an apocalypse is rather general, leading
some scholars to question its usefulness. Carey, for example, says "this modification has
proved too vague to be of much help." See Greg Carey, *Ultimate Things: An Introduction to
Jewish and Christian Apocalyptic Literature* (St. Louis: Chalice, 2005), 4.

of the recipients. More specifically, apocalypses offer encouragement, hope, and exhortation for the righteous, while providing warning and admonition for the unrighteous.[25]

The strength of the above definition lies in the fact that it is not an arbitrary construct imposed on the literature with which it deals. Instead, its methodological basis lies in a careful examination of all examples of apocalyptic literature that fall under its purview. It aims inductively to extract from the features of these writings a definition that fits the evidence.[26] It succeeds in doing so. In the present discussion we will accept this definition of *apocalypse* as satisfying the requirements of the available evidence:

> "Apocalypse" is a genre of revelatory literature with a narrative framework, in which a revelation is mediated by an otherworldly being to a human recipient, disclosing a transcendent reality which is both temporal, insofar as it envisages eschatological salvation, and spatial, insofar as it involves another, supernatural world. [An apocalypse is] intended to interpret present, earthly circumstances in light of the supernatural world and of the future, and to influence both the understanding and the behavior of the audience by means of divine authority.

Apocalypticism

The term *apocalypticism* refers to the attitudes, presuppositions, expectations, and beliefs that form the religious or cultural milieu of those belonging to movements similar to those that produce apocalypses. In the Jewish apocalypses such groups typically identify their own age as a time of impending violent upheaval, imminent divine intervention, and approaching eschatological vindication of a righteous remnant. This

---

25. For a helpful development of these literary functions in Jewish apocalypses see the following essay: Thomas J. Sappington, "The Factor of Function in Defining Jewish Apocalyptic Literature," *Journal for the Study of the Pseudepigrapha* 12 (1994): 83–123.

26. This seems to be the most prudent way to proceed. Anything else runs the risk of foisting preconceived requirements on the data. However, VanderKam sees something of a logical fallacy in this approach. He says, "There is a perhaps unavoidable element of circularity about such definitions in that the characteristics of texts which are intuitively or traditionally regarded as apocalypses constitute the definition which then determines the texts that are to be included in the genre." See James C. VanderKam, "The Prophetic-Sapiental Origins of Apocalyptic Thought," in *A Word in Season: Essays in Honour of William McKane*, ed. James D. Martin and Philip R. Davies, Journal for the Study of the Old Testament: Supplement Series, ed. David J. A. Clines and Philip R. Davies, vol. 42 (Sheffield: JSOT, 1986), 164.

remnant is sometimes portrayed as a disenfranchised group oppressed by their contemporaries, but not necessarily so.

Apocalypticism is a way of thinking. It is a mindset that looks to imminent divine intervention as the only solution to evils confronting a community that sees itself as righteous. The difference between *apocalypse* and *apocalypticism* is this: while *apocalypse* is a genre of literature and requires written expression, *apocalypticism* is essentially a way of thinking that may or may not produce a literature detailing such beliefs.

Apocalyptic Literature

The term *apocalyptic literature* is broader and more inclusive than the term *apocalypse*. While apocalyptic literature includes those writings that are specifically designated as apocalypses, it also includes related literature that shares certain characteristics with the apocalypse without qualifying for that more specific label. The term *apocalyptic literature* is broader and more inclusive; the term *apocalypse* is more narrow and restricted.

The expression *apocalyptic literature* refers to a type of writing that adopts to a significant degree the outlook of apocalypticism and portrays those themes through a vivid use of symbolic language. Apocalyptic literature tends to be rich in its **angelology**, vivid in its eschatological expectations, dire in its warning of cataclysmic judgment, and reassuring in its announcement of vindication for the righteous. Such writings may or may not take the form of an actual apocalypse. While an apocalypse is given over more or less entirely to such emphases, apocalyptic literature may incorporate other genres as well. In that sense the apocalyptic element does not stand alone.

Although in the Old Testament only the latter half of the book of Daniel qualifies as an apocalypse, there are other Old Testament writings that, at least in part, fall into the broader category of apocalyptic literature. Examples include portions of the books of Isaiah, Ezekiel, Joel, Zechariah, and various other writings as well.

Apocalyptic Eschatology

The message of Jewish apocalypses is usually eschatological in nature. As a rule, these writings deal with approaching events of the afterlife, whether regarding individual or corporate destiny for the righteous or the wicked. Of course, non-apocalyptic writings are sometimes eschatological in their emphasis as well. The message of the Old Testament prophets frequently focuses on eschatology, in addition to social ills that were contemporary to the time of the prophets. However, the eschatology of apocalyptic writings tends to be of a different sort when compared to the eschatology of the prophetic literature. The primary differences between the two have to do with the intensity of warning, the detail of description, and the manner of expression. The apocalypses tend to be more urgent in their appeal, more detailed in their descriptions of otherworldly events, and more given to the use of symbols and figures of speech than is the case with other writings.

The expression *apocalyptic eschatology* is therefore used to refer to a distinctive type of eschatology found in the apocalypses and related literature. This eschatology is characterized by God's sudden and perhaps violent breakthrough into human history in order to accomplish his purposes with mankind. This abrupt and irresistible display of divine power causes disruption of all that is normal or expected in the activity of human beings. It brings salvific deliverance for the faithful and cataclysmic judgment for their persecutors. It typically is described with a concentration of figurative language and symbolism.

Apocalyptic Discourse

The term *apocalyptic discourse* is used by some scholars to refer to the literary, ideological, and social characteristics of apocalyptic language.[27] This expression calls attention to the social context within which meaning is defined for adherents to a particular point of view. Out of such a social context various beliefs and traditions develop over time, informing the worldview and behavior of members of the group.

Such social discourse is characterized by certain *topoi* (or topics) that are influential in determining the convictions and way of life that find expression in a particular social structure. Carey finds in apocalyptic discourse the following eleven *topoi*: interest in an ultimate reality that is characterized by both temporal and spatial dimensions; use of visions and/or auditions to convey divine revelation regarding otherwise unknowable spiritual realities; emphasis on angelic or divine intermediaries as agents and interpreters of supernatural revelation; pervasive use of symbolic language for conveying revelatory information; use of pseudonymity as a literary device for enhancing the appeal and authority of a writing; descriptions of cosmic catastrophe brought about by divine intervention as a means of eschatological deliverance; **dualism** as a lens through which people, institutions, events, and time may be evaluated; determinism with regard to the course of history; emphasis on judgment and the afterlife; use of *ex eventu* **prophecy** to describe events that occurred prior to the writer's time; and speculation regarding cosmic bodies such as the sun, moon, and stars.[28] According to Carey, these eleven *topoi* play a significant role in framing apocalyptic discourse.

---

27. So, for example, Greg Carey, *Ultimate Things*, especially 1–15.
28. Ibid., 6–10.

Proto-Apocalyptic

The historical development of Jewish apocalyptic literature should be viewed as a continuum whose precise boundaries cannot be pinpointed. There is no specific moment at which apocalyptic literature can be said to begin, nor is there a specific moment at which this literature ceased to be. Prior to the appearance of apocalyptic literature as a fully developed genre there were texts that contained in seminal form ideas closely resembling those found in the later, more developed apocalypses. The expression *proto-apocalyptic* is used to describe those texts that foreshadow or anticipate in germ form ideas especially associated with later full-blown apocalypses.[29] These proto-apocalyptic elements are sometimes found embedded in otherwise non-apocalyptic writings.

In summary, we must distinguish between several related terms.

- *Apocalypse* is a genre of revelatory literature set in a narrative frame. In it an angel communicates to a human being otherwise inaccessible information concerning the supernatural world. This information has to do with eschatological salvation and realities of the supernatural world.

- *Apocalypticism* is the mindset, or worldview, associated with groups that produce apocalypses. It has to do especially with the eschatological expectations and beliefs of such communities.

- *Apocalyptic literature* is the written expression of the emphases that characterize apocalyptic communities, whether found in standalone compositions known as apocalypses or in sections of material assimilated into other genres of literature.

- *Apocalyptic eschatology* is a distinctive form of eschatology that reflects the characteristics found in the apocalypses, such as vivid descriptions of final judgment or vindication of the righteous.

- *Apocalyptic discourse* refers to the literary, ideological, and social characteristics of apocalyptic language.

- *Proto-apocalyptic* is an incipient form of apocalyptic ideas that anticipate what is found in the later apocalypses, where such ideas are given fuller and more complete expression.

---

29. Russell prefers the term *embryonic apocalyptic*, using an analogy borrowed from biology. See D. S. Russell, *Prophecy and the Apocalyptic Dream: Protest and Promise* (Peabody, MA: Hendrickson, 1994), 31.

TRAJECTORY OF DEVELOPMENT

By the end of the seventh century and the beginning of the sixth century B.C. an emphasis on apocalyptic motifs was developing within Judaism. Although at this stage such development was only in its incipient stages, apocalypticism would continue to take hold throughout the sixth century. The catalyst for this new approach may have been events connected to the upheaval caused by the Babylonian exile. Such factors as the cessation of the Israelite monarchy, the destruction of the Jerusalem temple in 586 B.C., the hardships of forced exile from the Jewish homeland, and the subsequent longings for divine intervention and restoration may all have contributed to the beginnings of Jewish apocalypticism.

The intertestamental period brought further developments in Jewish thinking and response to a world characterized by change and upheaval. By the third and second centuries B.C. a new genre of literature was growing in popularity in Judaism, and the genre proliferated during the second and first centuries. This period is characterized by the production of many extrabiblical Jewish apocalypses. These writings were similar in some ways to the Jewish literature that preceded them, and in other ways they were dissimilar.

The apocalypses can be divided into two categories, depending on whether they involve descriptions of an **otherworldly journey**.[30] First, some apocalypses are characterized by the description of a journey to the supernatural realm.[31] In these apocalypses an angelic intermediary escorts a human being on a journey to the spiritual world of the unseen, where the traveler is privileged to observe awe-inspiring sights that are completely out of the ordinary. Often the human recipient of such revelation is a famous biblical hero from the past, such as Abraham or Enoch. These otherworldly journeys take two very different forms. In some cases, the

---

30.   Here I am following Collins's analysis of the Jewish apocalypses. For elaboration see John J. Collins, "Introduction: Towards the Morphology of a Genre," in *Apocalypse: The Morphology of a Genre*, ed. John Joseph Collins, Semeia, vol. 14 (Missoula, MT: Scholars Press, 1979), 1–20.

31.   Himmelfarb has written extensively on the otherworldly journeys found in Jewish apocalyptic literature. See especially the following contributions: Martha Himmelfarb, *Tours of Hell: An Apocalyptic Form in Jewish and Christian Literature* (Philadelphia: University of Pennsylvania Press, 1983); idem, "The Experience of the Visionary and Genre in the Ascension of Isaiah 6–11 and the Apocalypse of Paul," in *Early Christian Apocalypticism: Genre, Social Setting*, ed. Adela Yarbro Collins, Semeia, vol. 36 (Decatur, GA: Scholars Press, 1986), 97–111; idem, "Heavenly Ascent and the Relationship of the Apocalypses and Hekhalot Literature," *Hebrew Union College Annual* 59 (1988): 73–100; idem, "Revelation and Rapture: The Transformation of the Visionary in the Ascent Apocalypses," in *Mysteries and Revelations: Apocalyptic Studies since the Uppsala Colloquium*, ed. James H. Charlesworth, Journal for the Study of the Pseudepigrapha: Supplement Series, ed. James H. Charlesworth, vol. 9 (Sheffield: Sheffield Academic Press, 1991), 79–90; idem, *Ascent to Heaven in Jewish and Christian Apocalypses* (Oxford: Oxford University Press, 1993).

traveler is escorted to the heavenly realm, where he observes scenes that have to do with the bliss of the righteous.[32] In other cases, the journey is not to heaven but to hell, where the scenes that are described concern vivid portrayals of misery, pain, and torture. Apocalyptic texts that describe otherworldly journeys thus share certain common emphases and goals. As Collins points out, the major themes of such literature have to do with an interest in establishing authority for a revealer or king, a curiosity about things otherwise unknowable, and an interest in eternal life.[33] Such features lend a certain predictability to the genre.

Second, some apocalypses lack a description of an otherworldly journey. Instead, they have other emphases that set them apart as a unified group of texts. Perhaps the most elaborate of these is the *Animal Apocalypse*, an apocalyptic text that probably dates to the second century B.C.[34] In the *Animal Apocalypse* Enoch presents to his son Methuselah an overview of world history extending from the time of Adam to the arrival of the messianic kingdom, including mention of such Old Testament figures as Abraham, Jacob, Moses, Saul, David, Solomon, and Elijah, all of whom are presented in terms of animal imagery. Adam, for example, is portrayed as a bull; Eve is a heifer; Noah is a white bull that becomes a human being; Israelites are sheep; Gentiles are wild animals; fallen angels are stars.

Jewish apocalypticism and the writing of apocalyptic texts continued until about the first century A.D., at which time Jewish interest in apocalypticism began to wane. Jewish writings of the following period (e.g., the Targumim, Midrashim, Tosephta, Mishnah, Talmud) show little interest in apocalypticism.[35] The reasons for this transition to a different form of Jewish literature are not entirely clear, although it probably had to do with the destruction of the Second Temple in A.D. 70 and the failure of the second Jewish revolt against the Romans in A.D.

---

32. The most famous of these apocalypses is the *Book of the Watchers*, which probably dates to the second or third century B.C. This text is a part (i.e., *1 Enoch* 1–36) of the larger composite work known as the *Book of Enoch*. Other examples of apocalypses that contain descriptions of similar journeys are the *Similitudes of Enoch*, which is also a part (i.e., *1 Enoch* 37–71) of the *Book of Enoch*, the *Testament of Abraham*, and the *Testament of Levi* (chapters 2–5).

33. John J. Collins, "Journeys to the World Beyond in Ancient Judaism," in *Apocalyptic and Eschatological Heritage: The Middle East and Celtic Realms*, ed. Martin McNamara (Dublin and Portland, OR: Four Courts, 2003), 22.

34. Other apocalyptic texts that lack description of an otherworldly journey include the *Apocalypse of Weeks* (*1 En.* 91:11–17; 93:1–10), *2 Baruch*, and *4 Ezra* (= *2 Esdras* 3–14).

35. Saldarini says, "Apocalyptic themes are not central to rabbinic literature nor are any passages extensive enough to form what might be called an apocalypse in the usual literary sense." See Anthony J. Saldarini, "The Uses of Apocalyptic in the Mishna and Tosepta," *Catholic Biblical Quarterly* 39 (1977): 396.

135.[36] These catastrophes were defining events for Judaism of that time. The destruction of the temple—along with continued intense persecution, loss of the priesthood, and expulsion of Jews from their ancient homeland—forced Judaism to seek new and alternative forms of religious expression. In the centuries that followed, Judaism largely left apocalypticism behind in preference for other genres.

SOCIAL WORLD OF APOCALYPTIC LITERATURE

Apocalyptic literature, for the most part, provides little in the way of direct information about the individuals or groups that produced this genre. Who exactly were the authors of these writings, and to what social setting did they align themselves? It would be helpful to know more about the social milieu out of which these writings came. Such information would perhaps provide insight as to why apocalyptic writers wrote as they did. It might also provide clues with regard to the proper interpretation of certain difficult sections found in these writings. However, most of these texts were either pseudepigraphical—falsely claiming to have been written by a famous hero of the past—or they were anonymous, providing no clue at all as to the identity of their author. It is only on the basis of careful analysis of the contents of these writings that it is possible to reconstruct the social setting out of which they came.

The German scholar Otto Plöger concluded that apocalyptic literature developed out of groups that saw themselves as marginalized and on the fringes of their social world.[37] According to him, such groups were usually disenfranchised, relatively powerless, and absent from strategic positions of leadership so far as the religious establishment was concerned. To some extent it was out of their frustrations with organized religion that they wrote apocalyptic literature. They believed that those in power had compromised their personal integrity and had introduced corruption and moral failure into religious observance. Apocalyptic writers sought vindication of the righteous remnant that had not gone along with such religious declension. They longed for divine judgment and punishment of the corrupt established order. They believed that such vindication was imminent and would soon come as a result of divine intervention.

---

36. Saldarini points to a ban by Rabbi Akiba in the second century on books that sought to imitate biblical writings, as well as concern over anything that might be construed as inciting rebellion after the painful Roman elimination of the Bar Kosiba (a.k.a. Bar Kokhba) revolt in A.D. 135, as playing a role in the demise of apocalyptic literature in the rabbinic period. See Anthony J. Saldarini, "Apocalypses and 'Apocalyptic' in Rabbinic Literature," in *Apocalypse: The Morphology of a Genre*, 187. See also Anthony J. Saldarini, "Apocalyptic and Rabbinic Literature," *Catholic Biblical Quarterly* 37 (1975): 348–58.

37. Otto Plöger, *Theocracy and Eschatology*, trans. S. Rudman (Richmond, VA: John Knox, 1968): 239.

Many scholars have agreed with Plöger in understanding apocalyptic communities to be disenfranchised and on the fringe of society. Cook, however, has advocated a very different approach to the social setting of ancient apocalyptic movements, rejecting what he calls the deprivation theory of Plöger and Hanson. According to him, such groups were not necessarily disenfranchised or powerless or living at the fringes of society. In many cases their members were actually powerful, influential, and within the mainstream of society. Cook calls attention to many apocalyptic groups throughout history that do not at all fit such a description. More importantly, he also directs attention to a number of biblical texts that can best be regarded as proto-apocalyptic and yet originate out of a priestly or mainstream setting. The key biblical texts to which he appeals are Ezekiel 38–39, Zechariah 1–8, Joel 2:1-11, and Joel 3–4.[38]

It seems best to acknowledge that our information regarding the social location of Jewish apocalyptic groups in antiquity is very limited. To what extent such groups were operating from inside or from outside accepted societal and religious structures is not always clear. It seems likely that apocalypticism was to be found in various social settings. In that case we should not without further evidence think that they were necessarily disenfranchised groups, although in some instances that may well have been the case.

CONCLUSION

In this chapter, we have laid a foundation for thinking about apocalyptic literature by defining our terms and probing certain methodological issues pertinent to the study of such material. We have attempted to answer the question: What is apocalyptic literature? We are now ready to consider some distinctive features of this literature that set it apart from other literature of its place and time. In the coming chapter we shall consider the purpose, main characteristics, and common themes that typify many biblical and extrabiblical texts.

---

38. Cook, *Prophecy and Apocalypticism*, 2.

2

MAJOR THEMES IN APOCALYPTIC LITERATURE

In order to get an overview of Jewish apocalyptic literature, this chapter will consider some representative texts drawn from the Old Testament, **intertestamental** Jewish literature, and the **Dead Sea scrolls**. This chapter will also summarize characteristic features of this literature and identify its major themes.

REPRESENTATIVE TEXTS

Old Testament apocalyptic literature belongs to a genre of Jewish writing that includes both canonical and non-canonical texts. For a proper understanding of this genre within the context of its historical development, neither of these groups of texts should be examined in isolation from the other. Each one provides background and illumination for the other. On the one hand, the study of canonical prophetic and apocalyptic texts illumines the origins and early stages of this genre, as well as helping to define its role and essential characteristics. On the other hand, the study of non-canonical apocalyptic texts provides insight into the growing popularity and proliferation of this genre in antiquity, testifying to its development and expansion in new historical contexts and religious settings. These non-canonical texts also provide a basis for understanding how such literature was read and why it appealed to so many readers during the intertestamental period. Familiarity with this larger corpus of apocalyptic writings is therefore helpful to biblical exegetes. We begin with an overview of the book of Daniel.

The Book of Daniel

Since the book of Daniel plays a central role in the discussion of Old Testament apocalyptic literature, a brief consideration of its message, purpose, major themes, and structure is appropriate.

Message. The overarching message of the book of Daniel is easily inferred from its content. In the first half of the book six episodes, mostly from the life of Daniel (chapters 1–6), stress the presence of God with his faithful people and his opposition to those who ignore his purposes. Several chapters emphasize the truth that, against all apparent odds, the Lord undertakes on behalf of his faithful servants. Other chapters call attention to the futility of arrogance that fails to acknowledge the sovereign Lord. Repeatedly these chapters describe the Lord as rewarding courage to face life-threatening dangers and as providing needed insight to explain enigmatic challenges. The message, then, is twofold. First, the Lord is with his faithful remnant, providentially supplying their needs and seeing them through the most trying of circumstances. Second, he resists the proud, and in due time he brings about their demise.

In the second half of the book (chapters 7–12) Daniel receives incredible visions that describe realities of this world and the world to come. These visions stress the fact that the Lord is in control of events of human history, moving all things toward the realization of his eternal kingdom. The visions point to imminent vindication of the righteous who are suffering for their faith. The message of these chapters is that the present world order is headed for divine judgment; the ultimate hope for the faithful remnant lies in divine intervention and apocalyptic deliverance.

Purpose. The book of Daniel is addressed to a community that should expect to suffer for their faith. They should not find this to be a cause for surprise, or an indication of divine abandonment. Instead, they should view religious crises as an indication of the presence of evil in the world. Deliverance will come in keeping with a timetable established by the sovereign Lord. The faithful remnant must take comfort in the realization that God is at work in the unfolding of human history, even though this may require that the righteous suffer for a time. He is in control of events rather than victimized by them. Right will eventually prevail, although there may be considerable pain to be endured prior to that time. The book of Daniel, through its historical stories and through its visionary revelations, holds out hope that God's purposes will be accomplished and that he has not forsaken his people. His kingdom will ultimately prevail.

Major Themes. The book of Daniel emphasizes several themes, which are repeatedly illustrated and sometimes directly articulated by various characters in the book. These themes point to an implied theology of the book of Daniel, which can be summarized in the following observations.

1. Faithfulness to God may be rewarded in extraordinary ways. Repeatedly in Daniel, heroic characters are faced with a dilemma that prompts them to choose a dangerous course of action due to their faith in God. Their actions illustrate an important lesson for the life of faith—namely, that resolution to do the right thing regardless of personal consequences meets with God's approval and blessing. This lesson is illustrated in a couple of ways in the book of Daniel.

First, reward for faithfulness applies to matters of personal piety. In chapter one, when Daniel is faced with the temptation to compromise his standards regarding defilement through dietary practices, he chooses to accept deprivation rather than risk ritual contamination. God rewards this decision, and that of his three friends as well, by prospering them beyond their expectation. As a result, Daniel and his friends were more successful in their career advancement than their colleagues, who did not share their personal convictions. In chapter three, Daniel's three friends are faced with a demand to compromise their religious integrity by worshipping a pagan statue. They refuse, choosing instead to accept punishment by death in a fiery furnace. To the surprise of observers, they are miraculously delivered by angelic intervention. The lesson is clear: God rewards the faithfulness of his people (Dan. 3:16–17, 28). In chapter six Daniel is miraculously delivered from the ravenous lions because of his unflinching exercise of personal religious practice. Rather than comply with an edict that required compromise of personal integrity he continued his normal practices and faced the consequences of his refusal to violate personal standards. According to Daniel 6:22, it is God who "shut the mouths of the lions." Again, the lesson is that God rewards the consistency of his faithful people. In chapter nine, when Daniel seeks to understand Jeremiah's prophecy concerning seventy years of exile, he first acknowledges God's justice in punishing his people for their sins. Seeking God's approval by confessing the sins of his people leads to illumination and understanding of Jeremiah's words. Confession and repentance are the path to divine approval and blessing.

Second, reward for faithfulness applies to matters of understanding divine revelation. Repeatedly Daniel is described as one who is able to provide extraordinary insight to enigmatic messages. When professional wise men fail to interpret dreams and visions, the king repeatedly summons Daniel. Without fail he delivers the needed interpretation. But Daniel's insight is due not to his own charismatic wisdom, but to the bestowal of divine insight. The lesson is that faithfulness to God leads to insight into God's revelation in a way that human wisdom alone cannot achieve.

2. Hubris against God may be judged in extraordinary ways. If faithfulness to God is rewarded in extraordinary ways, so pride and arrogance meet with God's disapproval. These are but two sides of the same coin. Several incidents in the book of Daniel forcefully illustrate this. In chapter four, when Nebuchadnezzar is overtaken by unwarranted pride over his accomplishments, God takes his sanity from him and reduces him to the level of an animal. For seven long years Nebuchadnezzar lacks intellectual competence sufficient for administering the affairs of his kingdom. Once his sanity is restored to him, Nebuchadnezzar concludes that "those who walk in pride he is able to humble" (Dan. 4:37).

This lesson was lost on a later Babylonian king who elevated himself in pride as Nebuchadnezzar had previously done. In chapter five, Belshazzar engages in reckless and idolatrous behavior, defiling the sacred vessels that Nebuchadnezzar had taken from the Jerusalem temple. As a result, the Lord sends a message inscribed on a palace wall that forewarns of Belshazzar's imminent demise. Daniel attributes Belshazzar's failure and resulting judgment to his not having learned from Nebuchadnezzar's fate: "But you, Belshazzar, his son, have not humbled yourself, though you knew all this" (Dan. 5:22). In chapter eleven, a king who "will exalt and magnify himself above every god" engages in relentless persecution of the faithful remnant. His venting is directed "against the God of gods," about whom he says "unheard-of things" advancing beyond all expectation (Dan. 11:36). The consequence of such hubris is a recurring theme in the book of Daniel.

These several accounts of arrogance and pride point to an important element of the theology of the book of Daniel. Insolence directed against God will be tolerated for only so long. The sovereign Lord will call all to account for their attitude toward divine authority.

3. Human history is an expression of divine sovereignty and control. Another major theme of the book of Daniel is the notion that human history advances along lines predetermined by God. History is not the accidental accumulation of circumstances and events. Quite the contrary. The Lord is mysteriously involved in human history, bringing to fruition his designs and intentions. This idea is affirmed by several scenarios described in the book.

First, through the events that befell them several characters are led to conclude that the rise and fall of human rulers are entirely in God's hands. As Daniel says, "He changes times and seasons; he deposes kings and raises up others" (Dan. 2:21; cf. 1:1). Nebuchadnezzar, restored to sanity in accord with God's promise, says, "He does as he pleases with the powers of heaven and the peoples of the earth. No one can hold back his hand or say to him: 'What have you done?'" (Dan. 4:35). Daniel, in rebuking Belshazzar for his pride, recalls that Nebuchadnezzar eventually "acknowledged that the Most High God is sovereign over all kingdoms on earth and sets over them anyone he wishes" (Dan. 5:21; cf. 5:26).

Second, the emergence of world powers is due to predetermination on the part of God. The book of Daniel emphasizes the notion that God has already determined what must happen, when it will occur, and under what circumstances it will take place. In chapters two and seven Daniel announces the emergence of four world empires, followed by the establishment of God's kingdom. The identity of these kingdoms and their rulers is anticipated through the medium of divine revelation. In chapter eight, a conflict between Persia and Greece is described in great detail. The chapter makes clear that these events were determined in advance of their occurrence. In chapter eleven the ongoing conflict between Ptolemaic and the Seleucid dynasties is outlined in detail, since it has been predestined by God. In chapter twelve specific periods of time, such as the 1,290 days and the 1,335 days, are mentioned in connection with the abomination of desolation (Dan. 12:11–12). These announcements are possible only because of divine predetermination.

Third, in chapter nine Daniel sets forth a prophecy of seventy "weeks" that summarize in three epochs events connected to the coming of an Anointed One (Dan. 9:20–27). These events are predetermined, including the demise of the one who sets up "an abomination that causes desolation" (Dan. 9:27). The sovereign Lord determines what will happen.

Fourth, the book of Daniel emphasizes the idea that God's kingdom will ultimately prevail over all human kingdoms. This is stressed in Daniel 2:44, which speaks of a heavenly kingdom that "will crush all those kingdoms and bring them to an end, but it will itself endure forever." This idea is acknowledged by king Darius, who says that Daniel's God "is the living God and he endures forever; his kingdom will not be destroyed, his dominion will never end" (Dan. 6:26). It is affirmed in Daniel's description of his night vision: "His dominion is an everlasting dominion that will not pass away, and his kingdom is one that will never be destroyed" (Dan. 7:14). The angelic explanation of this vision concludes with these words: "Then the sovereignty, power and greatness of all the kingdoms under heaven will be handed over to the holy people of the Most High. His kingdom will be an everlasting kingdom, and all rulers will worship and obey him" (Dan. 7:27). According to the book of Daniel, human history moves along lines determined in advance by God.

Structure. The structure of the book of Daniel reflects two complementary features of its literary organization. First, the structure can be analyzed from the standpoint of form and genre. In this regard, there are two major sections. The first section (chapters 1–6) is comprised of historical episodes taken mainly from the life of Daniel. The second section (chapters 7–12) consists of apocalyptic visions that Daniel is said to have received. While this division provides a helpful starting point, it does not take into account the relationship of the two sections.

Second, the structure may be analyzed from the standpoint of an underlying chiastic relationship discernible for chapters two through seven. From this perspective there are three sections. The first section (chapter 1) serves as an introduction to Daniel, who is the main character of the book. The second section (chapters 2–7) forms a **chiasm** in the book. Chapters two and seven correspond in that they set forth a revelation concerning four world empires to be followed by the kingdom of God. Chapters three and six correspond in that they set forth God's miraculous deliverance of his faithful servants from a fiery furnace or from a den of lions. Chapters four and five correspond in that they set forth divine judgment on human arrogance, as displayed by kings Nebuchadnezzar and Belshazzar. The third section (chapters 8–12) describes further revelations given to Daniel through visions. The chiastic structure is united by language in that Daniel 2:4b–7:28 is written in Aramaic, while the remaining chapters are written in Hebrew.

Old Testament Prophets

Certain passages in Old Testament prophetic literature point to an apocalyptic emphasis. Examples can be found mainly in Isaiah, Ezekiel, Zechariah, Joel, and Malachi. While they are not full-blown apocalyptic literature, these texts do reveal a developing apocalyptic emphasis.

Isaiah. In the so-called Isaiah Apocalypse found in Isaiah 24–27 the prophet warns of a time when the Lord will devastate the earth with inescapable judgment. It will be laid waste, devastated, and completely ruined (Isa. 24:1, 3). In spite of this destruction the prophet anticipates the Lord's deliverance of his people, as he wipes away their tears and removes their disgrace (Isa. 24:8). In this section Yahweh is portrayed as an all-powerful cosmic warrior who decisively overcomes the serpent Leviathan. In places this section employs **mythopoeic imagery** to describe the Lord's ultimate victory over the serpent. In Isaiah 27:1 the prophet says:

> In that day, the LORD will punish with his sword—his fierce, great and powerful sword—Leviathan the gliding serpent, Leviathan the coiling serpent; he will slay the monster of the sea.

This text vividly describes Yahweh as coming in vengeance to deal decisively with his longstanding adversary Leviathan.[1] With a terri-

---

1. For a comprehensive study of Leviathan, see K. William Whitney, *Two Strange Beasts: Leviathan and Behemoth in Second Temple and Early Rabbinic Judaism*, Harvard Semitic Monographs, vol. 63 (Winona Lake, IN: Eisenbrauns, 2006).

ble sword the Lord slays the mighty sea monster, described as a coiling serpent. This language has elements that are common to ancient Canaanite and Babylonian **mythology**, where one of the gods struggles against and decisively defeats a cosmic sea monster. Isaiah utilizes similar language about the figure of Leviathan to portray Yahweh's victory over evil. This language has much in common with later apocalyptic texts.[2]

Ezekiel. Although the book of Ezekiel is not overall an apocalyptic writing, it does contain sections whose diction moves beyond that of normal prophetic discourse. These sections resonate with apocalyptic language, calling to mind certain characteristics of the apocalypses. Such language flares up for a time in certain sections of Ezekiel and then eventually subsides, giving way to tones more typical of other prophetic literature. A few passages will illustrate this feature of Ezekiel's language and message.

The prophet Ezekiel was among the deportees that Nebuchadnezzar's military forces took captive to Babylon in 597 B.C. Writing to the exilic community of the sixth century B.C., Ezekiel describes unusual visions of God that he experienced while beside the Kebar River near the city of Babylon. In describing these visions Ezekiel uses elevated speech replete with figurative depictions of strange creatures that he saw in his visions. His language in these sections is similar to language found in portions of the book of Daniel. Ezekiel 1:4–9 illustrates some of these features.

> I looked, and I saw a windstorm coming out of the north—an immense cloud with flashing lightning and surrounded by brilliant light. The center of the fire looked like glowing metal, and in the fire was what looked like four living creatures. In appearance their form was human, but each of them had four faces and four wings. Their legs were straight; their feet were like those of a calf and gleamed like burnished bronze. Under their wings on their four sides they had human hands. All four of them had faces and wings, and the wings of one touched the wings of another. Each one went straight ahead; they did not turn as they moved.

---

2. As Millar points out, there is considerable disagreement among scholars concerning the genre of Isaiah 24–27. This section has been variously regarded as late postexilic apocalyptic literature, as preexilic prophetic judgment literature, as prophetic eschatological literature, as exilic (or early postexilic) proto-apocalyptic literature, and as early apocalyptic literature. See William R. Millar, *Isaiah 24–27 and the Origin of Apocalyptic*, Harvard Semitic Monographs, ed. Frank Moore Cross, vol. 11 (Missoula, MT: Scholars Press, 1976), 21.

Ezekiel's scene evokes the language of theophany. The prophet's reference to windstorm, immense clouds, flashing lightning, and brilliant light (v. 4) anticipates even stranger things to follow in the prophet's summary of his vision. He speaks of four living creatures that appear in a fire resembling glowing metal (v. 5), a motif later invoked by the author of the book of Revelation (Rev. 4:7). Though human in form, each of these creatures had four faces and four wings (v. 6). Under their wings were human hands (v. 8). Their faces were human-like (v. 10), but at the same time they were also lion-like, ox-like, and eagle-like (v. 10). Their appearance, the prophet says, resembled fiery coals or burning torches (v. 13). These unusual creatures were capable of incredible speed, and throughout all their movements they were accompanied by ever-present wheels with rims full of eyes (vv. 14–21). Over these creatures appeared a human-like figure enthroned and radiant in appearance (vv. 25–28).

This remarkable scene sets the stage for the divine commissioning of the prophet, which took place in 593 B.C. (Ezek. 1:1) and is described in Ezekiel 2. At that time Ezekiel was called to be Yahweh's prophetic spokesman to his people. In its use of symbolic language and its description of bizarre creatures, the language of Ezekiel 1 has much in common with later apocalyptic writings. However, the passage lacks certain other common features of apocalyptic literature, such as numerical **periodization** and stress on dualism. Its correspondence to later apocalyptic literature is limited and incomplete.

Yet another section using similar language is Ezekiel 38–39, which contains a lengthy prophecy against Gog. These chapters are perhaps the most familiar passage in the entire book. Once again Ezekiel uses language that anticipates the idiom of apocalyptic writings. In Ezekiel 38:17–23 the prophet describes Gog's attack on the land of Israel and the Lord's angry response to that attack.

> This is what the Sovereign LORD says: You are the one I spoke of in former days by my servants the prophets of Israel. At that time they prophesied for years that I would bring you against them. This is what will happen in that day: When Gog attacks the land of Israel, my hot anger will be aroused, declares the Sovereign LORD. In my zeal and fiery wrath I declare that at that time there shall be a great earthquake in the land of Israel. The fish of the sea, the birds in the sky, the beasts of the field, every creature that moves along the ground, and all the people on the face of the earth will tremble at my presence. The mountains will be overturned, the cliffs will crumble and every wall will fall to the ground. I will summon a sword against

> Gog on all my mountains, declares the Sovereign LORD.
> Every man's sword will be against his brother. I will ex-
> ecute judgment upon him with plague and bloodshed; I
> will pour down torrents of rain, hailstones and burning
> sulfur on him and on his troops and on the many nations
> with him. And so I will show my greatness and my holi-
> ness, and I will make myself known in the sight of many
> nations. Then they will know that I am the LORD.

The prophet's description of these events is ominous in tone. He warns that a great earthquake in the land of Israel will strike terror throughout the earth as the natural landscape and all things constructed on it undergo violent and devastating change. The prophet describes the Lord's coming judgment on Gog in alarming terms. The Lord says, "I will execute judgment upon him with plague and bloodshed; I will pour down torrents of rain, hailstones and burning sulfur on him and on his troops and on the many nations with him" (38:22). The total destruction of Israel's enemies is graphically portrayed in repulsive terms: "I will give you as food to all kinds of carrion birds and to the wild animals" (39:4). The description is shocking.

Depictions of divine judgment in striking terms such as these are common in later apocalyptic literature. The presence of such language in the book of Ezekiel suggests that the language of portions of this book, while lacking other common features of apocalyptic literature, is nonetheless moving to some degree in that direction. Ezekiel's language in this passage could be described as proto-apocalyptic.

Zechariah. The book of Zechariah has two major sections. The first section of the book consists of chapters 1–8, and the second section consists of chapters 9–14. There are features of apocalyptic literature in both parts of Zechariah, as can be seen from the following examples.

In Zechariah 1:7–6:8 the prophet describes eight night visions, repeatedly using language and motifs common to apocalyptic literature. For example, in this material there is frequent mention of angels (e.g., Zech. 1:9, 11, 12, 13, 14, 19 [Heb. 2:2]; 2:3 [Heb. 2:7]; 3:3, 5, 6; 4:1, 4, 5; 5:5, 10; 6:4, 5; cf. 12:8). This is a feature reminiscent of the detailed and elaborate angelology found in many Jewish apocalyptic writings. Throughout these visions there is also pervasive symbolism that employs language of picturesque analogy and comparison. We read, for example, of a rider on a red horse, behind which there also stood red, brown, and white horses (1:8). The prophet is mystified by this scene and has to inquire about the meaning of these strange things (1:9). The mysterious appearance of four horns leads to a similar request for explanation (1:18). Later the high priest Joshua is presented with a stone that is said to contain seven eyes (3:9). An angel must explain to the prophet the meaning of these seven eyes (4:10).

Likewise, the meaning of two olive branches beside two golden pipes pouring out golden oil puzzles the prophet until an angel explains that they represent servants of the sovereign Lord (5:7). There is also a large flying scroll that symbolizes a curse that extends across the land (5:1–2) and a woman in a basket representing wickedness, according to the angel's interpretation (5:7). Later four chariots come forth from two mountains of bronze; an angel explains that these chariots represent four spirits of heaven proceeding from the Lord's presence (6:1). In this first section of Zechariah there is also a strong messianic emphasis, focused on an individual figuratively called the Branch (3:8; 6:11–14; cf. 9:9–10; 12:8–10). The use of such symbolism is common in apocalyptic writings.

In the second section of Zechariah there is an emphasis on a coming messianic king. This king is portrayed as coming on a donkey— on a colt, the foal of a donkey (9:9). The New Testament sees the fulfillment of this text in the triumphal entry of Jesus into Jerusalem (Matt. 21:5; John 12:15). The prophet also describes a coming of the Lord to the Mount of Olives. This advent is said to cause a splitting of the Mount of Olives, resulting in water miraculously flowing out from Jerusalem in both summer and winter (14:4). A bit later the prophet speaks of divine judgment rendered against the enemies of Jerusalem. Zechariah 14:12–15 says:

> This is the plague with which the LORD will strike all the nations that fought against Jerusalem: Their flesh will rot while they are still standing on their feet, their eyes will rot in their sockets, and their tongues will rot in their mouths. On that day people will be stricken by the LORD with great panic. They will seize each other by the hand and attack one another. Judah too will fight at Jerusalem. The wealth of all the surrounding nations will be collected—great quantities of gold and silver and clothing. A similar plague will strike the horses and mules, the camels and donkeys, and all the animals in those camps.

Here the prophet describes an eschatological scene in which Yahweh intervenes in behalf of his people, bringing judgment on their enemies. The language is both startling and appalling. Zechariah speaks of rapidly rotting flesh, of eyes decomposing in their sockets, of tongues decaying in the mouths of their owners. There will be panic and violence among the inhabitants of the land. All of this is the result of a plague initiated by Yahweh himself.

Sudden divine intervention in human events accompanied by unusual cosmic effects is not uncommon in Jewish apocalyptic writings. Even though the book of Zechariah lacks other common features of apocalyptic literature and cannot be labeled an apocalypse as such, in places it clearly has an apocalyptic ring to it.

Joel. The prophet Joel, probably writing during the exilic or postexilic period, describes the approaching day of the Lord in terms of foreboding cosmic changes. His language has an apocalyptic ring to it. He says:

> And afterward, I will pour out my Spirit on all people. Your sons and daughters will prophesy, your old men will dream dreams, your young men will see visions. Even on my servants, both men and women, I will pour out my Spirit in those days. I will show wonders in the heavens and on the earth, blood and fire and billows of smoke. The sun will be turned to darkness and the moon to blood before the coming of the great and dreadful day of the LORD. And everyone who calls on the name of the LORD will be saved; for on Mount Zion and in Jerusalem there will be deliverance, as the LORD has said, even among the survivors whom the LORD calls (Joel 2:28–32).

The prophet signals a time when the bestowal of God's Spirit will extend to all, whether male or female, whether old or young, whether bond or free. This democratization of the bestowal of the Spirit, Joel says, will be accompanied by cosmic signs. There will be wonders in the heavens above and on the earth below. There will be blood, fire, and columns of smoke. The sun will be darkened, and the moon will appear blood-red. The day of Yahweh will bring deliverance for a faithful remnant that the Lord has called. Joel's prophecy is not fully apocalyptic, but the language anticipates language that later apocalyptic writers use in a more developed way.

Malachi. The book of Malachi is addressed to the fifth-century postexilic Jewish community. In this book the prophet denounces the grievous sins of his people, calls them to repentance and renewed faith in Yahweh, and warns them of judgment to come. His announcement of impending divine judgment is couched in language not unlike that of certain apocalyptic writings. According to the prophet, the Lord's coming will be preceded by the advent of a messenger who will prepare the way (3:1; cf. 4:5). This messenger is identified in the New Testament as John the Baptist (Matt. 11:10; Mark 1:2; Luke 1:76). In Malachi 4:1–3 the prophet describes the approaching day of the Lord in the following terms:

> "Surely the day is coming; it will burn like a furnace. All the arrogant and every evildoer will be stubble, and that day that is coming will set them on fire," says the LORD

Almighty. "Not a root or a branch will be left to them. But for you who revere my name, the sun of righteousness will rise with healing in its wings. And you will go out and frolic like well-fed calves. Then you will trample on the wicked; they will be ashes under the soles of your feet on the day when I act," says the LORD Almighty.

The emphasis found here on such motifs as fearful divine epiphany, fiery and consuming judgment, vindicating triumph of the righteous remnant, and inescapable punishment for the ungodly reflects themes that figure strongly throughout Jewish apocalyptic literature. By no stretch is the book of Malachi an apocalypse, but in an incipient way it does contain strands of apocalyptic motifs.

From these examples it is clear that Old Testament prophets such as Isaiah, Ezekiel, Zechariah, Joel, and Malachi sometimes used language that moves beyond common prophetic rhetoric. The seeds of apocalyptic language can be seen here. In these writers an incipient apocalypticism is present in germ form, situated within contexts that employ other forms of prophetic speech. Many later writers followed in the train of these prophets, expanding such motifs considerably.

Extrabiblical Jewish Apocalyptic Texts

During the intertestamental period Jewish literature shows an increasing interest in apocalyptic motifs. A significant corpus of extrabiblical apocalyptic writings developed during this time. The emphasis of this literature is similar to that of certain Old Testament texts. But in some ways it is also very different from Old Testament texts.

Types of Apocalypses. There are fourteen extrabiblical Jewish texts that satisfy the requirements of the definition of apocalypse adopted in chapter one. While these apocalypses have much in common, there are also important differences. They may be divided into two groups, depending on whether or not they describe a journey to the other world.[3] In those texts that contain no description of an otherworldly journey an angelic messenger grants to a human recipient a revelation regarding past or future events, but without a tour of heaven or hell. Texts that fall into this category are Daniel 7–12, the *Animal Apocalypse*, the *Apocalypse of Weeks*, *Jubilees* 23, *4 Ezra*, and *2 Baruch*.

In texts that have a description of an otherworldly journey an angelic messenger takes a human recipient of revelation on a journey through

---

3. Collins has proposed this twofold grouping. See John J. Collins, "The Jewish Apocalypses," in *Apocalypse: The Morphology of a Genre*, ed. John Joseph Collins, Semeia, vol. 14 (Missoula, MT: Scholars Press, 1979), 21–59.

heaven or hell. This person gains otherwise unattainable insight into experiences and conditions of the afterlife. Collins divides this type of apocalypse into three subcategories. (1) One type of apocalypse contains both an otherworldly journey and a review of history. The only text that belongs in this category is the *Apocalypse of Abraham* 15–32. (2) Some apocalypses contain both an otherworldly journey and/or political eschatology. The texts that belong in this category are the *Book of the Watchers*, the *Similitudes of Enoch*, the *Book of the Heavenly Luminaries*, *2 Enoch*, and the **Testament** *of Levi* 2–5. (3) Some apocalypses contain otherworldly journeys with only personal eschatology. The texts that belong in this category are *3 Baruch*, the *Testament of Abraham* 10–15 (8–12 in Recension B), and the *Apocalypse of Zephaniah*. As Collins points out, the spectrum of this literature ranges from apocalypses that are historical at the one end to apocalypses that are purely personal at the other end, with the remaining apocalypses occupying mediating positions somewhere along this continuum.[4]

Since Jewish apocalypses will be referred to rather frequently in the following discussion, we will summarize their contents and point out some features of their structure, themes, emphasis, and theology.

1. Book of Enoch. The *Book of Enoch* is a composite collection consisting of at least five separate compositions that have been grouped together. These components are as follows: (1) the *Book of the Watchers* (*1 En.* 1–36); (2) the *Similitudes of Enoch* (*1 En.* 37–71); (3) the *Astronomical Book* (*1 En.* 72–82); (4) the *Dream Visions* (*1 En.* 83–90); (5) the *Epistle of Enoch* (*1 En.* 91–108). In some cases there are subsets of distinctive material within these larger divisions. For example, the *Animal Apocalypse* (*1 En.* 85–90) is a part of the *Dream Visions* (*1 En.* 83–90), and the *Apocalypse of Weeks* (*1 En.* 93:1-10; 91:11-17) is a part of the *Epistle of Enoch* (*1 En.* 91–108).

The earliest portions of the *Book of Enoch* may date as early as the third century B.C. Other parts of this collection date to the first century A.D. This work is sometimes referred to as *Ethiopic Enoch*, since the only extant copy of the entire work is in Ethiopic. Our earliest manuscripts of portions of this work are Aramaic documents from Qumran, which suggests that the original language of the *Book of Enoch* may have been Aramaic. Its early date, its developed apocalypticism, and its widespread influence make this text important for understanding the growth and influence of Jewish apocalypticism during the intertestamental period.

2. Book of the Watchers (*1 Enoch* 1–36). The *Book of the Watchers* is a composite work that probably dates to the early second or perhaps late third century B.C. This work has three major sections. The first section (*1 En.* 1–5) provides a brief introduction to the book. Through angelic

---

4. Ibid., 23.

mediation Enoch is said to receive a revelation intended "not for this generation, but for a distant generation which will come" (*1 En.* 1:2). Enoch issues the following warning:

> And behold! He comes with ten thousand holy ones to execute judgment upon them, and to destroy the impious, and to contend with all flesh concerning everything which the sinners and the impious have done and wrought against him (*1 En.* 1:9).

The second section (*1 En.* 6–16) provides an account of fallen angels who desired sexual relationship with beautiful women (*1 En.* 6:2; cf. Gen. 6:1–4). Led by Semyaza and other angelic leaders, two hundred evil angels descend to Mount Hermon and become promiscuous with women (*1 En.* 6:1–7). From this illicit union are born giants whose height was three thousand cubits (*1 En.* 7:2). As a result of this corrupting influence Enoch says, "the world was changed" (*1 En.* 8:1). Michael and other good angels (i.e., Gabriel, Suriel, and Uriel) intercede on behalf of the earth (*1 En.* 9:1–11). But God decides to destroy the earth with a deluge, which will be followed by a restoration of the earth (*1 En.* 10:1–22). Enoch then announces this coming judgment to the evil angels (*1 En.* 13:1–3). When the angels appeal to Enoch to implore God on their behalf for forgiveness, he instead affirms their certain and imminent judgment. The evil angels will become evil spirits dwelling on the earth, forfeiting their former exalted state (*1 En.* 15:8–9).

In the third section (*1 En.* 17–36) angels take Enoch on a journey to the ends of heaven and earth, where he sees a prison reserved for the evil angels who sinned with women. He also sees the holy angels (i.e., Uriel, Raphael, Raguel, Michael, Saraqael, and Gabriel), who "keep watch" (*1 En.* 20:1–6), each with a specific area of responsibility.

3. *Similitudes of Enoch* (*1 Enoch* 37–71). The *Similitudes* (or *Parables*) *of Enoch* probably dates to the first half of the first century A.D. A growing consensus dates this text prior to the beginning of Jesus' ministry, in which case the *Parables of Enoch* may have influenced the early Jesus movement.[5] This work consists of three parables that are conveyed by Enoch "to those who dwell on the dry ground" (*1 En.* 37:5). Each parable is preceded by an introduction and followed by a conclusion.

According to the first parable (*1 En.* 38–44) Enoch is carried "off from the face of the earth" and set down "at the end of heaven" (*1 En.* 39:3), where he receives a vision concerning the righteous and the sin-

---

5. See James H. Charlesworth and Darrell L. Bock, *Parables of Enoch: A Paradigm Shift*, Jewish and Christian Texts in Contexts and Related Studies Series, ed. James H. Charlesworth, vol. 11 (London: Bloomsbury, 2013).

ners. Enoch gazes at multitudes standing before the Lord of Spirits, along with four angels (i.e., Michael, Raphael, Gabriel, and Phanuel). He sees "all the secrets of heaven" (*1 En.* 41:1), which largely consist of various cosmological insights disclosed to Enoch.

In the second parable (*1 En.* 45–57) Enoch receives revelation concerning sinners. One of the angels shows Enoch "all the secrets about that **Son of Man**, who he was, and whence he was, (and) why he went with the Head of Days" (*1 En.* 46:2). Of particular interest is the description of the Son of Man (*1 En.* 46:1–8). An angel informs Enoch that this is the one "with whom righteousness dwells"; he is the one who "will reveal all the treasures of that which is secret" (*1 En.* 46:3). He will execute judgment on the strong and powerful; he "will break the teeth of the sinners" (*1 En.* 46:4). Those who refuse to acknowledge the Lord of the Spirits will not experience resurrection; they "have no hope of rising from their resting-places" (*1 En.* 46:6). Enoch also receives revelation concerning the destinies of the righteous, the wicked, and the fallen angels. An angel explains to Enoch that four angels (i.e., Michael, Gabriel, Raphael, and Phanuel) will seize the hosts of Azazel and cast them into the lowest part of hell (*1 En.* 54:5).

According to the third parable (*1 En.* 58–69) Enoch views an eschatological scene that includes judgment of the two monsters Leviathan and Behemoth. Noah receives an explanation from Enoch regarding "all the secrets in a book and the parables which had been given to him" (*1 En.* 68:1). These are collected in "the words of the Book of the Parables." This revelation identifies by name the fallen angels and their leaders. It also includes a description of the fate of evil angels who sinned with women (*1 En.* 69:1–29). In the conclusion (*1 En.* 70–71) to the *Similitudes* "the spirit carried Enoch off to the highest heaven," where he views a heavenly scene attended by myriads of angels, some of whom are named (*1 En.* 71:9–13).

4. *Astronomical Book*, or *Book of Heavenly Luminaries* (*1 Enoch* 72–82). This work probably dates to the early second century B.C. In the *Astronomical Book* the angel Uriel guides Enoch to understand the itineraries of the luminaries of heaven. The movements of the sun (*1 En.* 72:2–37), the moon (*1 En.* 73:1–74:17), and the stars (*1 En.* 75:1–9) are explained to Enoch, as well as nature of the twelve winds (*1 En.* 76:1–14), the four directions (*1 En.* 77:1–4), the seven mountains (*1 En.* 77:5), the seven rivers (*1 En.* 77:6–9), and the waxing and waning of the moon (*1 En.* 78:1–17). Enoch writes these things for his son Methuselah, as well as further visions regarding astronomy and the calendar.

5. *Animal Apocalypse* (*1 Enoch* 85–90). The *Animal Apocalypse* (*1 En.* 85–90) is the larger of two sections that comprise *Dream Visions* (*1 En.* 83–90) of *1 Enoch*. The *Animal Apocalypse* probably dates to the second century B.C. It summarizes biblical history in the form of an allegory, describing biblical personages and nations under the guise of various animals. The account begins with the creation of Adam and continues to the time of eschatological judgment exercised by "the Lord of the sheep" on those who have sinned against God. Adam is represented as a bull, Eve as a heifer, and Noah as a white bull who "became a man" (*1 En.* 85:3–10). The angels who sinned with women are stars that fell from heaven and sired a monstrous race (*1 En.* 86:1–6). Good animals that return to the house of the Lord of the sheep are all transformed, becoming white bulls (*1 En.* 90:38). This transformation apparently indicates a return to the condition of Adam at the original creation.

6. Apocalypse of Weeks (1 Enoch 93:1–10; 91:11–17). The *Apocalypse of Weeks* (*1 En.* 93:1–10; 91:11–17) is but a small portion of the *Epistle of Enoch* (*1 En.* 91–108). [6] It probably dates to the early second century B.C. The *Apocalypse of Weeks* derives its name from its periodization of world history in a succession of ten so-called weeks (cf. the "seventy weeks" of Daniel 9:24–27). Enoch is said to be the seventh person to be born in the first of these ten weeks (*1 En.* 93:3). The weeks following are marked by times of iniquity as well as the appearance of righteous leadership. In the seventh part of the tenth week eternal judgment "will be executed on the Watchers" (*1 En.* 91:15)—that is, the angels who sinned by engaging in sexual relationship with women. [7] At this time "the first heaven will vanish and pass away, and a new heaven will appear, and all the powers of heaven will shine forever (with) sevenfold light" (*1 En.* 91:16). There will be "many weeks without number forever in goodness and in righteousness, and from then on sin will never again be mentioned" (*1 En.* 91:17).

7. Second Enoch. This work probably dates to the late first century A.D., although some scholars date *2 Enoch* much later. Since its extant manuscript attestation comes from Old Slavonic, this work is also known as *Slavonic Apocalypse of Enoch*. There are two recensions of the work, one much longer than the other.

Second Enoch expands the brief biblical account of the life of Enoch found in Gen. 5:21–32. It consists of two main parts. The first section (*2 En.* 1–68) describes Enoch's journey through the seven heavens. In the longer recension, Enoch sees the eighth, ninth, and tenth heavens as well. God instructs Enoch during this journey about the creation of

---

6. The order of presentation is problematic in the Ethiopic text, where the last three weeks appear before the first seven. This is apparently due to dislocation of *1 En.* 91:11–17 in the Ethiopic text; a Qumran Aramaic manuscript has the expected order. On the problem of dislocation of *1 Enoch* 91:1–17 see Matthew Black, *The Book of Enoch, or 1 Enoch: A New English Edition with Commentary and Textual Notes*, Studia in Veteris Testamenti pseudepigrapha, ed. A. M. Denis and M. de Jonge (Leiden: E. J. Brill, 1985), 287–89.

7. For a helpful treatment of the influence of the Watchers motif, see the following collection of essays: Angela Kim Harkins, Kelley Coblentz Bautch, and John C. Endres, ed., *The Watchers in Jewish and Christian Traditions* (Minneapolis: Fortress, 2014).

the world and the sin of Adam. Enoch returns to his earthly home and describes the revelation he received. The second section (*2 En.* 69–73) describes the lives of Enoch's descendants, Methusalam and Nir. The work concludes with a brief account of the Flood.

8. Book of Jubilees. *Jubilees* was probably written originally in Hebrew, and dates to the second century B.C. It is largely a paraphrastic retelling of Genesis and part of Exodus, sometimes with drastic alteration of the biblical text.[8] Chapter 23 of *Jubilees* stands out from the rest of the book in that it uses language that is apocalyptic in nature. Following an account of Abraham's death and burial, *Jubilees* 23 speaks of deteriorating conditions and shortening lifespan that will beset evil generations "until the day of the great judgment" (*Jub.* 23:11). The Lord will send a plague of judgment, which will be followed by a reversal of bad conditions, a lengthening of lifespan, and a restoration of peace and blessing. Moses is told to "write these words because thus it is written and set upon the heavenly tablets as a testimony for eternal generations" (*Jub.* 23:32).

9. Fourth Ezra (2 Esdras 3–14). *Fourth Ezra* describes a revelation received by Ezra in Babylon thirty years after the destruction of Jerusalem (i.e., 556 B.C.). However, the work was written much later than this, probably around A.D. 100.[9] The Babylonian destruction of Jerusalem recounted in this work is actually a foil for the Roman destruction of Jerusalem in A.D. 70.

Fourth Ezra consists of seven visions or dreams received by Ezra (or, Salathiel) while he was in Babylon. In the first vision (*4 Ezra* 3:1–5:20) the angel Uriel responds to Ezra's questions concerning the origin of sin and suffering. When Ezra asks for signs regarding future events, the angel discloses cosmic and terrestrial changes that will accompany these events. In the second vision (*4 Ezra* 5:21–6:34), the angel explains the fate of those who die before the completion of the present age. The angel also responds to Ezra's questions concerning when the first age will end and when the next age will begin. In the third vision (*4 Ezra* 6:35–9:25), the angel reveals to Ezra the destiny of the righteous and the unrighteous. The

---

8. Wintermute describes the relationship of the book of Jubilees to the corresponding biblical episodes with such verbs as "condensed," "omitted," "expurgated," "explained," "supplemented," and "radically recast." See O. S. Wintermute, "Jubilees (Second Century B.C.): A New Translation and Introduction," in *The Old Testament Pseudepigrapha*, vol. 2, Anchor Bible Reference Library (New York: Doubleday, 1985), 35.

9. Stone is probably correct in maintaining the essential unity of this work and rejecting source-critical analyses that view *4 Ezra* as a composite work clumsily assembled by a later editor. He says, "*4 Ezra* is clearly the work of a single, consummate literary craftsman. All explanations must start from this fact." See Michael E. Stone, "On Reading an Apocalypse," in *Mysteries and Revelations: Apocalyptic Studies since the Uppsala Colloquium*, ed. John J. Collins and James H. Charlesworth, Journal for the Study of the Pseudepigrapha: Supplement Series, ed. James H. Charlesworth, vol. 9 (Sheffield: Sheffield Academic Press, 1991), 72.

angel also speaks of the death of "my son the Messiah" after four hundred years. In the fourth vision (*4 Ezra* 9:26–10:59), Ezra sees a woman in mourning for her deceased son. The woman is transformed into a city, and the angel explains that this city is the heavenly Zion. In the fifth vision (*4 Ezra* 11:1–12:51), Ezra sees an eagle coming up from the sea with twelve feathered wings and three heads. A creature like a lion emerges from the forest and warns the eagle of its imminent demise. The angel identifies the eagle as "the fourth kingdom which appeared in a vision to your brother Daniel" (*4 Ezra* 12:11). The lion is identified as "the Messiah whom the Most High has kept until the end of days, who will arise from the posterity of David, and will come and speak to them" (*4 Ezra* 12:32).

In the sixth vision (*4 Ezra* 13:1–58), Ezra sees a man coming up from the sea with power to destroy his enemies. The angel explains that "this is he whom the Most High has been keeping for many ages, who will himself deliver his creation" (*4 Ezra* 13:26). This messianic figure is referred to as "my Son." In the seventh and final vision (*4 Ezra* 14:1–48), the angel instructs Ezra to select five men, to whom Ezra will dictate for forty days the contents of ninety-four books. Twenty-four of these books (i.e., the canonical writings of the Hebrew Bible) are to be made public by Ezra, but the other seventy books are reserved for "the wise among your people" (*4 Ezra* 14:46). These secret books are said to contain "the spring of understanding, the fountain of wisdom, and the river of knowledge" (*4 Ezra* 14:47).

10. Second Baruch. *Second Baruch* was probably written in the latter part of the first century A.D. Since the complete text of *2 Baruch* is extant only in Syriac, this text is also known as *Syriac Apocalypse of Baruch*. In structure, theme, and theology *2 Baruch* closely resembles *4 Ezra*.

Charles identifies seven sections in *2 Baruch*, all but one of them separated by fasts.[10] In the first section (*2 Bar.* 1:1–5:6), the Lord reveals to Baruch the coming destruction of Jerusalem by the Babylonians and the captivity of its inhabitants. In the second section (*2 Bar.* 6:1–8:3), angels descend from heaven to remove for safekeeping sacred objects taken from the temple prior to its destruction. In the third section (*2 Bar.* 9:1–12:5), Baruch laments the fall of Zion and warns Babylon of divine wrath that awaits her. In the fourth section (*2 Bar.* 13:1–20:5), Baruch is promised safety and preservation "until the consummation of the times" (*2 Bar.* 13:3). The Lord also responds to Baruch's questions regarding suffering of the righteous and prosperity of the wicked.

In the fifth section (*2 Bar.* 21:1–35:5), Baruch is promised a sign "at the end of days" (*2 Bar.* 25:1). The sign will be marked by twelve sepa-

10. R. H. Charles, ed., *The Apocrypha and Pseudepigrapha of the Old Testament in English, with Introductions and Critical and Explanatory Notes to the Several Books*, vol. 2 (Oxford: Clarendon, 1913), 474.

rate periods, each with "its own special characteristics" (*2 Bar.* 27:1). These periods will be followed by revelation of Messiah and final consummation. In the sixth section (*2 Bar.* 36:1–46:7) Baruch, in a vision, sees a vine and a cedar tree alongside a forest of other trees. These symbolize destruction of the kingdom that destroyed Zion and a succession of four empires (*2 Bar.* 39:3–5). The last of these will be destroyed by the messianic kingdom (*2 Bar.* 39:7). In the seventh section (*2 Bar.* 47:1–77:26), Baruch receives illumination regarding resurrection and the consummation of the world. The work concludes with "the letter of Baruch, the son of Neriah, which he wrote to the nine and a half tribes," urging them to faithfulness and trust in God (*2 Bar.* 78–86). After writing this letter, Baruch folds and seals it, ties it to an eagle's neck, and sends it to its intended recipients (*2 Bar.* 87).

11. Apocalypse of Abraham. This text probably dates to the first or second century A.D. It is extant only in an Old Slavonic translation. The *Apocalypse of Abraham* has two major sections. In the first section (*Apoc. Ab.* 1–8), the youth Abraham comes to realize that the idols worshiped by his father are subject to physical damage and permanent destruction. Abraham concludes that these idols cannot really be gods. Since his father crafted these idols, Abraham asks, "Is it not he rather who is god for his gods, because they come into being from his sculpting, his planning, and his skill?" (*Apoc. Ab.* 3:3–4). God then reveals himself to Abraham and tells him to leave his father's house to avoid the coming divine judgment. In the second section (*Apoc. Ab.* 9–32), the angel Iaoel transports Abraham to heaven. Abraham sees seven visions: a great light accompanied by a crowd of angels (*Apoc. Ab.* 15:5–7); an approaching fire making a loud noise (*Apoc. Ab.* 17:1–3); a fiery throne surrounded by awesome beings (*Apoc. Ab.* 18:1–14); expanses under the firmament (*Apoc. Ab.* 19:4–9); the earth and its inhabitants (*Apoc. Ab.* 21:2–7); the sins of the world (*Apoc. Ab.* 24:3–25:2); and the destruction of the temple (*Apoc. Ab.* 27:1–3).

12. Testament of Levi. The *Testament of Levi* is but one portion of a larger work known as the *Testaments of the Twelve Patriarchs*. It is probably of Jewish origin and likely dates to the first or second century B.C. In the apocalypse embedded in sections 2–5 of the *Testament of Levi,* the patriarch is transported through the seven heavens and given a guided tour by an angel. The first heaven is the lowest and gloomiest of the seven, since "it witnesses all the unrighteous deeds of men" (*T. Levi* 3:1). In the second heaven "are all the spirits of retribution for vengeance on the wicked" (*T. Levi* 3:2). The third heaven has "warrior hosts" who will punish the wicked on the day of judgment (*T. Levi* 3:3). The fourth heaven contains thrones and powers that offer praise to God continually. In the fifth and sixth heavens are angels who minister on the Lord's behalf. In the seventh heaven, which is the highest of all, "the Great Glory dwells, in the holy of holies, far above all holiness" (*T. Levi* 3:4). Levi witnesses an eschatological scene of judgment accompanied by various cosmic and terrestrial signs. The angel opens to Levi the gates of heaven, where he beholds the holy temple and the Most High sitting on a glorious throne. The angel returns Levi to earth and instructs him to take vengeance on Shechem, because of the rape of Dinah his sister (*T. Levi* 5:3).

13. Testament of Abraham. The *Testament of Abraham* describes Abraham's response to his impending death. Opinions on the date of this work range from the first century B.C. to the second century A.D. The *Testament of Abraham* has two major sections. One section focuses on a visit from Michael the archangel to inform Abraham, who is said to be "the Heavenly One's true friend" (*T. Ab.* 2:5), that his time to die has arrived. But Abraham refuses to cooperate. A second section focuses on a visit from Death to inform Abraham that his time to die has arrived. Using a bit of trickery, Death is successful.

14. Apocalypse of Zephaniah. This text probably dates to the first century B.C. or the first century A.D. Although surviving manuscripts are in Coptic, the work was probably written originally in Greek. In this work the angel of the Lord shows Zephaniah various scenes pertaining to his city. Zephaniah sees a number of visions: a vision of angels recording deeds of the righteous (*Apoc. Zeph.* 3:1–9); a vision of ugly angels responsible for the souls of the ungodly (*Apoc. Zeph.* 4:1–10); a vision of the heavenly city (*Apoc. Zeph.* 5:1–6); a vision of a great sea and the angel Eremiel in Hades (*Apoc. Zeph.* 6:1–17); a vision of the two manuscripts (*Apoc. Zeph.* 7:1–11). The work concludes with three successive trumpets announcing divine intentions.

15. Testament of Moses. Strictly speaking, the *Testament of Moses* is not an apocalypse. However, it has sufficient apocalyptic content to warrant its inclusion here. The date of the *Testament of Moses* is uncertain, partly because of its complex compositional history. Suggestions range from the second century B.C. to the first part of the second century A.D. In this testament, an aged Moses gives instructions to his successor Joshua regarding God's plans for the nation of Israel. Faithfulness to God's commandments will be rewarded, and disobedience will be punished. A faithful Levite named Taxo will arise who will prefer death to transgression of the Lord's commandments. Taxo's commitment to the God of Israel is clear: "Let us die rather than transgress the commandments of the Lord of lords, the God of our fathers" (*T. Mos.* 9:6). The heavens and earth will experience cataclysmic change, Gentiles will be punished, and Israel will be exalted. Moses encourages Joshua to overcome his personal feelings of inadequacy and to take comfort in God's just dealings with all people.

The extrabiblical apocalypses surveyed in the preceding summary provide valuable insight into the development of Jewish apocalypticism during the intertestamental period. This literature significantly shaped the religious thinking of at least some segments of Judaism during the third, second, and first centuries B.C.

Apocalypticism at Qumran

An Apocalyptic Community? Discovery of the Dead Sea Scrolls in 1947, and in the years following, led to the realization that among the writings prized by the **Qumran community** were extrabiblical texts with apocalyptic material. Perhaps the clearest example of Qumran interest in apocalyptic literature is the eleven fragmentary manuscripts of the *Book of Enoch* found at Qumran in September 1952.[11] Scholars are not agreed as to the degree to which this community entertained apocalyptic expectations.[12] Some specialists have described the Qumran community as an apocalyptic community.[13] According to these scholars, this group saw themselves as living on the threshold of eschatological fulfillment, awaiting salvific deliverance that would come through sudden divine intervention. Other scholars have questioned the apocalyptic identity of the Qumran community, insisting on a stricter use of the term *apocalyptic* that would exclude its applica-

11.   For a brief discussion of the Aramaic fragments of Enoch see Michael A. Knibb, *The Ethiopic Book of Enoch: A New Edition in the Light of the Aramaic Dead Sea Fragments*, vol. 2, *Introduction, Translation and Commentary* (Oxford: Clarendon, 1978), 6–15.

12.   In addition to the literature cited below, see especially the following contributions: John J. Collins, *Apocalypticism in the Dead Sea Scrolls*, The Literature of the Dead Sea Scrolls, ed. George Brooke (London and New York: Routledge, 1997); David Flusser, *Qumran and Apocalypticism*, trans. Azzan Yadin, Judaism of the Second Temple Period, vol. 1 (Grand Rapids and Jerusalem: Eerdmans and Magnes, 2007); Ida Fröhlich, "Pesher, Apocalyptical Literature and Qumran," in *The Madrid Qumran Congress: Proceedings of the International Congress on the Dead Sea Scrolls, Madrid 18–21 March, 1991*, ed. Julio Trebolle Barrera and Luis Vegas Montaner, Studies on the Texts of the Desert of Judah, ed. F. García Martínez and A. S. van der Woude, vol. 11,1 (Leiden/New York/Cologne: E. J. Brill, 1992), 295–305; Florentino García Martínez, *Qumran and Apocalyptic: Studies on the Aramaic Texts from Qumran*, Studies on the Texts of the Desert of Judah, vol. 9 (Leiden: Brill, 1992); Florentino García Martínez, "Apocalypticism in the Dead Sea Scrolls," in *The Continuum History of Apocalypticism*, ed. Bernard J. McGinn, John J. Collins, and Stephen J. Stein (New York and London: Continuum, 2003), 89–111; Carol A. Newsom, "Apocalyptic and the Discourse of the Qumran Community," *Journal of Near Eastern Studies* 49 (1990): 135–44; Al Wolters, "Apocalyptic and the Copper Scroll," *Journal of Near Eastern Studies* 49 (1990): 145–54; and Leo G. Perdue, "Continuing Streams: Apocalyptic Wisdom in Qumran," in *The Sword and the Stylus: An Introduction to Wisdom in the Age of Empires* (Grand Rapids and Cambridge: Eerdmans, 2008), 372–87.

13.   So, for example, Cross and (with qualification) Collins. See Frank Moore Cross, "The Early History of the Apocalyptic Community at Qumrân," in *Canaanite Myth and Hebrew Epic: Essays in the History of the Religion of Israel* (Cambridge: Harvard University Press, 1973), 326–42; John J. Collins, "Was the Dead Sea Sect an Apocalyptic Movement?," in *Archaeology and History in the Dead Sea Scrolls: The New York University Conference in Memory of Yigael Yadin*, ed. Lawrence H. Shiffman, Journal for the Study of the Pseudepigrapha: Supplement Series, ed. James H. Charlesworth, vol. 8 (Sheffield: JSOT Press, 1990), 25–51.

tion to this group. If this term were reserved only for writings that can properly be defined as apocalypses, it might be doubtful that the Qumran community was apocalyptic in nature, since the group did not actually produce an apocalypse. However, the presence of apocalypticism is not dependent on the production of written apocalypses. Once this distinction is accepted, it is difficult to avoid the conclusion that the Qumran community was an apocalyptic community.

Dead Sea Scrolls with Apocalyptic Elements. The Qumran community had an interest in apocalyptic writings and made use of these texts in formulating their own identity. It is not coincidental that four of the five composite sections that make up the *Book of Enoch* are attested in multiple copies at Qumran. The book of Daniel is attested in at least eight fragmentary manuscripts discovered at Qumran, one of which (4QDanᶜ) may date as early as the late second century B.C.[14] There is also 4QFlorilegium, which contains two citations from the book of Daniel (Dan. 11:32; 12:10) that are introduced by the formula "which is written in the book of the prophet Daniel" (אש[ר כתוב בספר דניאל הנביא). It is clear that the book of Daniel, like the *Book of Enoch*, was very important to the life of this community. One also finds apocalyptic emphases in certain of the sectarian scrolls that were prized by this group, such as the *Community Rule*, the *War Scroll*, and *New Jerusalem*. This community saw itself as living in times anticipated by the Old Testament prophets. The Habakkuk commentary offers an interpretation of that biblical book in light of current events unfolding in the life of the Qumran community. This community regarded itself as participating in the struggle between the sons of light and the sons of darkness. The covenanters of Qumran awaited divine deliverance that would rectify the injustices of the present world order and initiate a completely new beginning. Their worldview had much in common with the worldview found in Jewish apocalyptic texts of the intertestamental period.

Dimant identifies a number of Dead Sea scrolls that have material at least similar to that found in apocalyptic literature.[15] She divides these works into two groups based on their language, whether Hebrew or Aramaic. These texts contribute to our understanding of Jewish apocalypticism in the period immediately before and during New Testament times.

---

14. See Eugene Ulrich, "Daniel Manuscripts from Qumran. Part 2: Preliminary Editions of 4QDanᵇ and 4QDanᶜ," *Bulletin of the American Schools of Oriental Research* 274 (1989): 3–26.

15. See Devorah Dimant, "Apocalyptic Texts at Qumran," in *The Community of the Renewed Covenant: The Notre Dame Symposium on the Dead Sea Scrolls*, ed. Eugene Ulrich and James VanderKam, Christianity and Judaism in Antiquity Series, ed. Gregory E. Sterling, vol. 10 (South Bend, IN: University of Notre Dame Press, 1994), 191. The charts presented here are taken from Dimant's essay.

Hebrew Pseudepigrapha	
Jubilees	4Q176 19–20; 4Q216; 4Q218–224; 1Q17–18; 2Q19–20; 3Q5; 11Q12
Text close to *Jubilees*	4Q482–483
Pseudo-Jubilees	4Q217; 4Q225–227
Testament of Naphtali	4Q215
Words of Moses	1Q22
Moses Apocryphon	2Q21
Pseudo-Ezekiel	4Q385–388; 4Q391
Pseudo-Moses	4Q385a; 4Q387a; 4Q388a; 4Q389; 4Q390
Pseudepigraphic work	4Q459–460
Prophetic fragments	4Q522; 1Q25; 2Q23; 6Q10

Aramaic Texts	
Book of Giants	4Q203; 4Q530–532; 4Q533(?); 1Q23; 1Q24(?); 2Q26(?); 6Q8
New Jerusalem	4Q554–555; 1Q32; 2Q34; 5Q15; 11Q18
Visions of Amram	4Q543–548
Aramaic Levi	4Q213–214; 1Q21
Apocryphon of Levi	4Q537; 4Q540–541
Testament of Qahat	4Q542
Patriarchal Pseudepigraphon	4Q538–539
Aramaic Apocalypse	4Q246
Prayer of Nabonidus	4Q242
Proto-Esther (?)	4Q550
Daniel-Susanna	4Q551
(?) *Elect of God*	4Q534
Four Kingdoms Apocryphon	4Q552; 4Q553
Vision (?)	4Q556–558
Words of Michael	4Q529
Miscellaneous	4Q535–536; 4Q549

Tobit	4Q196–199
Genesis Apocryphon	1Q20
1 Enoch	Enoch: 4Q201–202; 4Q204–207; 4Q212; Astronomical Book: 4Q208–211

Several of these texts deserve special mention in light of their relevance to the study of Jewish apocalyptic literature.

Community Rule. This text was popular at Qumran, as indicated by the fact that twelve manuscripts of this document were found among the Dead Sea scrolls. The most complete and best preserved of these manuscripts is 1QS. While the *Community Rule* is not an apocalypse, columns 3 and 4 contain apocalyptic elements. The *Community Rule* probably dates to the second part of the second century B.C. According to this text two spirits influence the behavior of all mankind: the spirit of truth and the spirit of darkness. The sons of light are ruled by the Prince of Light; the sons of darkness are ruled by the Angel of Darkness. Truth and falsehood are engaged in an ongoing struggle: "Truth abhors the works of falsehood, and falsehood hates all the ways of truth" (1QS 4:17). This struggle will not continue indefinitely, for "God has ordained an end for falsehood" (1QS 14:18). The righteous will be vindicated and perfected.

War Scroll, or War of the Sons of Light against the Sons of Darkness. This work, designated 1QM, probably dates to the end of the first century B.C. Apocalyptic themes appear in columns 1 and 15–19, which warn of a final clash between the sons of light and the sons of darkness. This will be a time of great tribulation and distress for Israel. However, the people of God will be vindicated. They will gain victory over bands of the Kittim, who will be forever vanquished. The sons of the Covenant must be strong and persevere during their time of trial and tribulation. The King of Glory is with them. The author exclaims, "This is the day appointed by him for the defeat and overthrow of the Prince of the kingdom of wickedness, and he will send eternal succour to the company of his redeemed by the might of the princely Angel of the kingdom of Michael" (1QM 17:5–6).

New Jerusalem. This Aramaic text, the largest Qumran fragment of which is designated 5Q15, describes in detail the measurements of an eschatological Jerusalem. An angel leads the writer on a tour of this city, pointing out the dimensions of the city and its contents. The description resembles certain biblical passages, such as Ezekiel 40–48, Isaiah 54:11–12, and Revelation 21.

So far as is known, the Qumran community did not produce any apocalypses. Instead, its members looked to other sources for authoritative spiritual guidance. A major focus for them was the Hebrew

Scriptures, which they studied, copied, and preserved for posterity. Judging by the numbers of copies that have been preserved, Isaiah, Psalms, and Deuteronomy held special importance for them. Another source of spiritual guidance consisted of extrabiblical sectarian documents that governed life and conduct within this separatistic community, such as the *Community Rule*. These writings served to clarify and supplement the biblical writings. Members of the community also looked to their Teacher of Righteousness for an understanding of the present struggle between the sons of light and the sons of darkness. The documents they preserved show familiarity with apocalyptic ways of thinking.

CHARACTERISTIC FEATURES OF APOCALYPTIC LITERATURE

We will now consider some common features and themes found in Jewish apocalyptic literature. A few things should be kept in mind, so as not to distort the overall picture with regard to apocalyptic literature. First, not all features or themes described here will be found in every apocalyptic text. This literature is diverse, multifaceted, and from various time periods. This discussion should therefore not be thought of as a checklist of essential features to be found in all apocalyptic works. Second, the presence of a few of these characteristics is not in itself adequate reason for classifying the genre of a particular text as apocalyptic. Although these characteristics are commonly found in apocalyptic literature, they do not by themselves define what an apocalypse is. Their presence merely signals the possibility that a particular text may belong to this genre. Third, it is possible that such a listing of features and themes can give a wrong impression about the homogeneity of this literature. Apocalyptic texts are not all alike. In spite of striking similarities, there are significant differences among them.

The following six features of Jewish apocalyptic texts, to a large degree, characterize this genre: (1) a preference for literary rather than oral expression; (2) content that claims to be revelatory in nature; (3) an emphasis on dreams and visions as a means of receiving revelatory messages; (4) pseudonymous authorship that attributes material to a famous hero of the past; (5) an emphasis on hiddenness and secrecy; and (6) pervasive symbolism as a way of describing revelatory messages.

Literary Expression

An apocalypse represents first and foremost a genre of literature. In this distinctive form of writing, an ancient figure is portrayed as having received a divine revelation. In many cases this revelation is said to come through some sort of angelic mediation. The writer usually sets forth his revelation within a narrative framework that describes the attendant circumstances that accompanied the revelation. Through this narrative framework he hopes to tell a convincing and perhaps entertaining story, yet one that has a profound theological purpose. That purpose has to do with failures of the present world system and approaching divine judgment accompanied by salvific intervention on behalf of a faithful remnant. The writer may focus on past events of history, but he does so with an eye to the future. He is concerned to show where history is ultimately headed. He portrays how God will turn the present worldly crisis and cruel acts of human evil into a cataclysmic supernatural victory. The **apocalyptist** who assumes this theological role chooses to do so by a literary medium. He is a writer.

The Old Testament prophets, on the other hand, were largely social reformers who preached a message of warning with regard to social ills and injustices found within Israel or the neighboring cultures. On occasion these prophets looked to the future and announced what the God of Israel would do in days to come. Many prophets recorded their prophecies in written form for posterity, or others did so in their behalf. But their public ministries were mainly oral in nature. They preached sermons, delivered oracles, announced woes, pronounced judgments, presented accusations in the form of legal complaints, and much more. Sometimes they reduced their inspired presentations to manuscript or scroll, recording them for later generations. But they were first and foremost speakers who exhorted their audiences to action.

The same is true of early rabbinic tradition. The Jewish rabbis were teachers who relied on oral delivery to convey their instructions to devoted student audiences. Only at a later time was this traditional material codified in a written corpus known as the Talmud. The two major divisions of the Talmud, Mishnah and Gemara, provide insight into what illustrious rabbis of the past said and taught. A common format adopted for the presentation of this material is "Rabbi so-and-so said." Such quotations are often followed by citations from other rabbis as well. Rabbinic instruction in the earliest period was oral. Only later did students and admirers reduce these oral teachings to a written format in order to preserve them. By contrast, the communication medium of choice for apocalyptists was a written format rather than the spoken word. *A fundamental feature of apocalyptic literature is its literary expression.*

Revelatory Content

Apocalyptic literature was written with a revelatory purpose in mind. Its content concerns matters that are assumed to be inaccessible apart from divine revelation. Its subject matter appeals to the imagination and seeks to satisfy common curiosities that human beings have about the afterlife. It is understood that such things lie beyond the ability of the unaided human intellect to grasp fully. The apocalyptist professes to have a key for unlocking access to such information. He, or the ancient hero for whom he speaks, claims to have received a revelation that provides insight that others lack. It is this claim to special insight that gives apocalyptic literature an esoteric dimension. The apocalyptist professes to be the recipient of revelations that disclose and clarify events of the past, the present, and even the future.

Apocalyptic writers make such claims directly and without equivocation. The *Book of the Watchers*, for example, begins with the following claim:

> The words of the blessing of Enoch according to which he blessed the chosen and righteous who must be present on the day of distress (which is appointed) for the removal of all the wicked and impious. And Enoch answered and said, (There was) a righteous man whose eyes were opened by the Lord, and he saw a holy vision in the heavens which the angels showed to me. And I heard everything from them, and I understood what I saw, but not for this generation, but for a distant generation which will come (*1 En.* 1:1–2).

Other apocalyptic writers make similar claims regarding revelation. In the *Animal Apocalypse* Enoch says:

> And after this I saw another dream, and I will show it all to you, my son. And Enoch raised (his voice) and said to his son Methuselah, To you I speak, my son. Hear my words, and incline your ear to the dream-vision of your father (*1 En.* 85:1–2).

Enoch goes on to provide a sweeping survey of historical events presented as though he were prophetically announcing these events in advance of their fulfillment. However, the prophecy is *ex eventu*, written not by Enoch but by an author looking back on events that by his time had already transpired.

Occasionally apocalyptic writers claim that their revelation is an advance beyond that of Old Testament writers. In *4 Ezra* the angel who interprets Ezra's dream compares the revelation given to Ezra to that given to Daniel. The angel says,

> The eagle which you saw coming up from the sea is the fourth kingdom which appeared in a vision to your

> brother Daniel. But it was not explained to him as I now
> explain or have explained it to you (*4 Ezra* 12:11).

A conclusion can be drawn from such examples. *A basic feature of apocalyptic literature is its claim to divine revelation that the writer either appropriates for himself or attributes to a distant hero of the past for whom he speaks.* It is this revelatory quality that gives apocalyptic literature its putative authority and religious appeal.

Dreams and Visions

Apocalyptists claim to receive revelations through dreams and visions. In antiquity the subconscious state of mind that one experiences when asleep or in a trancelike state of mind was thought to be optimal for receiving revelation. The deity used the relative passivity of a human recipient to convey messages. Dreams therefore exercised powerful influence within cultures of the ancient Near East.[16] Interpreting the significance of such dreams was often the prerogative of a special caste of wise men who held powerful positions of political and religious influence.

In the *Animal Apocalypse* Enoch describes the revelation that he received in this way: "And this is the vision which I saw while I was asleep" (*1 En.* 90:40). Elsewhere a revelation comes to Enoch in the form of a dream (*1 En.* 85:1), or a dream-vision (*1 En.* 85:2), or a vision seen while in bed (*1 En.* 85:3). The recipient of revelation describes himself as "seeing" things while "looking with [his] eyes" in circumstances viewed "as [he] was sleeping" (*1 En.* 86:1). Things seen during such experiences are not tangible realities but imagined experiences. Such visionary experience may be the result of an intent and prolonged gaze. Enoch says, "And I looked until the time that [thirty-seven] shepherds had pastured (the sheep) in the same way, and, each individually, they all completed their time like the first ones" (*1 En.* 90:1).

Fourth Ezra describes visions that came to Ezra in the form of dreams as he slept (*4 Ezra* 11:1; 13:1). In a similar fashion Baruch exclaims, "And after this, behold, the heavens opened, and I saw (a vision), and strength was given me, and a voice was heard from on high" (*2 Bar.* 22:1). In the *Book of the Watchers* Enoch says, "(There was) a righteous man whose eyes were opened by the Lord, and he saw a holy vision in the heavens which the angels showed to me" (*1 En.* 1:2). In the *Similitudes of Enoch* parables come to Enoch in the form of visions (*1 En.*

---

16. For a comprehensive study see A. Leo Oppenheim, *The Interpretation of Dreams in the Ancient Near East, with a Translation of an Assyrian Dream-book*, Transactions of the American Philosophical Society, vol. 46 (Philadelphia: American Philosophical Society, 1956), 3.

37:1). In the *Testament of Levi* a revelation of the seven heavens comes as "sleep fell upon me" (*T. Levi* 2:5). References to dreams and visions form a common thread woven into the fabric of apocalyptic literature.

Such dreams could be terribly disturbing to the recipient, sometimes causing uncontrollable weeping, tremendous apprehension, or deep anxiety. They could be so frightening as to leave one in a shattered frame of mind. Ezra says, "Then I awoke, and my body shuddered violently, and my soul was so troubled that it fainted" (*4 Ezra* 5:14; cf. 12:3). In a similar way Enoch says,

> And I was asleep in the middle of them; and I woke up and saw everything. And this is the vision which I saw while I was asleep, and I woke up and blessed the Lord of righteousness and ascribed glory to him. But after this I wept bitterly, and my tears did not stop until I could not endure it: when I looked, they ran down on account of that which I saw, for everything will come to pass and be fulfilled; and all the deeds of men in their order were shown to me. That night I remembered my first dream, and because of it I wept and was disturbed, because I had seen that vision (*1 En.* 90:39–42).

Ezra describes his circumstances when a vision came to him in Babylon: "I was troubled as I lay on my bed, and my thoughts welled up in my heart" (*4 Ezra* 3:1). He describes his reaction following the vision: "Then I awoke, and my body shuddered violently, and my soul was so troubled that it fainted" (*4 Ezra* 5:14). As a result of the vision Ezra was left "in great perplexity of mind and great fear" (*4 Ezra* 12:3). Such language is not unlike that used in the book of Daniel to describe individuals who were recipients of divine communication (cf. Dan. 2:1, 3; 4:5, 19; 7:15, 28; 8:27; 10:7–9).

A common motif runs throughout these passages. Apocalyptists were not so much philosophers and rational thinkers who conducted research into the perplexities of life and subsequently wrote in calm cerebral fashion about their findings. They were visionaries whose dreams were understood to convey otherworldly realities that lay beyond the realm of normal human inquiry. They were dreamers who gazed into celestial realms. They were **seers** whose startling and bizarre visions brought surprising disclosures. *Dreams and visions play a prominent role in apocalyptic literature.*

Pseudonymous Authorship

Apocalyptists often made use of pseudonymity, attributing authorship of compositions to famous heroes of the past. These personalities were normally people well known from biblical history. However, apocalyptic writers supplied additional information about these individuals, describing their involvement in otherworldly activities. Sometimes these personalities were major figures of biblical history, such as Abraham or Moses. Other times they were figures who played a lesser role in biblical accounts, such as Enoch or Levi.

Regarding Enoch, the writer of Genesis makes an intriguing comment: "Enoch walked faithfully with God; then he was no more, because God took him away" (Gen. 5:24). The absence in Genesis of further explanation about Enoch's experience led to speculation with regard to what had happened to him. This speculation reached its apex in the *Book of Enoch*. One component of this text, the *Book of the Watchers*, begins this way:

> The words of the blessing of Enoch according to which
> he blessed the chosen and righteous who must be pres-
> ent on the day of distress (which is appointed) for the
> removal of all the wicked and impious (*1 En.* 1:1).

In what follows, Enoch explains the revelation that came to him concerning inappropriate angelic activity that resulted in divine judgment. Although the *Book of the Watchers* begins by referring to Enoch in the third person, a shift is quickly made and Enoch himself speaks in the first person. The reader is supposed to think that it is Enoch who is disclosing a revelation given to him by God. By attributing this work to Enoch, the writer apparently hopes to ensure that readers regard it as authoritative revelation. Other apocalyptic texts use the first person in a similar way.[17] *Pseudonymity is a common feature of Jewish apocalyptic literature.* Apocalyptists adopt this literary device as a way of enhancing the perceived authority of their writing.

Hiddenness and Secrecy

Apocalyptic literature was written with a particular audience in mind. That audience was an exclusive circle of devotees who belonged to an eschatological community. Often at the expense of persecution and disenfranchisement from society, they believed that they had received enlightenment concerning the struggle between good and evil. Apocalyptic literature was written for such an audience. It was not written for those on the outside. It did not attempt to speak in direct or easily understandable terms for the sake of those who might be curious but had not yet committed themselves to the movement.

---

17. Cf. *1 En.* 39:2–5; *1 En.* 85:1–2; *4 Ezra* 3:1–2; *2 Bar.* 1:1; 3:1; *T. Levi* 2:1–2, 7–8.

This literature was intended for the initiated, who preferred the indirect and allusive language of symbolism. Apocalyptic literature therefore has a certain opaqueness to it. Significant effort is required to understand its mysteries. Its interpretation is less than obvious. It has a hidden quality. In some cases its recipients are encouraged to seal it up, conceal its contents, and maintain secrecy about it. It was not intended for wide circulation among those whose interest was merely casual or minimal.

In *4 Ezra* the recipient of revelation is instructed to write down the revelation. Part of the revelation is to be made public, and part is to be kept secret. The Lord says to Ezra:

> I will light in your heart the lamp of understanding, which shall not be put out until what you are about to write is finished. And when you have finished, some things you shall make public, and some you shall deliver in secret to the wise (*4 Ezra* 14:25–26).

Later, the Lord gives instructions to Ezra:

> Make public the twenty-four books that you wrote first and let the worthy and the unworthy read them; but keep the seventy that were written last, in order to give them to the wise among your people. For in them is the spring of understanding, the fountain of wisdom, and the river of knowledge (*4 Ezra* 14:45–47).

The point is that while the twenty-four books of the Hebrew Bible may be read with profit by both those who are inside and those who are outside the community, the seventy books revealed to Ezra are only for those within the community. These books are hidden from the unworthy; they are reserved for the wise among Ezra's people. They are for those who are on the inside looking out, not for those who are on the outside looking in. *The meaning of apocalyptic books is hidden and secret.*

Pervasive Symbolism

Apocalyptic literature is characterized by abundant use of figurative language and symbolism. Writers of apocalyptic literature intended to bombard their readers with bizarre and sometimes grotesque imagery that appealed more to the imagination than to the intellect. This imagery is often difficult to understand. The following passage in the *Animal Apocalypse* at first seems hopelessly complicated and mind-boggling.

And that white bull who became a man went out from
that vessel, and the three bulls with him. And one of
the three bulls was white, like that bull, and one of
them (was) red as blood, and one (was) black; and that
white bull passed away from them. And they began to
beget wild animals and birds, so that there arose from
them every kind of species: lions, tigers, wolves, dogs,
hyenas, wild-boars, foxes, badgers, pigs, falcons, vul-
tures, kites, eagles and ravens. But amongst them was
born a white bull. And they began to bite one another;
but that white bull which was born amongst them begat a wild ass and a white bull with it, and the wild asses
increased. But that bull which was born from it begat a
black wild-boar and a white sheep; and that wild-boar
begat many boars, and that sheep begat twelve sheep.
And when those twelve sheep had grown, they handed
one of their number over to the asses, and those asses
in turn handed that sheep over to the wolves; and that
sheep grew up amongst the wolves (*1 En.* 89:10–13).

This complex story is likely to tax the patience of all but the most per-
sistent of readers. The symbolism is so pervasive, and the meaning so
elusive, that a casual reader will be tempted simply to give up and find
something easier to read.

However, there are enough interpretive clues embedded in the text to
suggest a coherent explanation. It is clear from even a casual reading that
this apocalypse is an allegory based on Old Testament history. Animal
imagery is used to portray biblical characters and to summarize biblical
events and history. What is not immediately clear is what each of the animals is intended to represent. The meaning of the main elements in this
passage seems to be as follows. After the Noachian flood, Noah's posterity began to repopulate the earth destroyed by the flood. The various
predatory and unclean animals mentioned by Enoch represent nations
that would prove to be hostile to Israel. The biting attributed to these
animals represents human violence such as characterized the postdiluvian
period. The white bull represents Abraham. He was the father of Ishmael
and Isaac, represented respectively by a wild donkey and another white
bull. The black wild-boar represents Esau (i.e., Edom); the white sheep
represents Jacob (i.e., Israel). The wolves represent the Egyptians who
enslaved the Israelites. The Israelites are represented by the sheep.

The *Animal Apocalypse* makes coherent sense if one has an interpretive
key for the figurative language and a general familiarity with the biblical
texts that provide the basis of this allegorical account. All we need is a sufficient number of clues concerning the identity of the animals that are de-

scribed and a familiarity with the biblical texts to which the apocalyptist alludes. But without such help, most readers would be at a loss to understand what is going on in such a complicated account.[18] It is the pervasive symbolism that creates this difficulty for reader-comprehension. *And pervasive symbolism is a regular feature of Jewish apocalyptic literature.*

MAJOR THEMES OF APOCALYPTIC LITERATURE

In addition to the characteristic features of apocalyptic literature considered in the preceding section, there are a number of major themes that frequently appear in this literature. We shall consider the following seven themes: (1) developed angelology; (2) ethical dualism; (3) deterministic outlook; (4) belief in an imminent crisis; (5) presence of a faithful remnant; (6) warning of divine judgment; and (7) anticipation of eschatological hope.[19]

Developed Angelology

Apocalyptic literature stresses the involvement of angels in the activities that it describes. This emphasis on angels is evident in the significant role they play as mediating agents in the communication of divine revelation.[20] Angels sometimes transport a human recipient on an otherworldly journey, or they respond to requests for interpretation of enigmatic visions and dreams. Apocalyptic writers felt free to proliferate names of angelic messengers and to provide details concerning angelic activities in a way that goes well beyond the limited information concerning angels found in the Hebrew Bible. The Old Testament mentions only two angels by name, Gabriel and Michael (Dan. 8:16; 9:21; 10:13, 21; 12:1). By contrast, extrabiblical apocalyptic texts mention dozens of angels by name. Apocalyptic writers also expanded the role of angels beyond what the biblical accounts indicate, describing in great detail angelic involvement in human activities. Nowhere is this emphasis on angelic activity more clear than in the *Book of Enoch*,

---

18. For a commentary on this and related Enochian texts see especially the following helpful treatments: Matthew Black, *The Book of Enoch, or 1 Enoch: A New English Edition with Commentary and Textual Notes*, Studia in Veteris Testamenti Pseudepigrapha, ed. A. M. Denis and M. de Jonge (Leiden: E. J. Brill, 1985); and Patrick A. Tiller, *A Commentary on the Animal Apocalypse of* 1 Enoch, Early Judaism and Its Literature, ed. William Adler, no. 04 (Atlanta: Scholars Press, 1993).

19. Such a list of characteristics could be amplified considerably, but little would be gained by doing so.

20. For a helpful treatment of the role of angels in interpreting human experiences see the following work: David P. Melvin, *The Interpreting Angel Motif in Prophetic and Apocalyptic Literature* (Minneapolis: Fortress, 2013).

which reflects a highly developed angelology. The following account in *1 Enoch* is based on Genesis 6:1–4, but with considerable embellishment with regard to angels.

> And it came to pass, when the sons of men had increased, that in those days there were born to them fair and beautiful daughters. And the angels, the sons of heaven, saw them and desired them. And they said to one another, Come, let us choose for ourselves wives from the children of men, and let us beget for ourselves children. And Semyaza, who was their leader, said to them, I fear that you may not wish this deed to be done, and (that) I alone will pay for this great sin. And they all answered him and said, Let us all swear an oath, and bind one another with curses not to alter this plan, but to carry out this plan effectively. Then they all swore together and all bound one another with curses to it. And they were in all two hundred, and they came down on Ardis which is the summit of Mount Hermon. And they called the mountain Hermon, because on it they swore and bound one another with curses. And these (are) the names of their leaders: Semyaza, who was their leader, Urakiba, Ramiel, Kokabiel, Tamiel, Ramiel, Daniel, Ezeqiel, Baraqiel, Asael, Armaros, Batriel, Ananel, Zaqiel, Samsiel, Sartael, . . . Turiel, Yomiel, Araziel. These are the leaders of the two hundred angels, and of all the others with them (*1 En.* 6:1–8).

This unholy union between fallen angels and women led to unrestrained violence on the earth, escalating bloodshed among men, and unprecedented wickedness that spread unchecked throughout the earth. The fallen angels, sometimes referred to figuratively as stars, perniciously taught human beings all sorts of inappropriate activity and esoteric skills that were subsequently put to wrong use. Enoch says,

> And Azazel taught men to make swords, and daggers, and shields and breastplates. And he showed them the things after these, and the art of making them: bracelets, and ornaments, and the art of making up the eyes and of beautifying the eyelids, and the most precious and choice stones, and all (kinds of) coloured dyes. And the world was changed. And there was great impiety and much fornication, and they went astray, and all their ways be-

came corrupt. Amezarak taught all those who cast spells and cut roots, Armaros the release of spells, and Baraqiel astrologers, and Kokabel portents, and Tamiel taught astrology, and [Asradel] taught the path of the moon. And at the destruction of men they cried out, and their voices reached heaven (*1 En.* 8:1–4).

As a result, the Lord announces that the earth will be destroyed by a deluge that will cover all the earth. Concerning the evil angel Azazel the Lord says,

> Bind Azazel by his hands and his feet, and cast him into the darkness: and split open the desert which is in Dudael, and throw him there. And throw on him jagged and sharp stones, and cover him with darkness; and let him stay there forever, and cover his face, that he may not see light, and that on the great day of judgement he may be hurled into the fire. And restore the earth which the angels have ruined, and announce the restoration of the earth, for I shall restore the earth, so that not all the sons of men shall be destroyed through the mystery of everything which the Watchers made known and taught to their sons. And the whole earth has been ruined by the teaching of the works of Azazel, and against him write down all sin (*1 En.* 10:4–8).

The putative activity of angels held a fascination for many Jewish apocalyptic writers. They viewed themselves not merely as interpreters of earlier sacred texts, limited by the information found in those texts. Rather, they understood themselves to be writing new revelation. They did not hesitate to expand and embellish biblical texts, supplying details that are conspicuously absent from them.

While the Old Testament affirms the existence of angels as part of God's created order, as a rule it does not provide elaborate details with regard to their activities. A bit of an exception to this general rule is found in Old Testament writings that adopt an apocalyptic orientation. The book of Zechariah, for example, stresses the role of angels as intermediaries between God and his prophetic spokesman. Angels figure prominently in explaining and interpreting divine mysteries revealed to Zechariah through a series of night visions (Zech. 1:7–6:8). Angels are also prominent in the book of Daniel. In fact, the angelology of this apocalyptic writing is more explicit than that of any other Old Testament book. The fourth figure in Daniel's fiery furnace, who is called by Nebuchadnezzar "a son of the gods" (Dan. 3:25), is later acknowledged to be an angel sent to protect Daniel's three friends (Dan. 3:28). Likewise, an angel appears to protect Daniel in the lion's den, shutting the mouth of the lions that otherwise would have killed him (Dan. 6:22). Two angels are the subjects of special attention in the book of Daniel: Gabriel, who provides Daniel with insight and illumination (Dan. 8:16; 9:21); and Michael, who serves as a protector for the people of Israel (Dan. 10:13, 21; 12:1).

Old Testament apocalyptic writings reflect a more developed angelology than what is found elsewhere in the Old Testament. However, this angelology is characterized by restraint when compared to that of extrabiblical apocalyptic writings.

Ethical Dualism

Apocalyptists tended to see the world in terms of black and white, with very little grey area in between. They viewed the world as reducible to polar opposites: light versus darkness, good versus evil, righteous versus unrighteous. In *4 Ezra* the Lord says to Ezra, "For this reason the Most High has made not one world but two" (*4 Ezra* 7:50). This dualism whereby everything can be sorted into polar categories is not merely numerical in nature. It has an ethical dimension, in that one of these categories is supremely good and the other is supremely evil. Ethical dualism permeates apocalyptic texts.

For apocalyptic writers there was no hope of significant improvement in the world from a moral or spiritual standpoint. Their pessimism was based on a belief that war was being waged between light and darkness; apart from divine intervention the situation would remain irreversibly bleak. The only hope for the righteous lies not in gradual improvement of their lot in this life, but in God's sudden and irresistible breaking into the human scene so as to bring judgment upon the ungodly and vindication for the righteous. All of human history can be summarized in dualistic terms of falsehood and truth. This theme surfaces in *2 Baruch*:

> For the Mighty One has indeed made known to you the sequence of the times that have passed and of those that are yet to be in the world, from the beginning of its creation right up to its consummation—times of falsehood and times of truth (*2 Bar.* 56:2).

According to this text, at the final judgment there will be only two groups of people, the faithful and the evil. As Baruch reminds the Lord:

> For at the consummation retribution will fall on those who have done evil for the evil they have done, and you

> will make glorious the faithful for their faithfulness. For
> those who are among your own you rule, and those who
> sin you root out from among your own (*2 Bar.* 54:21–22).

For apocalyptists, the world was a difficult place to be in, due to on-going conflict between good and evil, between the righteous and the unrighteous. There simply was no way to escape the implications of that conflict. On the other hand, for the apocalyptist there was a sense in which the ultimate issues of this cosmic struggle were reducible and simple. Evil and darkness may wage fierce and costly war against good and light, but in due time the good would prevail.

Ethical dualism figures significantly in the theology of the book of Daniel. According to Daniel, this dualism operates in two spheres. On the earthly plane, the people of God are engaged in a struggle against destructive forces of evil that seek their ruin and annihilation. The righteous can resist the progress of this evil, but they cannot entirely overcome it in this life. On a spiritual plane, angelic forces are also engaged in conflict with opposing forces of evil. The resistance of these spiritual forces is so strong that it can even cause delay in the fulfillment of the angelic mission (Dan. 11:13). According to the book of Daniel, the ultimate resolution of this struggle between good and evil will come only through divine intervention and judgment (Dan. 12:1–3).

Deterministic Outlook

Apocalyptic literature reflects belief in a sovereign God who has predetermined the course of human history. Apocalyptists typically believed that the course of history was settled and fixed. It was not alterable. The triumph of evil over good in this life was only apparent. God permitted bad things to happen, but in his timing vindication and judgment would inevitably come. In the *Testament of Moses,* Moses says, "[H]e chose and appointed me, and prepared me from the foundation of the world, to be the mediator of his covenant" (*T. Mos.* 1:14).

A common notion that surfaces in this regard is that of periodization, or the belief that world history consists of fixed periods of times that must run their course prior to the final consummation. Numerical symbolism plays an important role in this belief.[21] Numbers such as three, four, seven, ten, and twelve are often used in this literature with special significance.

---

21. Russell refers to the apocalyptic use of symbolic numbers for describing historical epochs as "allegorical arithmetic." See D. S. Russell, *The Method and Message of Jewish Apocalyptic, 200 BC–AD 100,* Old Testament Library, ed. Peter Ackroyd, et al. (Philadelphia: Westminster, 1964), 195–202.

The schemes adopted for such ideas vary among the apocalyptic writers. In the *Apocalypse of Weeks* periodization consists of ten successive weeks. According to this text, Enoch was born "the seventh in the first week" (*1 En.* 93:3). The second week was characterized by great wickedness, and at the end of the third week "a man will be chosen as the plant of righteous judgment; and after him will come the plant of righteousness forever" (*1 En.* 93:5). In the fourth week a law will be made with a fence, and in the fifth week a house and a kingdom will be built (*1 En.* 93:6–7). In the sixth week, the house of the kingdom will be burnt with fire (*1 En.* 93:8). In the seventh week "an apostate generation will arise" (*1 En.* 93:9). The eighth week will be one of righteousness, with the wicked being "handed over into the hands of the righteous" (*1 En.* 91:12). Judgment of the wicked will take place in the ninth week, and in the tenth week the wicked angelic Watchers will be judged, followed by the vanishing of the first heaven and the appearance of a new heaven (*1 En.* 91:14–15). These ten weeks will be followed by an unspecified number of weeks, which the writer characterizes in this way: "After this there will be many weeks without number for ever in goodness and in righteousness, and from then on sin will never again be mentioned" (*1 En.* 91:17).

Some apocalyptic works follow a different scheme of periodization. The *Apocalypse of Abraham* speaks of four ascents of time, an hour of the age, twelve periods of the impious age, and the twelve hours on earth (*Apoc. Ab.* 28:4–29:2; 30:2). A different approach is adopted in *4 Ezra*, where the progress of history is expressed in terms of twelve divisions. According to this text the Lord says to Ezra, "For the age is divided into twelve parts, and nine of its parts have already passed, as well as half of the tenth part; so two of its parts remain, besides half of the tenth part" (*4 Ezra* 14:11–12). The future as well as the past must run a predetermined course without alteration. According to *2 Baruch*, the future "will be divided into twelve separate periods," each with its own characteristics (*2 Bar.* 27:1–15). The first of these periods "will see the beginning of the troubles" (*2 Bar.* 27:1), and the twelfth period will be followed by "the final consummation" (*2 Bar.* 27:15). The angel tells Baruch that "the Mighty One has indeed made known to you the sequence of the times that have passed and of those that are yet to be in the world, from the beginning of its creation right up to its final consummation" (*2 Bar.* 56:2). All of these things have been determined, Baruch is told, from the beginning of creation (*2 Bar.* 56:3).

Yet another approach to periodization is described in *2 Enoch*. This text puts forth a scheme that takes as its starting point the days of the creative week described in Genesis 1. Since in the Lord's sight a thousand years are like a day (Ps. 90:4), the writer of *2 Enoch* concludes that human history would run its course for six thousand-year days, following which there would be a seventh-day millennium of rest and then the eternal state. The following passage sets forth this understanding of history.

> On the eighth day I likewise appointed, so that the eighth day might be the first, the first-created of my week, and that it should revolve in the revolution of 7000; [so that the 8000] might be in the beginning of a time not reckoned and unending, neither years, nor months, nor weeks, nor days, nor hours [like the first day of the week, so also that the eighth day of the week might return continually] (*2 En.* 33:1–2).

Apocalyptists tended to emphasize the fixed nature of human history. According to them, all things were moving toward a final goal the nature and timing of which have been determined by God. They tended to have a deterministic outlook with regard to everything that has taken place in the past or will take place in the future. They often viewed history as determined by a specific and unalterable number of periods. Since God had predetermined these things, they must run their course according to the divine plan. There was no possibility that human beings might frustrate or interfere with this previously determined scheme.

In the book of Daniel determinism is nowhere more clearly seen than in the prophecy of the seventy weeks (Dan. 9:24–27), which provides a numerically structured plan for the fulfillment of divine purposes. According to this prophecy, God has predetermined elements of history as epochs of specific duration which must run their appointed course. Determinism is also an important part of Daniel's scheme of four world empires, which are described in detail in Daniel 2 and 7. The basic assumption behind these familiar structures is that God has predetermined events of human history and that human resistance to that plan is futile.

Imminent Crisis

Apocalyptic writers tended to think that the last days were imminent. These writers pointed to signs that indicated the nearness of terrible days to come. The implied message for readers was that they should prepare themselves for what was about to transpire. In *4 Ezra* these times would be accompanied by unusual cosmic signs and strange terrestrial phenomena. The author of this text calls attention to the following events:

> And the sun shall suddenly shine forth at night,
> and the moon during the day.
> Blood shall drip from wood,
> and the stone shall utter its voice;

the peoples shall be troubled,
and the stars shall fall (*4 Ezra* 5:4–5).

Many other signs of the end–time crisis are also mentioned in *4 Ezra*, including retrieval of fish from the Dead Sea, widespread chaos, frequent and unexpected fires, wild beasts roaming freely, women giving birth to monsters, salt waters appearing unexpectedly in fresh-water sources, friends warring against friends, an absence of reason and wisdom, and unbounded increase in evil (*4 Ezra* 5:7–9).

Many of the Old Testament writers also anticipate an impending crisis that will be accompanied by cosmic change of unparalleled magnitude. Portions of Isaiah, Ezekiel, Zechariah, Joel, and Malachi, for example, address this matter. Apocalyptic writers believed that such a crisis could neither be hastened nor delayed, as it was entirely in God's control. They stress that readers should take the coming crisis seriously and prepare themselves for it, since it is unavoidable.

Faithful Remnant

Although apocalyptists acknowledged that desperate times had arrived in the struggle of light against darkness, they also believed that there was a faithful remnant that resisted evil and sought to serve God. This faithful remnant rejected the social and religious *status quo* and refused to conform to the apostate culture around them. However, this remnant was a minority. In the words of *4 Ezra*, "I said before, and I say now, and will say it again: there are more who perish than those who will be saved, as a wave is greater than a drop of water" (*4 Ezra* 9:15–16). The same writer says that "the righteous are not many but few, while the ungodly abound" (*4 Ezra* 7:50). Ezra is also told that "the Most High made this world for the sake of many, but the world to come for the sake of few" and that "many have been created, but few shall be saved" (*4 Ezra* 8:1, 3). The righteous are likened to a single grape picked from a cluster.

> So I considered my world, and behold, it was lost, and my earth, and behold, it was in peril because of the devices of those who had come into it. And I saw and spared some with great difficulty, and saved for myself one grape out of a cluster, and one plant out of a great forest. So let the multitude perish which has been born in vain, but let my grape and my plant be saved, because with much labor I have perfected them (*4 Ezra* 9:21–22).

In spite of the falling away of the majority, this faithful remnant will ultimately prevail and be vindicated. Ezra is told:

> And it shall be that whoever remains after all that I
> have foretold to you shall himself be saved and shall
> see my salvation and the end of my world. And they
> shall see the men who were taken up, who from their
> birth have not tasted death; and the heart of the earth's
> inhabitants shall be changed and converted to a differ-
> ent spirit (*4 Ezra* 6:25).

Since the righteous will ultimately prevail, they need not be concerned about their persecutors or focus on the difficulties they face. They should instead ready themselves for the world that is to come. As the angel says to Baruch:

> Rejoice in the suffering you now endure: why concern
> yourselves about the downfall of your enemies? Make
> yourselves ready for what is reserved for you, and prepare
> yourselves for the reward laid up for you (*2 Bar.* 52:6–7).

The remnant theme is a feature of apocalyptic literature pointing to eventual reversal of the injustices of this life. In a sense, this reversal was seen as a solution to the problem of evil. Oppression of the righteous by the wicked is bearable because the righteous will finally prevail.

Remnant theology forms a part of the underpinning of the book of Daniel. Standing in opposition to the enemies of God's people is a group referred to as "those who are wise." Though subject to per-secution and physical harm, they will "be refined, purified and made spotless until the time of the end," according to Daniel 11:33–35. This remnant is promised a bright future in Daniel 12:3: "Those who are wise will shine like the brightness of the heavens, and those who lead many to righteousness, like the stars forever and ever."

Divine Judgment

Jewish apocalyptic literature places an emphasis on divine judgment, which is seen as the final antidote to injustice in this world. The wicked may prosper and gain ascendancy over the righteous in this life, but they must face God's judgment in the next life. This emphasis on divine judgment can be seen in a number of apocalyptic texts. According to *4 Ezra*, the Lord described judgment to Ezra in the following manner:

> Behold, the days are coming, and it shall be that when
> I draw near to visit the inhabitants of the earth, and
> when I require from the doers of iniquity the penalty
> of their iniquity, and when the humiliation of Zion is

complete, and when the seal is placed on the age which is about to pass away, then I will show these signs: the books shall be opened before the firmament, and all shall see it together (*4 Ezra* 6:18–20).

The timing of such judgment and vindication is a matter that curious minds cannot resist. Ezra wants to know when these things will happen. He is informed that judgment will take place after the time when "my son the Messiah shall die, and all who draw human breath" (*4 Ezra* 7:29). The Lord says to Ezra:

And the Most High shall be revealed upon the seat of judgment, and compassion shall pass away, and patience shall be withdrawn; but only judgment shall remain, truth shall stand, and faithfulness shall grow strong. And recompense shall follow, and the reward shall be manifested; righteous deeds shall awake, and unrighteous deeds shall not sleep. Then the pit of torment shall appear, and opposite it shall be the place of rest; and the furnace of hell shall be disclosed, and opposite it the paradise of delight (*4 Ezra* 7:33–36).

For the ungodly such judgment will result in suffering, grief, and torment. The Lord says to Ezra:

And if it is one of those who have despised his law, and who have hated those who fear God—such spirits shall not enter in to habitations, but shall immediately wander about in torments, ever grieving and sad (*4 Ezra* 7:79–80).

The author of *2 Baruch* encourages his audience to focus their attention not on this present world, where injustices and suffering abound, but on the age to come, where wrongs will be made right. He says:

For the Most High will assuredly speed up his times,
and he will assuredly bring on his seasons.
And he will assuredly judge those who are in his world,
and will truly punish all men,
in accordance with their hidden works.
And he will assuredly examine (their) secret thoughts,
and what is stored away in the innermost recesses of their being,
and he will expose and censure (them) openly (*2 Bar.* 83:1–3).

Similarly, the first parable of the *Similitudes of Enoch* describes the consequences of the future judgment. He says:

> When the community of the righteous appears, and the sinners are judged for their sins and are driven from the face of the dry ground, and when the Righteous One appears before the chosen righteous whose works are weighed by the Lord of the Spirits, and (when) light appears to the righteous and chosen who dwell on the dry ground, where (will be) the dwelling of the sinners, and where the resting-place of those who have denied the Lord of Spirits? It would have been better for them if they had not been born. And when the secrets of the righteous are revealed, the sinners will be judged and the impious driven from the presence of the righteous and the chosen (*1 En.* 38:1–3).

The second parable of the *Similitudes of Enoch* speaks of vindication for the righteous who have been martyred. Enoch says:

> And in those days I saw the Head of Days sit down on the throne of his glory, and the books of the living were opened before him, and all his host, which (dwells) in the heavens above, and his council were standing before him. And the hearts of the holy ones were full of joy that the number of righteousness had been reached, and the prayer of the righteous had been heard, and the blood of the righteous had been required before the Lord of Spirits (*1 En.* 47:3).

The prophets in general, and the apocalyptic writers in particular, warn of impending judgment on the ungodly. This theme is especially prominent in apocalyptic texts. A striking example appears in Daniel 7:9–10, where one called the Ancient of Days takes his seat in an otherworldly court scene. Myriads standing before the judge await their sentence as "the court was seated and the books were opened" (v. 10).

Passages like these attest to a belief that divine judgment should be expected in the future. That judgment will call the wicked to account for their actions and will decree punishment for the same. The judgment will also vindicate the righteous and reward them for their commitment to God's ways.

Eschatological Hope

Given their rejection of the *status quo* and their acknowledgment of the ascendancy of evil in the present world order, it might be tempting to think that apocalyptists were entirely pessimistic in their outlook. This conclusion would be unfair. Apocalyptic writers also articulate an eschatological hope. In their belief the solution to the present predicament faced by the righteous lay in the future, not the present. Apocalyptic writers looked to that future reality for hope. The coming future order would be diametrically different from the present. It would bring about the removal of sin and error; it would reveal truth in a new way. Ezra is told:

> For evil shall be blotted out and deceit shall be quenched; faithfulness shall flourish, and corruption shall be overcome, and the truth, which has been so long without fruit, shall be revealed (*4 Ezra* 6:27–28).

This hope sets the righteous apart from the ungodly; they have no such hope. As Ezra says:

> O sovereign Lord, behold, you have ordained in your law that the righteous shall inherit these things, but that the ungodly shall perish. The righteous therefore can endure difficult circumstances while hoping for easier ones; but those who have done wickedly have suffered the difficult circumstances and will not see the easier ones (*4 Ezra* 7:17–18).

Unlike the righteous, the ungodly despair of hope for the future. As the angel says to Baruch:

> You too will be preserved till the time of (the coming of) the sign which the Most High will provide for those on earth at the end of days. And this shall be the sign—when a stupor seizes those on earth and they are assailed by all kinds of misfortune and adverse circumstances. And when they say as a result of their sufferings, The Mighty One has no longer any interest in the earth, then, when they have given up hope, the time will come (*2 Bar.* 25:1–40).

The *Apocalypse of Weeks* anticipates the removal of the former world order and the appearance of a glorious new order without sin. Eschatological hope is described in this way:

> And the first heaven will vanish and pass away, and a
> new heaven will appear, and all the powers of heaven
> will shine forever (with) sevenfold light. And after this
> there will be many weeks without number for ever in
> goodness and in righteousness, and from then on sin
> will never again be mentioned (*1 En.* 91:17).

Similar scenes of eschatological hope are described in the book of Daniel as part of the expectation shared by the faithful remnant. As the angel Michael informs Daniel, "Multitudes who sleep in the dust of the earth will awake: some to everlasting life, others to shame and everlasting contempt. Those who are wise will shine like the brightness of the heavens, and those who lead many to righteousness, like the stars for ever and ever" (Dan. 12:2–3).

From such passages it seems clear that in spite of its negative assessment of the present religious situation, the apocalyptic message was one of anticipation and hope for the future. The ungodly could look forward only to judgment and punishment. But the righteous could endure present suffering and persecution in the awareness that their future would be for them something far better.

CONCLUSION

This chapter has summarized the contents of biblical and extrabiblical Jewish apocalypses in order to provide an overview of the structure and approach taken in these texts. It has also considered the presence of apocalypticism at Qumran, as indicated by some of the Dead Sea Scrolls. It has illustrated from pertinent ancient texts six features of Jewish apocalyptic literature. These features include the following: its literary rather than oral expression, its revelatory content, its emphasis on dreams and visions, its use of pseudepigraphy as a literary technique, its emphasis on hiddenness and secrecy, and its pervasive use of symbolism and figurative language.

This chapter has also considered seven major themes found in apocalyptic texts. These major themes include the following: a highly developed angelology, an emphasis on dualism that stresses the conflict between good and evil, a deterministic outlook based on the sovereignty of God, an emphasis on imminent crisis, the concept of a faithful remnant, coming divine judgment for punishment of evil and vindication of the righteous, and eschatological hope for the future. With this profile in mind, we are ready to tackle issues related to the interpretation of apocalyptic texts.

3

PREPARING FOR INTERPRETATION OF APOCALYPTIC LITERATURE

AS WE HAVE SEEN FROM THE PRECEDING discussion, Jewish apocalyptic literature appears in a wide range of historical settings. Its origins and development were complex. It had its main roots in Old Testament prophetic literature, although other influences played a significant role in its development as well.[1] Apocalyptic literature has certain similarities to material found in some of the Old Testament prophets, such as Isaiah, Ezekiel, Zechariah, and Joel. However, prophetic themes and theological emphases were modified, expanded, and taken in new directions as apocalyptic literature developed. This literature thrived during the intertestamental period, where we encounter a sizable group of writings that were very popular and influential within sectarian Jewish communities. Apocalyptic literature declined in influence among Jewish communities after the first century A.D. However, these texts (and others like them) continued to be preserved, read, and transmitted by various Christian communities during the apostolic and post-apostolic periods.

This chapter will call attention to some background areas for Old Testament expositors who intend to work closely with the biblical text in its original languages. Our focus will be on the book of Daniel, since

---

1. These conclusions are discussed more fully in the Appendix, "Antecedents of Apocalyptic Literature."

it contains the only real apocalypse in the Old Testament. The main question entertained in this chapter is this: How does one prepare for the interpretation of apocalyptic texts? Of particular interest in this regard are certain exegetical procedures and available tools that play a helpful role in modern exposition of the book of Daniel. The following five areas come under consideration here: (1) comprehending figurative language; (2) learning from **reception history**; (3) evaluating issues of textual transmission; (4) working with the original languages; and (5) benefiting from previous studies.

COMPREHENDING FIGURATIVE LANGUAGE

Since figurative language is used to some extent throughout the Bible, biblical exegetes must be prepared to recognize figures of speech and properly interpret them. Figurative language is especially common in apocalyptic literature, whose writers often prefer indirect and oblique descriptions of events or persons over direct and straightforward statements. A full treatment of figurative language employed in apocalyptic literature is well beyond the scope of the present volume. However, familiarity with a select handful of figures will be useful for the exposition of apocalyptic texts. Here we will briefly consider five figures of speech: **simile**, **metaphor**, **metonymy**, **hypocatastasis**, and **synecdoche**.

Simile

Through the use of simile an author seeks to clarify a less familiar item by likening it to a more familiar item. By reflecting on the identified characteristics of the more familiar item, one gains a better understanding of certain features or characteristics of the less familiar item. It is taken for granted that the two items are not identical in all particulars; they are similar only with regard to some shared feature or characteristic to which an author or speaker wishes to call attention. Simile is easy to spot in literature because of its use of comparative words such as "like" or "as." The name *simile* in fact derives from the Latin word *similis*, which means "like" or "similar." In Hebrew and Aramaic the preposition -כ ("like," "as"; cf. Heb. כמו) is the most common marker for simile. Examples of simile in the book of Daniel include the following.

> Then the iron, the clay, the bronze, the silver and the gold were all broken to pieces and became *like chaff* [כעור] on a threshing floor in the summer (Dan. 2:35).

> Finally, there will be a fourth kingdom, strong *as iron* [כפרזלא]—for iron breaks and smashes everything—and

as iron [כפרזלא] breaks things to pieces, so it will crush and break all the others (Dan. 2:40).

He was driven away from people and ate grass *like the ox* [כתורין]. His body was drenched with the dew of heaven until his hair grew *like the feathers of an eagle* [כנשרין] and his nails *like the claws of a bird* [כצפרין] (Dan. 4:33).

In the time of your father he was found to have insight and intelligence and wisdom *like that of the gods* [כחכמת אלהין] (Dan. 5:11).

He lived with the wild donkeys and ate grass *like the ox* [כתורין] (Dan. 5:21).

The first was *like a lion* [כאריה], and it had the wings of an eagle. I watched until its wings were torn off and it was lifted from the ground so that it stood on two feet *like a human being* [כאנש], and the mind of a human was given to it (Dan. 7:4).

Those who are wise will shine *like the brightness of the heavens* [כזהר הרקיע], and those who lead many to righteousness, *like the stars* [ככוכבים] for ever and ever (Dan. 12:3).

In each of these examples, simile is used to clarify some feature or characteristic of the topic under discussion. Use of this figure of speech brings vividness to the description and clarity to the intended meaning. By thinking through the points of comparison, the reader arrives at a better grasp of the reality to which the writer is pointing.

Metaphor

The terms *metaphor* and *metaphorical language* are often used in a broad and inclusive sense to refer to almost any figure of speech. In this discussion we will use the term *metaphor* in a more restrictive sense to refer to a particular type of figurative language. In metaphor a writer or speaker uses equative language to indicate that one thing *is* in some sense another thing. The intended correspondence, however, is limited in scope. It holds true only within parameters established by the context in which the metaphor occurs.

Although metaphor yields an interpretation similar to that of simile, the semantic structure is different. In metaphor, the word of likeness employed by simile (i.e., "as" or "like") is absent. Instead, metaphor makes a statement of identification or clarification using equative language in the form of "x *is* y." The name *metaphor* is suggestive of its meaning. It derives from the Greek word μεταφέρω, which means "to carry" (φέρω) one thing "with" (μετά) another. One item is said to "be" another, with the implied understanding that the second thing explicates but does not necessarily exhaust the meaning of the former. Metaphor simply identifies a noteworthy feature or characteristic of the other entity to which a speaker or writer wishes to draw attention.

Metaphors and similes can be used to express the same idea. The difference between them has more to do with structure and authorial preference than with intended meaning. For example, in emphasizing the ephemeral nature of human existence, Isaiah 40:7 employs a metaphor: "Surely the people *are* grass" [אָכֵן חָצִיר הָעָם]. But when this passage is cited in 1 Peter 1:24, the writer instead employs a simile: "all people are *like* grass" [πᾶσα σὰρξ ὡς χόρτος]. The specific rhetorical feature varies in these two biblical examples in that one is metaphor and the other is simile; however, the meaning is the same. Grass and people are alike in that while both may prosper and flourish for a time, they are both subject to physical decline and eventual death. In either case, the use of simile or metaphor makes the statement more vivid, picturesque, and memorable than it would be otherwise. Examples of metaphor in the book of Daniel include the following.

> You *are* that head of gold (Dan. 2:38).

> The four great beasts *are* four kings that will rise from the earth (Dan. 7:17).

> The fourth beast *is* a fourth kingdom that will appear on earth (Dan. 7:23).

> The ten horns *are* ten kings who will come from this kingdom (Dan. 7:24).

> The shaggy goat *is* the king of Greece, and the large horn between his eyes *is* the first king (Dan. 8:21).

In each of these examples, metaphor is used to clarify a point concerning the item under discussion. Use of this figure of speech contributes to the description provided by the biblical author, as well as clarifies the interpretation of the item to which reference is made. While English prefers to use a linking verb (i.e., a form of "to be") in expressing metaphor, Hebrew and Aramaic prefer to use a nominal clause, leaving the verb to be inferred.

Metonymy

Metonymy is a figure of speech that uses substitution in order to imply rather than directly state a relationship between two items. Unlike simile (which says that one thing is *like* another) or metaphor (which says that one thing in some sense *is* another), metonymy uses just a single item, substituting the stated thing for the thing that is actually intended. In metonymy the named item only partially accounts for the meaning that the writer has in mind. For example, the familiar adage "the pen is mightier than the sword" contains two metonymies. The word "pen" is a metonym standing for literature produced by use of the pen, and the word "sword" is a metonym standing for violence brought about by use of deadly instruments. The intended meaning is that incisive literature that appeals to the mind, in the end, achieves more than can be accomplished by the exercise of brute force. In that sense "the pen is mightier than the sword." A statement that at first may seem to be ridiculous, in that pens are not by nature mightier than swords, turns out instead to have profound meaning. But grasping such meaning requires at least a basic understanding of the way in which metonymy works.

The name *metonymy* derives from two Greek words, μετά and ὄνο-μα. Taken together, these two words suggest the idea of "naming" (ὄνομα) one thing "with" (μετά) another. Metonymies can be of four distinct types: (1) metonymy of adjunct, which replaces the intended topic with a reference to a more limited or specific feature pertaining to the topic; (2) metonymy of subject, which replaces the intended specific feature with a reference to a broader topic pertaining to the feature; (3) metonymy of cause, which replaces the intended effect of an action with a statement of its cause; and (4) metonymy of effect, which replaces the intended cause of an action with a statement of its effect. In metonymy the item that is mentioned is actually present in some way in the circumstances being described, although that item does not exhaust the meaning that the author had in mind when he used it. The interpreter must therefore recover the item that is not directly mentioned in order to grasp fully the writer's intention. For that reason, the figure of metonymy is often more difficult to recognize and properly interpret than is the case with either simile or metaphor.

In the following examples from the book of Daniel, "head" is a metonymy of adjunct representing one's physical life; "hand" is a metonymy of adjunct representing power or control; "throne" is a metonymy of adjunct representing all that constitutes royal authority; "heart" is a metonymy of adjunct representing mental decision making; "ships" is a metonymy of adjunct representing seagoing military forces comprised

of warriors; and "sword" is a metonymy of adjunct representing any
life-threatening military instrument of harm.

> The king would then have *my head* [ראשי] because of you
> (Dan. 1:10).

> No one can hold back *his hand* [בידה] or say to him: "What
> have you done?" (Dan. 4:35).

> But you did not honor the God who holds *in his hand* [בידה]
> your life and all your ways (Dan. 5:23).

> I watched the ram as he charged toward the west and the north
> and the south. No animal could stand against it, and none could
> rescue *from its power* [lit., "from his hand," מידו] (Dan. 8:4).

> The ram was powerless to stand against it; the goat knocked it to
> the ground and trampled on it, and none could rescue the ram
> *from its power* [lit., "from his hand," מידו] (Dan. 8:7).

> Now, O Lord our God, who brought your people out of Egypt
> *with a mighty hand* [ביד חזקה] and who made for yourself a name
> that endures to this day, we have sinned, we have done wrong
> (Dan. 9:15).

> The king of the North will return to his own country with great
> wealth, but *his heart* [ולבבו] will be set against the holy covenant
> (Dan. 11:28).

> *Ships* [ציים] of the western coastlands will oppose him, and he
> will lose heart (Dan. 11:30).

> Those who are wise will instruct many, though for a time they
> will fall *by the sword* [בחרב] or be burned or captured or plun-
> dered (Dan. 11:33).

> He will also invade the Beautiful Land. Many countries will fall,
> but Edom, Moab and the leaders of Ammon will be delivered
> from *his hand* [מידו] (Dan. 11:41).

With all such metonymies, interpreters must make a transition from
the item named to the item intended but not specifically mentioned.
The process of interpretation is not complete until one makes this transition and can articulate the intended meaning.

Hypocatastasis

Like metonymy, hypocatastasis is a figure of speech that uses substitution in order to imply rather than directly state a relationship between two items. Unlike metonymy, in hypocatastasis the item that is stated need not actually be present in the circumstances that are described. For example, when the psalmist says "many bulls [פרים] surround me" (Ps. 22:12 [13]) or "dogs [כלבים] surround me" (Ps. 22:16 [17]), he uses figurative language to refer to his human enemies. Bulls or dogs were not actually present in the circumstances that he describes. The language is evocative in nature. Readers in the ancient Near Eastern world were familiar with the threat that such animals could pose to human beings and were able to make the mental transfer required by the figure of speech. By substituting dogs or bulls for human enemies, the psalmist vividly captures the mortal danger that his adversaries represented. Like dogs or bulls, his enemies were violent, vicious, and extremely dangerous.

Hypocatastasis can be used to express the same thought that can be conveyed equally well by other figures of speech. For example, in Jeremiah 49:19 the prophet uses a simile to refer to the military forces led by the king of Babylon: "*like a lion* [כאריה] coming up from Jordan's thickets." But in Jeremiah 4:7 the prophet uses hypocatastasis to express the same idea: "*A lion* [אריה] has come out of his lair." In both cases, the king of Babylon is the implied referent. Although the choice of a particular figure of speech in these two passages varies between simile and hypocatastasis, the intended meaning is the same.

Failure to grasp the significance of a figure of speech used by a speaker or writer can lead to serious misunderstanding of the words employed. For example, when Jesus said to beware of the "leaven" [τῆς ζύμης] of the Pharisees and Sadducees, his disciples wrongly thought he was referring to loaves of bread (Matt. 16:6–12). Consequently, they missed the point that leaven had been substituted for erroneous teaching. Likewise, when Jesus spoke of destroying the "temple" [τὸν ναὸν τοῦτον] and raising it up again in three days, many who heard him wrongly concluded that he was referring to the Jerusalem temple (John 2:19–22). They did not grasp the fact that the word "temple" was used here for "body" and that Jesus was predicting his own resurrection. In both cases, interpretation was skewed by failure to understand the significance of the figurative language that was employed.

The term *hypocatastasis* is suggestive of its meaning. It derives from three Greek words: "under" (ὑπό), "down" (κατά), and "standing" (στᾶσις). Ancient Greek rhetoricians used this word to refer to an intended meaning that "stands down under" the word actually used by a writer. In other words, there is an implied comparison. Like metonymy, hypocatastasis is less obvious than simile or metaphor tend to be. When this figure of speech is used, the interpreter's work remains unfinished until the hypocatastatic element is fully recovered and accounted for in the exposition of the text.

Hypocatastasis is common in the book of Daniel, both in nominal and in verbal form. Examples of nominal hypocatastasis in this book include the following:

> You have been weighed on the **scales** [במאזניא] and found wanting (Dan. 5:27).

> In my **vision** at night I looked, and there before me were the four **winds of heaven** [רוחי שמיא] churning up **the great sea** [לימא רבא] (Dan. 7:2).

> Four great **beasts** [חיון], each different from the others, came up out of **the sea** [ימא] (Dan. 7:3).

> The first was like a lion, and it had **the wings of an eagle** [וגפין די נשר]. I watched until **its wings** [גפיה] were torn off and it was lifted from the ground so that it stood on two feet like a human being, and the mind of a human was given to it (Dan. 7:4).

> And there before me was a second **beast** [חיוה], which looked like a bear. It was raised up on one of **its sides** [ולשטר], and it had three **ribs** [עלעין] in **its mouth** [בפמה] between **its teeth** [שני]. It was told, 'Get up and eat your fill of **flesh** [בשר]!' (Dan. 7:5).

> After that, I looked, and there before me was another beast, one that looked like a leopard. And on **its back** [גבה] it had four **wings** [גפין] like those of a bird. This beast had four **heads** [ראשין], and it was given authority to rule (Dan. 7:6).

> After that, in my vision at night I looked, and there before me was a fourth **beast** [חיוה]—terrifying and frightening and very powerful. It had large iron **teeth** [ושנין]; it crushed and devoured its victims and trampled underfoot whatever was left. It was different from all the former **beasts** [חיותא], and it had ten **horns** [וקרנין] (Dan. 7:7).

> While I was thinking about **the horns** [בקרניא], there before me was another **horn** [קרן], a little one, which

came up among them; and three of the first **horns** [קַרְנַיָּא] were uprooted before it. This **horn** [בְּקַרְנָא] had eyes like the eyes of a man and a mouth that spoke boastfully (Dan. 7:8).

As I looked, thrones were set in place, and the Ancient of Days took his seat. His **clothing** [לְבוּשֵׁהּ] was as white as snow; **the hair of his head** [וּשְׂעַר רֵאשֵׁהּ] was white like wool. **His throne** [כָּרְסְיֵהּ] was flaming with fire, and **its wheels** [גַּלְגִּלּוֹהִי] were all ablaze (Dan. 7:9).

In the vision recounted in these verses from Daniel 7, Daniel sees in visionary form certain realities that are presented in figurative terms. The meaning of the figurative elements is clear from the second half of Daniel 7, where an angelic spokesman interprets for Daniel the main elements of this vision. The beasts that are described in vv. 2–9 represent successive empires. The wings on the beast suggest swiftness of military conquest. The favored side of the second beast apparently represents the dominant element in a composite empire consisting of two national entities. The mouth and teeth which are said to devour flesh are figures of speech used to describe military conquest of weaker empires. The heads speak of rulers who exercise authority and provide direction for their empires. The teeth of the dreadful fourth beast represent its awesome ability to overcome weaker empires and crush them. The horns of that beast represent various rulers, and the little horn is a particularly powerful ruler who is able to dispose of lesser rulers. The seats, the clothing, the wheels, and the thrones are figures of speech used to describe august royal authority and power. By thinking through the implications of figurative language we reach a clearer and more precise understanding of the biblical text.

Beneath each of the elements named in Daniel's vision there is a corresponding reality that the interpreter must sort out and identify. In order to do this he must first recognize the particular figures of speech that are used. Failure to acknowledge the presence of figurative language may lead to serious misunderstanding of the text. After locating the figurative language in a text, the interpreter should classify the figures according to their structure and intent. Does a given figure of speech fall into the category of metonymy, hypocatastasis, simile, metaphor, or something else? Finally, the interpreter should transform these figures into corresponding prose statements that clearly articulate their intended meaning in nonfigurative language. The more concentrated and pervasive figurative language becomes in a text, the greater the role that analysis of figurative language must play in the exegetical process.

Synecdoche

Synecdoche is a figure of speech in which either the whole of an entity stands for only a part thereof, or a part of an entity stands for its whole. The Greek derivation of the name is suggestive of its meaning: "to draw out" (δέχομαι) [something] "with" (σύν) [something else]. The most common synecdoche in biblical literature is the word "all." In many places the whole that is identified stands for only a part thereof. For example, according to Luke 2:1 (NRSV) a decree was issued that "all the world" [πᾶσαν τὴν οἰκουμένην] was to be taxed. However, "world" is this context is limited to the population of the Roman Empire. The intended significance of "all" is something less than exhaustive. In such cases it is important that interpreters rightly understand the intention of an author and not press the language beyond its proper limits.

Examples of synecdoche in the book of Daniel include the following:

> Before they reached the bottom of the den the lions overpowered them and broke *all their bones* [וכל גרמיהון] (Dan. 6:24).

> *All Israel* [וכל ישראל] has transgressed your law and turned aside, refusing to obey your voice (Dan. 9:11).

> [W]hen he has become strong through his riches, he will stir up *all* [הכל] against the kingdom of Greece (Dan. 11:2).

Interpretive Tools

In addition to the figures of speech discussed above, many other figures are used in the Old Testament. Further inquiry into the complexities of figurative language and its rhetorical functions will prove beneficial for biblical interpreters who wish to think through how such language works. For help with interpretive issues related to the analysis of figurative language, exegetes will find the following resources to be useful:

Bullinger, E. W. *Figures of Speech Used in the Bible, Explained and Illustrated.* London: Eyre & Spottiswoode, 1898. Reprint, Grand Rapids: Baker, 1968. An old but still useful inventory of several hundred figures of speech used in the Bible, illustrated by numerous examples drawn from both the Old and the New Testaments.

Caird, G. B. *The Language and Imagery of the Bible.* London: Gerald Duckworth, 1980. Reprint, Grand Rapids: Eerdmans, 1997. A standard work treating figurative language used in the Bible.

Sandy, D. Brent. *Plowshares and Pruning Hooks: Rethinking the Language of Biblical Prophecy and Apocalyptic.* Downers Grove, IL: InterVarsity, 2002. A perceptive examination of the way prophetic and apocalyptic language works in the process of communication.

LEARNING FROM RECEPTION HISTORY

Given the difficulties of interpreting a book like Daniel or Revelation, it is not surprising that the history of interpretation of these books is littered with bizarre and fanciful explanations. The common denominator for many of these explanations is that they failed to materialize in the way their advocates claimed would happen. Students of the history of biblical interpretation must therefore learn to navigate their way through a great deal of expositional clutter and chatter. One commentator refers to the history of interpretation of Daniel's seventy weeks (Dan. 9:24–27) as the "Dismal Swamp of O.T. criticism."[2] He has good reason for doing so. On the basis of that passage many conflicting interpretations have been put forth, most of them with little solid exegetical foundation. The reception history of Daniel's seventy weeks really is a dismal swamp.

However, the swamp is not limited to that passage alone. Many other biblical texts have also been victims of poor exegesis and strained interpretation. In some cases, these texts have been tortured so as to make them say things contrary to their intention. Perhaps the greatest temptation that confronts interpreters of apocalyptic literature is that of going beyond what the text actually says and indulging in reckless and harmful speculation. The history of interpretation testifies to the frequency and futility of such efforts.

Examples of Faulty Interpretation

Two examples will illustrate the problem. The first example concerns the horrendous events of the Second World War. It is not surprising that many who lived through those terrible times, particularly those who were closest to their horror and devastation, wondered if they were living out apocalyptic events described in the Bible. Some Bible readers even wondered if there was significance to the spelling of Adolf Hitler's name. If one assigns numerical values to the successive letters of the Roman alphabet, whereby /a/ equals 100, /b/ equals 101, and so

---

2. James A. Montgomery, *A Critical and Exegetical Commentary on the Book of Daniel*, International Critical Commentary, ed. S. R. Driver, A. Plummer, and C. A. Briggs (Edinburgh: T. & T. Clark, 1927), 400.

forth, the numerical value of *Hitler* is 666, a number that according to Revelation 13:18 has apocalyptic significance. Some Bible readers took this correlation to be confirming evidence that the German Führer was an end-time figure portrayed in Scripture. Others looked to *Il Duce* of Italy for this role, linking Benito Mussolini to apocalyptic texts that were understood to describe a Roman leader of the end-time.[3] At one time such ideas had popular appeal. However, with the end of the war it became clear that such connections lacked the end-time significance that had been attributed to them. Faulty exegesis had led to unfounded speculation and erroneous conclusions.

A second example concerns the attachment of eschatological significance to the days of the creative week. According to Genesis 1–2, God accomplished his creative purposes in six days and then rested on the seventh day. By taking each day to correspond to a thousand-year period of time (cf. Ps. 90:4), some writers argued that the history of the world would continue for six thousand-year "days," which would be followed by a thousand-year "day" of millennial rest (cf. Rev. 20:1–3). The history of the world would thus correspond to the days of the creative week as described in the book of Genesis. This is an ancient view. It is found, for example, in the first-century Christian writing known as the *Epistle of Barnabas*.[4] This view also appealed to some popular movements in modern times, leading to speculation that the coming of Christ would occur at the end of the twentieth century. Unfortunately, such misuse of biblical texts is not uncommon.

Lesson for Interpreters

What lesson should one learn from such failures? The lesson is that the allure to engage in speculative theories equating contemporary events with biblical prophecy should be resisted. Too often, devotees of such failed theories simply return to the drawing board and look for minor adjustments that allow for slight revision of their theories. They fail to acknowledge that the problem is much greater than one of minor details that require adjustment. The entire approach is wrongheaded, in that apocalyptic texts should not be forced to answer things that they were not intended to answer. To think otherwise leads to bad exegesis, which may be followed by disillusionment, cynicism, and even discredit of the biblical text when such predictions fail to materialize. The lesson offered by the history of interpretation is that expositors err, sometimes grievously so, when they go beyond what the biblical text

3. See D. Brent Sandy, "Did Daniel See Mussolini? The Limits of Reading Current Events into Biblical Prophecy," *Christianity Today*, February 8, 1993, 36.

4. *Ep. Barnabas* 15:3–7 (cf. *2 En.* 33:1–2).

affirms, or when they seek to wrestle out answers to questions concerning which the biblical texts themselves are either altogether silent or at best unclear. It is better to accept the limits of our knowledge and to grant humility a proper role in the exegetical process.

EVALUATING ISSUES OF TEXT

The text of the book of Daniel presents special challenges to the expositor. The issues can be sorted into two broad categories: language and text.

Problems of Language

First, there is the issue of bilingualism. Unlike most of the Old Testament, the original language of which is Hebrew, the book of Daniel (like the book of Ezra) is written in two languages. Roughly half of this book is in Hebrew, while the other half is in Aramaic.[5] Many suggestions have been offered as to why Daniel is written in two languages, but none of them is without problems. The bilingualism of Daniel may have to do with the early transmission history of this book. The stories about Daniel may at one time have circulated separately from most of the visions. When the material was brought together the original languages were retained. Although these two languages are similar in that they are both northwest Semitic languages, Hebrew and Aramaic are distinct languages and not just dialects of the same language. A modern approximation of this relationship can be seen in the similarity between German and Dutch, or Spanish and Portuguese, or Swedish and Finnish. Exegesis of the book of Daniel in its original languages requires a working knowledge of both Hebrew and Aramaic.

Problems of Text

A second issue concerns the state of the printed text found in *BHS* (i.e., *Biblia Hebraica Stuttgartensia*), which is presently the edition of the Hebrew Bible most widely used in academic settings. Since ancient manuscripts and versions do not always agree about the precise wording of the text, expositors must be prepared to engage in the practice of text criticism in order to ascertain the earliest and best form of the text. Although the Hebrew and Aramaic manuscripts that comprise the **Masoretic text** are uniform in their text-type, they are relatively

---

5. For Daniel 1:1–2:4a the language is Hebrew. In Daniel 2:4b–7:28 the language shifts to Aramaic. Following this Aramaic section, the language returns to Hebrew in Daniel 8:1–12:13.

late, coming from the medieval period. Earlier witnesses to the Old
Testament text come primarily from two sources: the Dead Sea Scrolls
and the ancient versions. These sources sometimes reflect readings that
are different from those of the Masoretic text.

There are at least eight fragmentary manuscripts of the book of
Daniel among the Dead Sea Scrolls.[6] With the exception of chapter
twelve, portions of all chapters of the book of Daniel are represented by
these manuscripts. The change of language from Hebrew to Aramaic
and from Aramaic to Hebrew occurs exactly as in the Masoretic text.
One of these Qumran manuscripts, 4QDan[c], probably dates to the
late second century B.C. The other seven manuscripts date to the first
century B.C. or the first century A.D. The Daniel manuscripts from
Qumran in general reflect a text which is quite close to that of the
Masoretic text. There are no surprising readings in these manuscripts
that call for major textual change in our present Hebrew/Aramaic text.
On the contrary, this evidence indicates how well the text of Daniel has
been transmitted to our modern world.

The most important of the ancient versions are the Greek, the Syriac,
and the Latin. Because these versions were translated directly from a
Hebrew/Aramaic text, they are known as primary versions. Certain
other ancient versions were translated from the Greek Septuagint;
they are known as daughter versions. For text-critical purposes, the
most important of the ancient versions is the Greek. There are two
very different Greek versions of the book of Daniel: Theodotion and
the Old Greek. Although it is fairly close to the Masoretic Hebrew
text, Theodotion provides a number of variant readings that are supe-
rior to the Masoretic text. The Old Greek (or Septuagint) is at times
very different from both the Hebrew Masoretic text and Theodotion.
These differences are most apparent in Daniel 4–6. Some critics have
supposed that differences in the Old Greek are due to a paraphrastic
translation technique adopted by the Greek translator, who supposedly
took excessive liberties with the text. This view is probably incorrect.
It is more likely that the Greek translator faithfully rendered a Hebrew/

---

6. These manuscripts from Qumran are as follows: (1) 1QDan[a] contains Daniel 1:10–17; 2:2–6
    and dates to the middle of the first century A.D.; (2) 1QDan[b] contains Daniel 3:22–28; 27–30
    and dates to A.D. 20–50; (3) 4QDan[a] contains Daniel 1:16–20; 2:9–11, 19–49; 3:1–2; 4:29–30;
    5:5–7, 12–14, 16–19; 7:5–7, 25–28; 8:1–5; 10:16–20; 11:13–16 and dates to the middle of the
    first century B.C.; (4) 4QDan[b] contains Daniel 5:10–12, 14–16, 19–22; 6:8–22, 27–29; 7:1–6,
    11 [?], 26–28; 8:1–8, 13–16 and dates to the middle of the first century A.D.; (5) 4QDan[c]
    contains Daniel 10:5–9, 11–16, 21; 11:1–2, 13–17, 25–29 and probably dates to the late second
    century B.C.; (6) 4QDan[d] is badly deteriorated and contains only five partial lines in its largest
    fragment; (7) 4QDan[e] consists of five very small fragments from chapter nine, none with more
    than one complete word; (8) pap6QDan contains Daniel 8:16–17 [?], 20–21 [?]; 10:8–16;
    11:33–36, 38 and dates to the middle of the first century A.D.

Aramaic text that itself was different from our Hebrew or Aramaic manuscripts of the book of Daniel. It appears that early on, the text of Daniel circulated in two very different text-forms. The text-form that we find in Theodotion eventually prevailed, while the text-form found in the Old Greek saw only limited circulation. For text criticism of the book of Daniel, the Old Greek tends to be less helpful than Theodotion or the other available textual resources.

Two other ancient versions are important for text-critical purposes. First, there is the Syriac version. The standard Syriac version of the Old Testament is known as the Peshitta (i.e., the "simple" version). The Peshitta probably dates to the second century A.D., although most manuscripts of the Peshitta date only to about the sixth century or later. The Peshitta often aligns with the Masoretic text, but this is not always the case. Its textual variants are an important pool of readings that deserve close attention. Second, there is the Latin version. The Latin Vulgate was translated from a Hebrew/Aramaic text in the fifth century A.D. by the well-known scholar Jerome. As a resident of Bethlehem who was in touch with the Jewish community in Jerusalem, Jerome no doubt had access to early manuscripts of the Hebrew Bible. The Vulgate is therefore an authority that should not be neglected in text-critical work.

When these witnesses (i.e., Hebrew/Aramaic manuscripts and ancient versions) disagree among themselves with regard to the precise wording of the biblical text, the expositor is called upon to make a decision concerning the original form of the text. Several factors may provide some guidance in this process. First, one should not entertain a bias for (or against) any one form of text. While the Masoretic text is reliable overall, this generalization is of little help in arbitrating particular text-critical problems. Even the best manuscripts contain scribal error. Preference should not automatically be given to the Masoretic text to the neglect of other ancient witnesses. Its evidence must be weighed and evaluated along with other ancient evidence. Second, **external evidence** (i.e., actual manuscripts and versions) has priority over readings favored on the basis of **internal evidence** alone (i.e., subjective reasoning about causes of error and their solution). Textual criticism should be based primarily upon readings that are attested in the external evidence. Otherwise, one runs the risk of inventing textual readings that never actually existed in history. Third, when deciding which reading among those that are attested is preferable, internal evidence plays a significant role. Here the so-called canons of text criticism come into play. The most important of these canons are the following:

- The more difficult reading (*lectio difficilior*) is to be preferred over the easier reading, since copyists tended to make things easier rather than more difficult.

- The reading that best explains the origin of the other readings is to be preferred, since there are genetic relationships between manuscripts.

- The reading with wide geographical support is to be preferred over a reading that is attested only in a local area, since local texts often took on certain idiosyncrasies.

- The shorter reading (*lectio brevior*) is to be preferred over the longer reading, since scribes tended to add clarifying words or phrases.

Although these canons are sound rules of thumb that are based on observable scribal tendencies, they all have exceptions. They must be used judiciously, in light of other considerations that might also pertain to particular texts.

Important textual variants for the Hebrew Bible have been collected in the critical apparatus of *BHS*.[7] Expositors should begin text-critical investigation with the apparatus of *BHS*, consulting other textual resources as needed. Variants that affect exegesis should be evaluated on the basis of both their external support and their internal strength. One should be wary of conjectural emendations of the text that have no external support in the form of Hebrew/Aramaic manuscripts or ancient versions, although on rare occasion it may be necessary to resort to such proposals. Variants that commend themselves on the basis of external and internal support may be adopted in preference to readings in the Masoretic text that may lack adequate support.

Space does not permit a detailed discussion of the procedures of text criticism. However, the following guidelines apply: (1) Exegetes should develop a general understanding of the history of transmission of the Old Testament text, since that will provide a framework for understanding how textual problems were prone to develop. (2) They should develop familiarity with the major textual witnesses, since that will help them to assign weight to the various witnesses. (3) They should also develop a grasp of sound text-critical methodology, since method will determine how one approaches textual problems.

---

7. This edition, which has been in use for several decades now, is presently undergoing a revision. The new edition is known as *BHQ* (*Biblia Hebraica Quinta*). Like *BHS*, *BHQ* is a **diplomatic edition** of the eleventh-century Leningrad Codex. However, its critical apparatus is more complete, up to date, and user-friendly than that of *BHS*. The biblical text is accompanied by a textual commentary that deals with significant textual variants for each biblical book. At the time of this writing, the Daniel fascicle for *BHQ* has not yet appeared. The following fascicles of *BHQ* are presently available: Megilloth (2004), Ezra–Nehemiah (2006), Deuteronomy (2007), Proverbs (2008), the twelve Minor Prophets (2010), Judges (2011), Genesis (2015).

Textual Resources

Those who wish to investigate text-critical issues will find the following resources to be helpful. (Here and elsewhere, the focus is on English-language resources.)

Brotzman, Ellis R., and Eric J. Tully. *Old Testament Textual Criticism: A Practical Introduction*. 2nd ed. Grand Rapids: Baker, 2016. A helpful general introduction to Old Testament text criticism, with special attention to the book of Ruth.

Elliger, K., and W. Rudolph, eds. *Biblia Hebraica Stuttgartensia*. Stuttgart: Deutsche Bibelstiftung, 1977. For the time being, still the standard one-volume edition of the Hebrew Bible. *BHS* is a diplomatic edition of the Leningrad Codex (Ms B19A), which dates to A.D. 1008. In addition to the text of the Hebrew Bible, *BHS* also contains the Masorah Parva (i.e., small Masorah) and a limited critical apparatus.

McCarter, P. Kyle. *Textual Criticism: Recovering the Text of the Hebrew Bible*. Guides to Biblical Scholarship: Old Testament. Philadelphia: Fortress, 1986. A good introduction to Old Testament text criticism, with many examples of scribal error in manuscripts of the Hebrew Bible and suggestions regarding their correction.

Tov, Emanuel. *Textual Criticism of the Hebrew Bible*. 3rd ed. Philadelphia: Fortress, 2012. The best one-volume introduction to Old Testament text criticism. It provides a good overview of the history of the text, illustrations of types of scribal error, and an introduction to text-critical methodology.

Tov, Emanuel. *The Text-Critical Use of the Septuagint in Biblical Research*. 3rd ed. Winona Lake, IN:, Eisenbrauns, 2015. A useful introduction to the proper role of the Septuagint in text criticism of the Hebrew Bible.

Wonneberger, Reinhard. *Understanding BHS: A Manual for the Users of Biblia Hebraica Stuttgartensia*. Trans. Dwight R. Daniels. 2d ed. Subsidia biblica, vol. 8. Rome: Pontifical Biblical Institute, 1990. The operating language of the critical apparatus in *BHS* is Latin. Wonneberger's work provides a key to the Latin abbreviations found in the apparatus, as well as suggestions on the use of this apparatus.

Würthwein, Ernst. *The Text of the Old Testament: An Introduction to the* Biblia Hebraica. 3rd ed. Revised and expanded by Alexander Achilles Fischer. Translated by Erroll F. Rhodes. Grand Rapids and Cambridge: Eerdmans, 2014. A standard introduction to text criticism of the Old Testament, recently revised and brought up to date.

WORKING WITH ORIGINAL LANGUAGES

Exegesis should be based on critical editions of ancient texts in their original language. For the Old Testament this means, above all, the Hebrew text. For exegetical work in the books of Ezra or Daniel, it also means the Aramaic text. An expositor should know where to go to find reliable information on the biblical languages. Here we will consider selected tools for studying Old Testament vocabulary, grammar, and syntax.

Bible Study Software[8]

Those who work extensively with biblical texts should invest in software for personal computers that is designed to make study of Scripture more accurate, comprehensive, and efficient. The following programs, listed in alphabetical order, are sophisticated, powerful, and fairly intuitive to use. All of these programs provide tagged electronic texts of the Bible that can be easily searched for retrieval of complex information, such as morphological parsing and statistics pertaining to word usage. These programs also provide a selection of additional electronic tools for Bible study. One of them is a Windows-based program; the others will run on both PC and Mac platforms. Serious students of Scripture cannot afford to be without one of these programs.

> *Accordance.* This is a flagship program for detailed analysis of biblical texts. It is superb for comprehensive searching and morphological analysis of electronic texts. In terms of intuitive ease of use, *Accordance* is unexcelled. A wide variety of resources is available. Users first buy a basic package and then purchase modules containing additional resources, depending on their particular needs.

---

8. See Appendix 1 ("Computer and Internet Resources for Old Testament Exegesis") in Edward M. Curtis, *Interpreting the Wisdom Books: An Exegetical Handbook* (Grand Rapids: Kregel, forthcoming), for a more extensive discussion of electronic resources, along with suggestions for their use.

BibleWorks. This program has a powerful search engine that is capable of both simple and complex analysis of electronic texts performed almost instantly. In addition to the basic program, one can add other resources to suit the needs of individual users. This program has more than two hundred Bible translations in forty languages.

Gramcord for Windows. *Gramcord* is a powerful electronic program for doing grammatical and syntactical research in Greek, Hebrew, and English biblical texts. By adding various additional resources (Greek or Hebrew grammars, dictionaries, texts, etc.) to the base package, *Gramcord* can be expanded to fit particular research needs and interests.

Logos Bible Software. In addition to standard resources for studying biblical texts, *Logos* provides electronic texts of many primary resources for the Hebrew Bible and the Greek New Testament (lexica, grammars, etc.). *Logos* also provides thousands of other searchable electronic resources (monographs, commentaries, etc.). Depending on the particular needs of users, *Logos* is available in various packages that are bundled to include the tools that are most likely to be helpful. As an electronic library for biblical research, *Logos* is unsurpassed.

Lexical Resources

Expositors must determine, as accurately as possible, the meanings of words used in the biblical text. A starting point for this process is a good lexicon. For biblical Hebrew and Aramaic there are several standard lexical resources that are especially helpful.

Brown, Francis, S. R. Driver, and Charles A. Briggs, eds. *A Hebrew and English Lexicon of the Old Testament, with an Appendix containing the Biblical Aramaic*. Oxford: Clarendon Press, 1907. A standard lexicon that provides an amazing amount of philological detail in a single volume. BDB lists the entries on the basis of verbal root rather than alphabetically, which sometimes leads to linguistic analysis that is debatable as well as creating an environment that is not user friendly for beginning students. Although BDB has served Old Testament students well for more than a century, it is now out of date and should not be relied upon exclusively.

Clines, David J. A., ed. *The Dictionary of Classical Hebrew*. 9 vols. Sheffield: Sheffield Academic Press, 1993–2016. A massive dictionary covering not only biblical Hebrew, but also the Hebrew of ben Sira, the Dead Sea Scrolls, and ancient inscriptions. A strength of *DCH* is its analysis of the usage of words appearing in classical Hebrew. Here it excels. A disadvantage is that it excludes data drawn from the cognate Semitic languages. Biblical Aramaic is not included in this dictionary.

Koehler, Ludwig, and Walter Baumgartner, eds. *The Hebrew and Aramaic Lexicon of the Old Testament.* Trans. M. E. J. Richardson, 2 vols. Leiden: Brill, 2001. This is the best up-to-date lexicon in English for biblical Hebrew and Aramaic. Entries are arranged by alphabetical order, making *HALOT* easier to use than BDB. It provides excellent analysis of the usage of Hebrew and Aramaic vocabulary. It also includes relevant data from cognate Semitic languages. If one is able to have only one lexicon for Old Testament studies, this is the lexicon to have.

Vogt, Ernst, ed. *A Lexicon of Biblical Aramaic, Clarified by Ancient Documents.* Translated and revised by J. A. Fitzmyer. Rome: Gregorian and Biblical Press, 2011. Vogt's lexicon originally appeared (1971) in Latin. Fitzmyer translated this important work into English and brought it up to date.

Grammatical Resources: Hebrew

Expositors must also determine the meaning of phrases, clauses, and sentences. For this, a grasp of grammar and syntax is essential. One should be prepared to make use of standard resources for grammatical study of the biblical text. For biblical Hebrew, there are several useful treatments of grammar and syntax. The following works provide reliable help for grammatical issues that affect Old Testament exegesis:

Arnold, Bill T., and John H. Choi. *A Guide to Biblical Hebrew Syntax.* Cambridge: Cambridge University Press, 2003. A helpful summary of the main categories of Hebrew syntax, illustrated by many examples.

Joüon, Paul. *A Grammar of Biblical Hebrew.* Trans. and rev. T. Muraoka. Subsidia biblica, vol. 27. Rome: Pontificio Istituto Biblico, 2006. The best up-to-date reference grammar for biblical Hebrew. Muraoka has thoroughly revised and updated Joüon's 1923 grammar, which was written in French.

Kautzsch, E., ed. *Gesenius' Hebrew Grammar.* Trans. A. E. Cowley. 2nd English ed. Oxford: Clarendon, 1910. A standard tool widely used throughout the twentieth century for study of biblical Hebrew. Gesenius was a nineteenth-century master of Hebrew grammar and syntax. Although still widely used, this grammar is out of date.

Waltke, Bruce K., and M. O'Connor. *An Introduction to Biblical Hebrew Syntax.* Winona Lake, IN: Eisenbrauns, 1990. The best intermediate treatment of biblical Hebrew syntax. This work presents categories of Hebrew syntax, provides numerous (though sometimes debatable) examples from the Hebrew Bible, and interacts extensively with the secondary literature.

Williams, Ronald J. *Williams' Hebrew Syntax.* 3rd ed. Rev. John C. Beckman. Toronto: University of Toronto Press, 2007. A helpful treatment of Hebrew syntax. The second edition of Williams's work on Hebrew syntax appeared in 1976. Beckman revised Williams's work, expanded it, and brought it up to date.

Grammatical Resources: Aramaic

Students of the Aramaic portions of Daniel will occasionally want to consult a reliable grammar. The following works are especially useful. A few introductory grammars are included here for those who may not have studied Aramaic previously.

Greenspahn, Frederick E. *An Introduction to Aramaic.* Corrected 2d ed. SBL Resources for Biblical Study, ed. Marvin A. Sweeney, no. 46. Atlanta: Scholars Press, 2007. A helpful introductory grammar. It adapts the biblical Aramaic texts to the progress of users, gradually introducing more difficult elements of grammar and syntax. This means that the biblical texts have been revised and adjusted to correspond to the progress of the grammar; it is not until the final section on Daniel 7 that one actually encounters unrevised biblical Aramaic texts.

Johns, Alger F. *A Short Grammar of Biblical Aramaic.* Rev. ed. Andrews University Monographs, vol. 1. Berrien Springs, MI: Andrews University Press, 1972. A helpful grammar designed "to meet the needs of the typical theological seminary student" (v, Preface). It assumes some knowledge of Hebrew. The following companion work is also available: James N.

Jumper, *An Annotated Answer Key to Alger Johns's* A Short Grammar of Biblical Aramaic (Berrien Springs, MI: Andrews University Press, 2003).

Rosenthal, Franz. *A Grammar of Biblical Aramaic.* 7th ed. Porta linguarum orientalium, ed. Werner Diem and Franz Rosenthal, no. 5. Wiesbaden: Otto Harrassowitz, 2006. Probably the most widely used introductory grammar of biblical Aramaic. It presupposes no knowledge of Hebrew. It does not discuss syntax separately, since "few beginning students of a language ever take the trouble of reading the portion of the grammar dealing with syntax" (1).

Schuele, Andreas. *An Introduction to Biblical Aramaic.* Louisville: Westminster John Knox, 2012. A helpful introduction to biblical Aramaic, with treatment of both morphology and syntax. A few reading selections from extrabiblical Aramaic are included in the appendices. The small size of Aramaic font used in the original printing will cause difficulty for many users. The work has been reissued in a larger format to address this problem.

Van Pelt, Miles V. *Basics of Biblical Aramaic: Complete Grammar, Lexicon, and Annotated Text.* Grand Rapids: Zondervan, 2011. A basic introduction to biblical Aramaic that includes an annotated text of the Ezra and Daniel passages.

BENEFITING FROM PREVIOUS STUDIES

In addition to collections of primary sources, there is a large corpus of secondary literature dealing with Jewish apocalypticism and related topics. This bibliography is divided into the following categories: primary sources for apocalyptic texts (in English translation); general works on apocalyptic literature; essays from symposia on apocalypticism; apocalyptic literature and the Dead Sea Scrolls; preaching apocalyptic literature; bibliographical help on pseudepigraphical literature.

Primary Sources for Apocalyptic Texts

The biblical apocalypses (i.e., the book of Daniel in the Old Testament and the book of Revelation in the New Testament) should be studied within their historical, religious, and cultural settings.

Rather than viewing them in isolation from this background, it is best to relate these writings to the context out of which they came. In order to accomplish this, the primary sources of apocalyptic literature are essential. Although specialists will work with these texts in critical editions based on original languages, translations are available for the use of nonspecialists. The following works present Jewish apocalyptic literature in accessible English translations, along with helpful introductions that discuss such matters as authorship, date, and structure. Reading the primary sources firsthand will give one a feel for apocalyptic literature that cannot be attained from reading secondary literature alone.

> Charles, R. H., ed. *The Apocrypha and Pseudepigrapha of the Old Testament in English, with Introductions and Critical and Explanatory Notes to the Several Books.* 2 vols. Oxford: Clarendon, 1913. Prior to the publication of Charlesworth's edition, this was the standard collection of the Old Testament apocryphal and pseudepigraphical literature in English. The first portion treats Old Testament apocryphal books. The second portion treats non-canonical Jewish literature written between 200 B.C. and A.D. 100. Extensive notes and discussions are found throughout. Charles has sometimes been criticized for adopting a too-free approach with regard to textual emendation. Although there is much useful material in this edition, it is now out of date.

> Charlesworth, James H., ed. *The Old Testament Pseudepigrapha.* 2 vols. Anchor Bible Reference Library. Garden City, NY: Doubleday, 1985. A fairly up-to-date collection of Old Testament pseudepigraphical writings. The first volume covers apocalyptic literature and **testaments**. The second volume covers the following areas: expansions of the Old Testament and legends; wisdom and philosophical literature; prayers, psalms, and odes; fragments of lost Judeo-Hellenistic works. Copious notes and critical discussions appear throughout. This is the best source for Old Testament pseudepigraphical literature in English translation.

> Reddish, Mitchell G., ed. *Apocalyptic Literature: A Reader.* Nashville: Abingdon, 1990. An anthology that provides representative selections from both Jewish and Christian apocalyptic texts. A brief introduction discusses matters of text, date, and historical background for each selection. This is a good place to begin reading apocalyptic texts; from here one can move to more detailed presentations.

General Works on Apocalyptic Literature

There is a substantial amount of secondary literature dealing with various aspects of Jewish apocalyptic literature. The following selections provide help with a variety of issues pertaining to this literature. These works will help one gain an overview of the nature of the apocalyptic genre and a grasp of major views regarding its history, origins, and characteristics.

> Carey, Greg. *Ultimate Things: An Introduction to Jewish and Christian Apocalyptic Literature*. St. Louis: Chalice, 2005. This helpful volume treats features of what the author calls apocalyptic discourse—that is, the literary, ideological, and social aspects of apocalyptic language. It covers both biblical and extrabiblical apocalyptic literature for both Old and New Testaments.

> Collins, John J. *The Apocalyptic Imagination: An Introduction to Jewish Apocalyptic Literature*. 3rd ed. Grand Rapids: Eerdmans, 2016. Discusses issues related to the study of the apocalyptic genre and surveys the contents and higher-critical issues of various apocalyptic texts. There is an especially helpful chapter on the relationship of Qumran to apocalypticism.

> Collins, John J. *Daniel, with an Introduction to Apocalyptic Literature*. Forms of the Old Testament Literature, ed. Rolf Knierim and Gene M. Tucker, vol. 20. Grand Rapids: Eerdmans, 1984. Provides a brief introduction to the genre of apocalyptic literature, and a form-critical evaluation of the book of Daniel on a chapter-by-chapter basis. Helpful bibliographies appear throughout. A glossary at the end of the book provides useful definitions and/or summaries of genre-related terms.

> Collins, John J., ed. *The Origins of Apocalypticism in Judaism and Christianity*. The Encyclopedia of Apocalypticism, vol. 1. New York: Cassell & Continuum, 1998. This is the first of a three-volume encyclopedia dealing with various aspects of apocalypticism. Taken together, the essays found in these volumes provide a comprehensive overview of apocalypticism, although this volume is not an encyclopedia in the normal sense of the word.

> Collins, John J., ed. *The Oxford Handbook of Apocalyptic Literature*. Oxford: Oxford University Press, 2014. A collection of twenty-eight essays arranged in five sections: the literary and phenomenological context; the social function of apocalyptic

literature; literary features of apocalyptic literature; apocalyptic theology; and "apocalypse now."

Cook, Stephen L. *The Apocalyptic Literature*. Interpreting Biblical Texts, ed. Gene M. Tucker. Nashville: Abingdon, 2003. A helpful general survey of issues pertaining to the study of apocalyptic literature.

Frost, Stanley Brice. *Old Testament Apocalyptic: Its Origins and Growth*. London: Epworth, 1952. An old but still useful consideration of the historical roots of apocalyptic literature and its characteristics, with thorough discussions of both biblical and extrabiblical examples of apocalyptic literature. Frost regards apocalyptic literature as a development out of prophecy.

Gruenwald, Ithamar. "Jewish Apocalyptic Literature." In *Principat*, ed. Wolfgang Haase, 89–118. Aufstieg und Niedergang der römischen Welt: Geschichte und Kultur roms im Spiegel der neuren Forschung II, ed. Hildegard Temporani and Wolfgang Haase, vol. 19.1. Berlin and New York: Walter de Gruyter, 1979. Surveys issues related to the rise of Jewish apocalyptic literature, such as connections to prophetic literature, angelology, pseudepigraphy, relationship to the "the outside books," status in relation to prophecy, status in relation to the Apocrypha, view of history, and eschatology.

Hanson, Paul D. *The Dawn of Apocalyptic*. Philadelphia: Fortress, 1975. An examination of antecedents of apocalyptic literature as displayed in prophetic writings such as Third Isaiah, Ezekiel, and Second Zechariah, together with an identification of mythic themes found in apocalyptic literature. Hanson sees apocalyptic literature as precipitated by a sixth-century rift between rival factions of a Zadokite-dominated temple party on the one hand, and a visionary element which had resisted the Zadokite temple program on the other hand.

Koch, Klaus. *The Rediscovery of Apocalyptic: A Polemical Work on a Neglected Area of Biblical Studies and Its Damaging Effect on Theology and Philosophy*. Translated by Margaret Kohl. Studies in Biblical Theology, 2d series, ed. Peter Ackroyd, James Barr, et al., vol. 22. Naperville, IL: Alec R. Allenson (1970). A survey of scholarship dealing with the origins and nature of apocalyptic literature. It is an appeal to restore the apocalyptic genre to a more central role in modern biblical studies.

McGinn, Bernard J., John J. Collins, and Stephen J. Stein, eds. *The Continuum History of Apocalypticism*. New York and London: Continuum, 2003. This volume derives from a larger three-volume work entitled *The Encyclopedia of Apocalypticism* (New York and London: Continuum, 1998). Its three divisions mirror those earlier three volumes: the origins of apocalypticism in the ancient world; apocalyptic traditions from late antiquity to ca. 1800 C.E.; apocalypticism in the modern age. Twenty-five essays treat various aspects of apocalypticism from the time of its origins up to modern times.

Murphy, Frederick J. "Apocalypses and Apocalypticism: The State of the Question." *Currents in Research: Biblical Studies* 2 (1994): 147–79. A helpful overview of recent research (up to 1994) on topics related to apocalypses and apocalypticism. Murphy divides his discussion into the following categories: definitions; genre; worldview; social movements; origins; the nature of apocalyptic discourse.

Rowland, Christopher. *The Open Heaven: A Study of Apocalyptic in Judaism and Early Christianity*. New York: Crossroad, 1982. A study of apocalypticism, dealing with such issues as the meaning of the term *apocalyptic*, the content of apocalypses, the origins of apocalypses, the esoteric tradition in early rabbinic Judaism, and apocalyptic in early Christianity. This work is based on the author's doctoral dissertation completed at the University of Cambridge.

Rowley, H. H. *The Relevance of Apocalyptic: A Study of Jewish and Christian Apocalypses from Daniel to the Revelation*. Revised ed. Greenwood, SC: Attic Press, 1963. Surveys apocalyptic literature from the last two centuries B.C. (i.e., Daniel, *1 Enoch*, *Book of Jubilees*, *Testaments of the Twelve Patriarchs*, *Sibylline Oracles*, *Psalms of Solomon*, the Zadokite work, Qumran scrolls) and apocalyptic literature of the first century A.D. (i.e., *Assumption of Moses*, *2 Enoch*, *Life of Adam and Eve*, *4 Ezra*, *Apocalypse of Baruch*, *Ascension of Isaiah*, *Apocalypse of Abraham*, *Testament of Abraham*, Little Apocalypse of the Gospels, and Revelation).

Russell, D. S. *The Method and Message of Jewish Apocalyptic, 200 BC–AD 100*. Old Testament Library, ed. Peter Ackroyd, James Barr, Bernhard W. Anderson and James L. Mays. Philadelphia: Westminster, 1964. A comprehensive survey of Jewish apocalyptic literature, although it is now dated. Russell describes the milieu and the contents of apocalyptic literature; discusses the method and characteristics of Jewish apocalyptic literature; and examines the message of Jewish apocalyptic literature.

Sacchi, Paolo. *Jewish Apocalyptic and Its History*. Translated by William J. Short. Journal for the Study of the Pseudepigrapha: Supplement Series, ed. James H. Charlesworth and Lester L. Grabbe, vol. 20. Sheffield: Sheffield Academic Press, 1996. Sacchi is a leading figure in contemporary Italian research on Jewish apocalyptic literature. This volume presents in English translation a number of his previously published essays. Several of these essays deal with the *Book of Enoch* or the problem of evil.

Essays from Symposia on Apocalypticism

Over the past decades several academic symposia have convened to discuss problems and issues related to apocalyptic literature. Many of the papers presented at these meetings have been very influential in the ongoing study of this literature.

Collins, John Joseph, ed. *Apocalypse: The Morphology of a Genre*. Semeia, vol. 14. Missoula, MT: Society of Biblical Literature, 1979. During the 1970s the Apocalypse Group of the Society of Biblical Literature Genres Project studied apocalyptic literature from the period 250 B.C.–A.D. 250.

Collins, Adela Yarbro, ed. *Early Christian Apocalypticism: Genre, Social Setting*. Semeia, vol. 36. Decatur, GA: Society of Biblical Literature, 1986. Throughout much of the 1980s a group of scholars met at annual meetings of the Society of Biblical Literature to study the apocalyptic genre, with special attention to early Christianity.

Collins, John J., and James H. Charlesworth, eds. *Mysteries and Revelations: Apocalyptic Studies since the Uppsala Colloquium*. Journal for the Study of the Pseudepigrapha: Supplement Series, ed. James H. Charlesworth, vol. 9. Sheffield: JSOT Press, 1991. A collection of essays originating in a symposium held in 1989 at the Society of Biblical Literature meeting in Anaheim, California.

Hellholm, David, ed. *Apocalypticism in the Mediterranean World and the Near East: Proceedings of the International Colloquium on Apocalypticism, Uppsala, August 12–17, 1979*. Tübingen: J. C. B.

Mohr (Paul Siebeck), 1983. A collection of thirty-four essays (in English, German, or French) dealing with various issues in apocalypticism. These essays were originally papers presented at the 1979 Uppsala conference.

Apocalyptic Literature and the Dead Sea Scrolls

Some of the Dead Sea Scrolls preserved by the Qumran community give evidence of apocalypticism. This apocalyptic interest has been examined in a number of modern works, among them the following.

Collins, John J. *Apocalypticism in the Dead Sea Scrolls*. Literature of the Dead Sea Scrolls, ed. George Brooke. London and New York: Routledge, 1997. Considers the following topics in light of the Dead Sea Scrolls: the definition of apocalypticism; Daniel, *Enoch*, and related literature; creation and the origin of evil; the periods of history and the expectation of the end; messianic expectation; the eschatological war; resurrection and eternal life; the heavenly world; the apocalypticism of the scrolls in context.

García Martínez, Florentino. "Apocalypticism in the Dead Sea Scrolls." In *The Continuum History of Apocalypticism*, ed. Bernard J. McGinn, John J. Collins and Stephen J. Stein, 89–111. New York and London: Continuum, 2003 [originally published in John J. Collins, ed., *The Origins of Apocalypticism in Judaism and Christianity*, Encyclopedia of Apocalypticism, vol. 1 (New York: Continuum, 1998), 162–92]. Argues that Qumran writings reflect an apocalyptic tradition that is both similar to and different from other apocalyptic traditions. The author treats the following areas: the origin of evil and the dualistic thought of the Qumran sect; the periods of history and the expectation of the end; communion with the heavenly world; the eschatological war.

Preaching Apocalyptic Literature

Public proclamation of apocalyptic literature for a lay audience presents special problems for expositors in terms of how exactly to go about this task. It is probably safe to say that many preachers do not even attempt a systematic exposition of apocalyptic texts. The following works, written from a variety of perspectives, offer suggestions on how best to do this.

Ashcraft, Morris. "Preaching the Apocalyptic Message Today." *Review and Expositor* 72 (1975): 345–56. Articulates factors that should be taken into consideration when preaching from apocalyptic portions of the Bible. Ashcraft suggests that too much stress on explaining the "props" of apocalyptic literature may keep the audience from understanding the overall plot. He sets forth some major apocalyptic themes from the book of Revelation that can enrich contemporary preaching.

Block, Daniel I. "Preaching Old Testament Apocalyptic to a New Testament Church." *Calvin Theological Journal* 41 (2006): 17–52. Proposes the following strategies for preaching the message of the book of Daniel: respect the genre of the book; recognize the historical significance of Daniel; recognize form and structure; recognize the source of Daniel's revelations; recognize major theme; recognize theological message. He concludes with some principles for studying and preaching the book of Daniel.

Fee, Gordon D. "Preaching Apocalyptic? You've Got to Be Kidding!" *Calvin Theological Journal* 41 (2006): 7–16. A brief reflection on literary features of apocalyptic literature and suggestions for preaching through the book of Revelation, preferably in a thirteen-week series.

Jonaitis, Dorothy. *Unmasking Apocalyptic Texts: A Guide to Preaching and Teaching*. New York and Mahwah, NJ: Paulist Press, 2005. Discusses the nature of apocalyptic literature and reflects on teaching and preaching apocalyptic texts of both the Old and the New Testaments. Jonaitis offers sermon outlines for texts taken from Isaiah, Ezekiel, Zechariah, Daniel, 1 and 2 Thessalonians, the Synoptic Gospels, and the book of Revelation.

Jones, Larry Paul, and Jerry L. Sumney. *Preaching Apocalyptic Texts*. St. Louis: Chalice, 1999. Stresses the importance of preaching apocalyptic material, but cautions against overly literalistic approaches. About two-thirds of the book consists of sermons based on the following texts: Daniel 7; 1 Thessalonians 4:13–5:11; Mark 13; Revelation 5; and Revelation 14. In each case there is a brief section dealing with exegesis of the passage in question, followed by two sermons on the passage.

Bibliographical Help on Pseudepigraphical Literature

Those who undertake scholarly study of apocalyptic literature will benefit from the following extensive bibliographies covering most topics related to the **pseudepigrapha**.

DiTommaso, Lorenzo. *A Bibliography of Pseudepigrapha Research,* *1850–1999.* Journal for the Study of the Pseudepigrapha: Supplement Series, ed. Lester L. Grabbe and James H. Charlesworth, vol. 39. Sheffield: Sheffield Academic Press, 2001. This massive work of more than a thousand pages provides bibliographical help for research in the pseudepigrapha and related literature.

DiTommaso, Lorenzo. *The Book of Daniel and the Apocryphal Daniel Literature.* Studia in Veteris Testamenti Pseudepigrapha, ed. Michael Knibb, Henk Jan de Jonge, Jean-Claude Haelewyck, and Johannes Tromp, vol. 20. Leiden and Boston: Brill, 2005. A very comprehensive bibliographic tool with more than a thousand pages. The coverage focuses on the period from 1850 to 1999, although some material outside these limits has been included as well.

CONCLUSION

In this chapter we have considered ways to prepare for the interpretation of apocalyptic literature. We have identified five areas that deserve special attention. First, a good grasp of the nature of figurative language and the ways in which it communicates is essential. Second, it is important to learn from the history of biblical interpretation so as not to repeat the mistakes of the past. Third, interpretation should take into account issues and problems of textual transmission for the Old Testament text. Fourth, expositors should work with the original languages of the Old Testament if at all possible. Fifth, interpreters should develop a familiarity with previous studies of apocalyptic literature so as to benefit from the helpful work that others have done in this area. Preparation in these areas will prove to be beneficial in interpreting Old Testament apocalyptic literature.

4

INTERPRETING APOCALYPTIC LITERATURE

IS IT POSSIBLE TO UNDERSTAND THE BIBLE in a thorough way with little or no concern for its linguistic, historical, and cultural contexts? Can Scripture be fully grasped with little or no thought given to the intricacies of how figurative language and poetry work? Should the Bible be read in a way that isolates it from the social, religious, and political world out of which it first emerged? The answers to these questions will be obvious to some readers and less so to others. To some extent, it comes down to a question of how clearly we should expect the Bible to answer the questions that we pose to it. A related concern is whether we are even asking the right questions to begin with.

Many Christian believers hold to a doctrine of perspicuity of Scripture. In general terms, this doctrine articulates a belief that the Bible is clear and unambiguous in its ability to communicate spiritual truth. As a result of this clarity, an untrained reader or even a child can comprehend the essence of the biblical message. This is because the Bible presents an overarching metanarrative regarding human sin and divine salvation that is readily grasped and easily understood, at least in terms of the big picture.

However, perspicuity does not apply equally to all parts of the Bible. While much of the teaching of Scripture is transparent, not everything in the Bible is so clear as to be easily grasped. Many portions of Scripture are extremely difficult to understand. Even biblical writers themselves acknowledge this fact. The author of 2 Peter, for example, admits that he found some things in the writings of the apostle Paul very difficult to understand. He even complained of ignorant and unstable people who wrestled with and distorted certain statements found not only in the Pauline corpus but elsewhere in the Scriptures as well (2 Pet. 3:16).

While it is true that the big-picture message of the Bible is clear and simple enough for even a child to grasp, it is also true that there are many things in the Bible that are very difficult to understand. It is therefore a good idea to approach Scripture with a humility that doggedly seeks to come to grips with the text as fully as possible, while at the same time acknowledging that there are many things in the Bible that we may never fully comprehend in this life.

Apocalyptic literature is one of the most difficult genres found in the Bible. It abounds in figurative language—language that is often opaque and difficult to grasp. Such language is capable of being exploited and misinterpreted by those who misunderstand this genre or foist upon it unwarranted expectations. How then should we approach apocalyptic literature? Are there any guidelines for responsible interpretation that can set us on a path of accurate exposition of this distinctive form of writing?

GUIDELINES FOR INTERPRETATION

This chapter takes up some general principles that offer help in understanding Old Testament apocalyptic literature, focusing especially on the book of Daniel. Some of these guidelines apply equally to all genres of biblical literature. Others more specifically address concerns that especially surface in connection with apocalyptic texts. In most cases, these guidelines represent the collective wisdom of many expositors over many centuries of biblical research and exposition. While these guidelines will not answer every question of curiosity that might surface in the study of these texts, they will point us in the right direction. They may on occasion even serve as stop signs, preventing expositors from heading down the wrong path. Unfortunately, interpreters are sometimes tempted to read into texts things that are not really there, rather than drawing from the text things that are there but may previously have escaped notice. There is a huge difference between these two practices. The following guidelines will help expositors to avoid the bad and practice the good when it comes to the interpretation of apocalyptic literature.

Interpreting Grammatically and Historically

A fundamental principle for scholarly interpretation of any ancient writing is that texts are best understood within the context of their original language(s) and their original historical setting(s). In biblical studies this concern has led to the formulation of what is sometimes called the grammatical-historical method. Such an approach is an essential part of scholarly inquiry into the meaning of an ancient text. This applies equally to biblical and extrabiblical literature. When texts are divorced from their linguistic and historical contexts, they are apt either to be completely misunderstood (at worst) or to be only partly understood (at best). In the following discussion we will apply this principle to the study of Daniel 7–12.

The rationale for studying the Bible in its original languages lies partly in the fact that translation inevitably requires a level of interpretation. All translations are, to some extent, mini-commentaries on the biblical text. Translators often find it necessary to build interpretation into a translation so as to make the translation readable and serviceable for its intended audience. This is appropriate and to some extent unavoidable. Reading the ancient text in its original language enables one to separate this layer of interpretation from what the text actually says. Consequently, a basic goal of every interpreter should be to determine as accurately as possible what the text says in its original language, as opposed to what readers and interpreters may have presumed it says. Only after this has been done to the fullest possible extent should one move on to the level of interpreting what the text means by what it says.

Three areas come into play in working with the original languages of the book of Daniel: grammar, syntax, and vocabulary. With regard to grammar, interpreters of the book of Daniel need to have a working knowledge of the morphology of both Hebrew and Aramaic. They need not be experts in these areas, but they do need to understand the basic grammatical forms of the language and their significance. The most crucial element in this regard, and perhaps the most difficult to learn well, is the verb. The Semitic verbal system differs appreciably from that of Indo-European languages, which means that for many students it will seem nonintuitive and unlike that of western languages they may have studied previously. An ability to recognize the verbal stems and conjugations, and an ability to interpret accurately their significance, are essential for the interpreter.

By analyzing the syntax of a text, interpreters are able to improve their understanding of what the ancient writers said. At this stage, interpreters may not yet know what the text *means*, but they will have a clearer understanding of what the writer did or did not say. Crucial in this regard is a grasp of the syntax of the verb, the noun, and clauses. Interpreters of the book of Daniel will need to have familiarity with standard grammatical tools that summarize the syntax of biblical Hebrew and Aramaic.[1] Understanding the syntactical options enables an interpreter to reach valid conclusions with regard to the meaning of the text.

---

1. Some of these grammatical and lexical tools were identified in chapter 3.

With regard to vocabulary, interpreters of the book of Daniel will want to make effective use of the standard lexical resources for biblical Hebrew and Aramaic. These resources offer immense help in determining how words are used in the biblical text and what precisely these words mean. An interpreter should also have a basic understanding of how to do lexical research—a skill that is usually acquired through formal academic training in these languages. A grasp of this methodology and familiarity with the available lexical tools permit the expositor to engage in lexical research independently, as the need arises.

Working with the original languages of the Bible is an attainable and realistic goal for expositors who have had the opportunity to pursue formal biblical training. The effort required for this pursuit is repaid many times over by its practical results. Interpreters are thereby enabled to draw close to the biblical text and to separate what the text actually says from faulty interpretations that may run aground on the reef of the original languages. Familiarity with the biblical text in its original languages provides a solid foundation for exegetical and theological interpretation of the text.

The historical context of an ancient text is no less important. Modern interpreters need to be aware of the historical background to which biblical writers may allude or which they may take for granted. The authors of Scripture often assume familiarity with such information on the part of their readers. Since they were living in the midst of these circumstances, there was no need for biblical writers to give their readers a history lesson regarding such things. Modern readers, however, do not have this advantage. They are removed from the historical setting of the text by thousands of years. Consequently, they must be more deliberate in recovering this historical background.

In the case of the book of Daniel, interpreters should have a general grasp of the history of the ancient Near East, particularly with regard to the Neo-Babylonian Empire and its kings and the Achaemenid Persian Empire and its leaders.[2] Much of what the Babylonians did, from the time of Nebuchadnezzar till the collapse of the Neo-Babylonian Empire to the Persians in 539 B.C., has a bearing on events described in the book of Daniel. Likewise, what the Persians did, from the time of Cyrus the Great till the fall of Persia in the fourth century to the Greek conqueror Alexander the Great, has a bearing on events described in the book of Daniel. What the **Ptolemies** and the **Seleucids** did during the third and second centuries B.C. also has a bearing on events described in the book

---

2. The following resources provide helpful information on historical backgrounds for the book of Daniel: Edwin M. Yamauchi, *Persia and the Bible* (Grand Rapids: Baker Book House, 1990); and D. J. Wiseman, *Nebuchadrezzar and Babylon* (Oxford: Oxford University Press, 1985).

of Daniel. One cannot fully grasp portions of the book of Daniel without at least some understanding of the history of these times.

The first guideline for interpreting apocalyptic literature, then, is to interpret this literature in accord with the grammar and syntax of its original text and in light of the historical backdrop against which its stories are told. To do this effectively, interpreters should prepare themselves with a working knowledge of the original languages. They should also gain a general understanding of the history of the times during which the events of the text occurred. Such an approach will help them to avoid many problems associated with the exposition of these texts.

Attending to Issues of Genre

Not all Old Testament literature belongs to the same genre. Depending on the genre of a text, different factors may come into play in the exegetical process. The narrative texts of Samuel or Kings, for example, are very different from the poetic texts of laments or praise psalms. Oracles of salvation are very different from legal texts, and announcements of judgment are not the same as wisdom literature. It is therefore important that expositors identify the genre of the text with which they are working. The genre of a passage provides clues as to how the language of that passage is to be understood.

As pointed out in chapter one, apocalyptic literature is a distinct genre. It has a picturesque and graphic dimension that appeals to the imagination in a way that straightforward narrative texts may not do, at least to the same degree. Figurative language is used to heighten the impact of apocalyptic descriptions on their readers. Sometimes these figures conjure up fantastic and bizarre images that correspond to nothing known in the natural world. Strange animals appear with multiple heads. These animals may have unnatural appendages or body parts with unnatural composition, such as land beasts that display feathered wings or have iron teeth. Fierce creatures that are nonexistent in nature may be used to portray human empires notorious for their reckless and destructive practices. A statue comprised of various metals and having odd proportions may be used to summarize successive periods of human history characterized by gradual decline and eventual collapse. Powerful beasts with strange horns may engage in fearsome conflict with other creatures that appear no less strange. One may encounter a weird lion with wings like a bird, an awkwardly balanced bear leaning to one side, a leopard with four heads and two pairs of wings on its back, and other strange animals having as many as ten horns on a single head. One may read of a majestic throne ablaze with fire at the very time a glorious occupant sits on it, unaffected by the river of fire that proceeds forth from the throne. One may find a contentious ram engaging in conflict with a hairy goat, leaving in its wake a path of awesome destruction. The world of apocalyptic literature bristles with strange images and arresting scenes that captivate the imagination and rivet the attention of an empathetic reader. Often the meaning of such figurative language is anything but obvious.

Such descriptions in the book of Daniel create a powerful image in the mind of the reader, even if these pictures are sometimes grotesque or ridiculous in terms of anything known from natural science. Such language implicitly signals that the genre of the book of Daniel is very different from that of books such as Joshua or Judges. It would be a mistake to embark on interpreting such texts without giving special attention to considerations of genre. The genre of apocalyptic literature consciously and deliberately utilizes these bizarre images in order to appeal to the imagination of the reader and to create a more effective and lasting impression than might be the case with a less symbolic presentation. The apocalyptic genre must be appreciated for its vividness and uniqueness, but it must be explained on its own terms and in light of its own intentions. Expositors must not press such texts in directions that these texts do not wish to take us. A basic principle of interpretation is that expositors must understand the characteristics of the genre with which they are dealing and must be sensitive to the expectations and requirements of that genre.

Locating Interpretive Clues

Although apocalyptic texts can be puzzling and elusive, it is safe to assume that the authors of such texts wished to be understood. Apocalyptists had a message that they regarded as important, and they wished to communicate that message to their audience. They had a reason for writing. Their message was not necessarily intended for everyone. Apocalyptists usually wrote in an esoteric fashion for a select audience that shared their theological point of view. They intended to be understood by that audience. Their purpose was not to tease readers by enticing them to reflect on figurative imagery for which there was no reasonable explanation. No matter how obscure the details of the apocalyptic message might seem at first reading, with patience and diligence it is possible to grasp the essential points of this message. In light of the popularity of apocalyptic writings in the intertestamental period it is safe to say that many readers did generally understand these texts, or at least they thought they did. But in order to understand such literature readers must locate interpretive clues that provide guidance for the interpretation. Sometimes these clues are embedded in the text itself; sometimes they are found outside the text.

The book of Daniel often provides interpretive guidance that is located right in the biblical text itself. Daniel 7 provides an example of this. In the first section of this chapter (vv. 1–14) an apocalyptic scene begins with the emergence from the sea of four strange and frightening animals, the last of which has ten horns. In the midst of these horns there appears an unusual horn—one that is able to see and talk. As Daniel tries to grasp the significance of this **vision**, a scene of celestial judgment appears, complete with an august figure seated on a blazing throne with wheels and a fiery river flowing forth from before it. Readers immediately recognize that there is a great deal of symbolism and figurative language here. But what does it mean? At first not even Daniel himself understood the significance of what he had seen in the vision (vv. 15–16). It seems clear that without a clue to set one on the proper path, interpretation would necessarily be speculative and inconclusive.

In the second section of Daniel 7 (vv. 15–27) the main features of the vision are explained. Here it becomes clear that the four terrible animals described in the first part of the chapter represent a succession of world empires that would exercise a negative influence on the people of Israel. According to the interpretation that is provided, the fourth of these empires would be particularly foreboding for the people of Israel, and would precipitate terrible and dreadful events impacting the people of God. Only through divine intervention would deliverance of the righteous and judgment of the wicked finally come. While the interpretation provided in vv. 15–27 is limited in terms of specific historical corroboration, this section does provide an interpretive key that points the reader in the right direction.

A further key is found in the correlation between chapters 2 and 7 of the book of Daniel. Nebuchadnezzar's dream of the statue in chapter 2 conveys essentially the same information regarding four world empires as the vision found in chapter 7. In Daniel 2:36–45 the metals of Nebuchadnezzar's image are explained as representing four successive empires that begin with Babylon (v. 38) and are eventually superseded by a divinely initiated kingdom that will never pass away (v. 44). These two chapters thus complement one another—a feature that aids in the interpretation. With the identity of the first empire specifically given as Babylon, interpreters can use extrabiblical historical sources in order to fill in the gaps regarding the following empires.

Sometimes the most helpful interpretive clues are not resident in the text itself. Instead, help must be sought outside the text. An example of this is found in Daniel 11. Much of this chapter describes individuals who are referred to simply as "the king of the North" and "the king of the South." Is it possible to identify the referents of this phraseology more specifically, and perhaps even date these mysterious kings to a specific period of time? The answer is "yes." Many commentaries on Daniel 11 provide precise and detailed information about various Ptolemaic and Seleucid kings of the third and second centuries B.C. who are confidently identified as the intended referents of this chapter. Although their names are not given in Daniel 11, we know these kings by name from extrabiblical historical sources. They are individuals such as Ptolemy I Soter (323–285 B.C.), who is the "king of the South" referred to in Daniel 11:5; Seleucus I Nicator (311–280 B.C.), who is one of his commanders referred to in Daniel 11:5; Ptolemy II Philadelphus (285–246 B.C.), who is the "king of the South" described in Daniel 11:6; Antiochus II Theos (261–246 B.C.), who is the "king of the North" described in Daniel 11:6. Various others are described as well, including Antiochus IV Epiphanes (175–164 B.C.), who is the "contemptible person" who plays an especially prominent role in the latter half of Daniel 11.

How is it possible to make these identifications in such specific terms, given the fact that these names do not actually appear in the biblical text? The answer is that our clue in this case is taken from extrabiblical historical records. The match between Daniel's description of various kings of the north and kings of the south and the various Seleucid and Ptolemaic rulers of this period is so precise that we can feel confident in these equations. These are the individuals that the book of Daniel obliquely refers to as kings of the north and kings of the south. However, were it not for the secular historical records, it would not be possible to make the correlations in identity that bring clarity to the interpretation of Daniel 11. The needed clues of correspondence are outside the biblical text rather than within it. Readers of the biblical text must look to secular history for help in establishing the identity of the historical figures and events in question.

The lesson highlighted by such examples is clear. Readers of apocalyptic texts must learn to watch for interpretive clues that point to the proper understanding of the biblical text. Sometimes these clues are embedded in the text itself, and sometimes they are found outside the text. The greater the degree of correspondence between these two sources of information, the greater may be our confidence that we are properly interpreting the text.

Focusing on Macrostructure

In apocalyptic literature the level of detail provided in figurative analogies is usually greater than the level of detail provided in their interpretation. Not every feature in an illustration necessarily has a corresponding feature in the interpretation. It is often the macrostructure of a passage that is most important for interpretation, more so than its microstructure. One must therefore be careful not to press the details of a given illustration beyond their intended function. Some details are supplied in an illustration merely to provide a full and robust mental picture that appeals to the imagination of the reader. It is possible that not all of these particulars have a corresponding meaning in the interpretation. Some interpreters of the book of Daniel get bogged down in a search for correspondence for all of the details found in a dream or vision. This can lead to fanciful and arbitrary interpretation of the biblical text. Interpreters should keep in mind that their purpose is to present to their audience what the biblical text means to say—nothing more and nothing less. There is often an enticement to go beyond the text, drawing conclusions that biblical authors never intended and in fact would be surprised to know about. Faithful biblical interpretation distinguishes between what the text affirms and speculative conclusions that lack adequate mooring in the text. Good interpretation emphasizes the former and avoids the latter.

It is not surprising that when the biblical text sets forth interpretations of Daniel's dreams and visions, not every item is accounted for or explained. For example, in Daniel 7 only a terse explanation is offered for the four animals of vv. 2–7. The text succinctly states, "The four great beasts are four kings that will arise from the earth" (Dan. 7:17). But what about the various additional details that are mentioned in the text? What do the eagle wings on the first animal represent (v. 4), or the three ribs in the mouth of the bear (v. 5), or the four wings on the leopard (v. 6)? We are not explicitly told what they represent. Only the last of these four animals is explained in greater detail, and even there not every detail is accounted for. We must be careful about attempting to be overly specific with the details that are mentioned concerning these animals. The wings of the first beast probably imply swiftness of movement and rapidity of conquest; the ribs in the mouth of the bear probably imply conquest of three other unnamed nations. But such conclusions should be held rather lightly.

Interpreters should also resist the temptation to attribute significance to details that are unmentioned in the interpretation that appears in the text. For example, nothing is made of the tail of the lion, nor is specific significance assigned to its feet (v. 4). The same is true of the spots of the leopard (v. 6). These features are at least implicitly present in the illustration but play no role in the interpretation. The reason is simple. If pressed, the language of analogy eventually breaks down. Illustrations usually correspond to their referent only to a point, after which the correspondence tapers off and no longer matters in the larger scheme of things. The principle to grasp here is that one should focus on the macrostructure of apocalyptic texts and not attempt to interpret the language of illustration more minutely or exhaustively than the context requires. At the level of microstructure it is possible for readers to invent interpretations that the author never intended. Such proposals are usually irrelevant, and perhaps even harmful, to proper exegesis of the text.

Accepting the Limits of Figurative Language

Figurative language is an effective and colorful tool of communication. It enlivens speech and writing and often produces mental images that linger in the memory longer than might be the case with more matter-of-fact statements. For good reason biblical writers make extensive use of symbolism and figurative language in apocalyptic literature. It helps readers visualize and better understand complex ideas of culture, history, and theology. However, figurative language is limited in the degree to which it corresponds to reality. A few examples will serve to illustrate this point.

In Genesis 11:4 the inhabitants of the earth say, "Come, let us build ourselves a city, with a tower that reaches *to the heavens*" (cf. Deut. 1:28). It is not likely that these builders really thought they were capable of making a tower that could reach to the heavens. This is the language of **hyperbole**; the builders deliberately exaggerated in order to emphasize the greatness of their anticipated achievement. In Joel 2:31 [Heb. 3:4] the prophet speaks of the moon being turned to *blood*. But this is the language of **hypocatastasis**. By "blood" the prophet means that the moon will have a reddish or blood-like color, a perception brought about by certain atmospheric conditions. In John 12:19 the writer reports that "*the whole world* has gone after" Jesus. But this is synecdoche. Here "the world" means not every last person in the world but all kinds of people, and lots of them. In Psalm 23:1 the psalmist says "The LORD is my *shepherd*." But the comparison implied in this metaphor is limited to the point being made by the psalmist. There are some things true of shepherds that are not true of the Lord. In Psalm 63:7 the psalmist says "I sing in the shadow of your *wings*." But God has no wings. This is the language of **zoomorphism**, whereby a physical feature of a bird is attributed to God or order to emphasize his loving care and protection. In Luke 16:29 Jesus says "they have *Moses and the Prophets*." But by the time these words were spoken, Moses and the prophets had been dead for centuries. This is the language of metonymy. Jesus is referring to the Old Testament Scriptures, that is, the writings of Moses and the prophets. His audience did not have the living persons of Moses and the prophets, but they did have the Scriptures that these famed heroes of the past had written.

In dealing with the language of apocalyptic literature we must accept the limits of figurative language and not attempt to draw more from such language than was intended by its author. By pressing such language in an overly literal fashion it is possible to miss a writer's point or misrepresent him entirely. The language of symbolism can lose its effectiveness and become a playground for interpretational gymnastics that wind up distorting rather than illumining the text.

Respecting the Silence of the Text

Biblical texts in general, and apocalyptic texts in particular, do not always tell us everything we might wish to know. This fact has implications for how we do exegesis. To exegete a text means *to draw forth* (Greek, ἐξηγέομαι) from that text all that is there, so as to make its meaning transparent and clear—especially for those who may lack the skills of exegesis. By disposition and training, exegetes are inclined to squeeze from the text every last drop of meaning. However, if not held in check, this tendency can easily lead to eisegesis. Instead of drawing out from the text what is there, one pours into the text things that do not belong there. Some interpreters present as exegesis observations that they have in fact imposed on the text—assertions that in some cases are actually contrary to the meaning of the text. Exegesis all too easily can fall prey to eisegesis. This problem is especially evident in places where biblical texts do not readily yield answers to the questions we pose of them. Unfortunately, there are times when the biblical text is completely silent with regard to matters for which we would like an answer. This is especially true in areas of eschatology and apocalyptic literature. Faithful interpretation means that we respect the silence of the biblical text and refuse to go beyond what the text itself affirms. Where the text is silent, we must learn to live with that silence.

PITFALLS OF INTERPRETATION

More so than almost any other portion of the Old Testament, apocalyptic literature presents an opportunity for readers to respond in various ways that are not productive. At one end of the spectrum are readers who are put off by the pervasive symbolism and the obscure language of apocalyptic writings. In some cases, these readers choose to avoid this literature altogether, despairing of the possibility of properly understanding it. At the other end of the spectrum are readers who enthusiastically embrace apocalyptic literature and pursue it with deep interest. These readers sometimes stray into reckless speculation when it comes to interpreting these texts. Various other reactions to apocalyptic literature fall in between these two extremes. Consequently, interpreters must be alert to a number of pitfalls along the path to understanding apocalyptic literature. Some of these pitfalls are discussed in what follows.

Unnecessary Ignorance

Much confusion has beset the interpretation of apocalyptic texts over the centuries. As a result, some modern readers have drawn the conclusion that such texts represent a miry swampland in which readers find it difficult to get their bearings and find their way due to the difficulty of the terrain. Consequently, the response of some readers has been simply to avoid apocalyptic literature altogether. For fear of failing, they choose to be ignorant of these writings. Instead, they focus their efforts on other portions of the Bible thought to be less challenging or problematic. Such a response is perhaps understandable. However, it is unnecessary.

Apocalyptic texts are not nearly as difficult or indecipherable as some seem to think. The author of the only apocalypse in the New Testament clearly intended for his writing to be read and understood. At the outset of the book of Revelation the author says, "Blessed is the one who reads aloud the words of this prophecy, and blessed are those who hear it and take to heart what is written in it, because the time is near" (Rev. 1:3). The author of this text did not think that his writing was incomprehensibly difficult. He pronounced blessing on those who read his message and who joined him in anticipation of the events described in this prophecy. In a similar way, the author of the book of Daniel expected that his message would be understood by his readers. The angel Michael reassures Daniel with these words: "Now I have come to explain to you what will happen to your people in the future, for the vision concerns a time yet to come" (Dan. 10:14). Later, an angelic herald explains to Daniel, "None of the wicked will understand, but those who are wise will understand" (Dan. 12:10). While a certain amount of apprehension is understandable in the study of apocalyptic literature, there is no good reason to avoid these writings or choose to remain ignorant of their contents.

Misplaced Certainty

At the other end of the spectrum, far removed from those who choose to remain ignorant of apocalyptic texts, are those who are overly confident in their ability to explain this literature. In some cases they exude a brash, swashbuckling attitude that has no hesitation in adopting interpretations that few scholars have ever held in the history of exegesis. Such confidence is misplaced. Few things are more essential for an interpreter of apocalyptic literature than a humility that admits the limits of our knowledge and refuses to go beyond the clear data of the text. While much in apocalyptic literature is clear and unambiguous, many details in these texts remain uncertain. To pretend otherwise is not a characteristic of responsible exegesis.

Manipulation of Details

One approach adopted by some interpreters of apocalyptic literature involves manipulation of textual details so as to fit a scheme that was predetermined in advance. Rather than allowing the ancient text to speak for itself, these readers force upon the text a grid that actually muzzles the voice of the text. Illustrations of this pitfall may be found in both past and present attempts at exegesis. For example, with the rise of Islam in the seventh century, some Jewish and Christian interpreters explained portions of the book of Daniel in light of the perceived threat of Muslim influence. According to these interpreters, the little horn of Daniel 8 was a prophetic reference to the spread of Islam.

Such a view is even found in one of the great manuscripts of the Hebrew Bible. The so-called Leningrad Codex, which dates to A.D. 1008, was copied by a Jewish scribe who identified himself in a colophon found at the end of the manuscript. In that colophon the scribe dates his manuscript, using five different systems of dating. One of these calculations includes a reference to Daniel's little horn, interpreted as a reference to Islam: "This is the year 399 of the reign of the little horn." It is clear that in this scribe's understanding, Daniel's little horn was a reference to the rise of Islam, which began four centuries prior to the scribe's own time and in his day was perceived as a threat to Judaism. Such an interpretive viewpoint was apparently common in Jewish circles during the medieval period, since the scribe of the Leningrad Codex felt no need to explain his otherwise cryptic reference to the book of Daniel.

Other readers have attempted to relate events in the book of Daniel to the rise of the papacy. For example, Doukhan maintains that Daniel's 1,335 days (Dan. 12:12), 1,290 days (Dan. 12:11), and 2,300 "evenings and mornings" (Dan. 8:14) refer respectively to A.D. 508 (when Clovis, King of France enabled the papacy to implement political power), 1798 (when papal power was diminished through the rise of secular philosophy), and 1844 (when Jesus allegedly entered the heavenly sanctuary and the time of waiting began).[3] Such views are possible only if certain details of the ancient text are manipulated so as to achieve a predetermined result.

The message of apocalyptic literature often focuses on how the conflict between good and evil will eventually be resolved. These writings hold out hope for the faithful, who are provided with encouragement to expect divine intervention on their behalf. In its own unique way this literature presents an understanding of human history and encourages an eschatological hope. To attempt to extract from these writings

---

3. See Jacques B. Doukhan, *Daniel: The Vision of the End*, rev. ed. (Berrien Springs, MI: Andrews University Press, 1989), especially 49–55.

prophecies about the rise of Islam or the emergence of the papacy is to distort their message of salvific hope. It is to reduce this message to an esoteric blueprint for religious history that is far removed from the provenance of this literature. Such distortion is a trap that interpreters must carefully avoid.

Creation of Arbitrary Timetables

During his incarnation, Jesus spoke of a time when he would return in power and glory. Although his first advent was characterized by lowliness and humiliation, he promised that his second advent would be characterized by strength, glory, and power. The apostles maintained a strong belief in the return of Jesus, as is clear from the New Testament writings. The early disciples of Jesus had come to expect a future return of their Lord, just as he had instructed them to do. It was natural for them to wonder about the timing of that eagerly anticipated event. Would it take place soon, perhaps even in their lifetime? Or would there be an extended period of prolonged silence and apparent delay? According to the book of Acts, just prior to his ascension to heaven Jesus's disciples urged him to disclose the time of his return. They asked him pointedly, "Lord, are you at this time going to restore the kingdom to Israel?" (Acts 1:6). Jesus's answer was equally pointed and clear: "It is not for you to know the times or dates the Father has set by his own authority" (Acts 1:7).

Two conclusions may be drawn from this exchange. First, the disciples were right to anticipate the return of this beloved one who was about to leave them. His absence would create a void that could only be rectified by his return. Second, the timing of that event was something that was beyond their ability to ascertain. The fact of his return was for them a given. But when it would occur was unknowable.

Believers have often failed to take seriously Jesus's answer to the question of the timing of his return. In an odd twist of fate, many have concluded that in fact they could know the time or date of Jesus's second coming. Ironically, they reached their conclusions regarding the date of Christ's return on the basis of biblical texts. In the early church such predictions were sometimes based on the alleged correspondence between the creative-week of Genesis 1 and a putative millennial-week understanding of human history. Just as creation took six days of labor that were followed by a seventh day of rest, so human history would be limited to six one-thousand-year periods that would be followed be a millennial seventh day of rest. If this view were correct, it would be possible to know approximately when Jesus would return. Others saw in the seven churches of the book of Revelation a pattern of historical epochs for the church age which could be dated approximately by correlating them to church history. Adherents of this view understand the Laodicean church to correspond to the present generation, implying that the return of Christ must therefore be soon. Others worked with the interpretation of specific biblical texts, claiming to calculate the return of Christ on the basis of the 2,300 days of Daniel 8:14, for example.

The specifics of such calculations vary considerably.[4] The common denominator, however, is a belief that it is possible to know the very thing that Jesus said could not be known—namely, the time of his predicted return. The history of biblical interpretation is littered with timetables that attracted great attention for a brief time and then drifted into oblivion, as it became obvious that they were as incorrect as the ones that preceded them. The lesson is clear: Apocalyptic literature does not disclose such information, and it is a mistake to attempt to draw out of these texts information that they do not intend to disclose.

CONCLUSION

This chapter has considered six basic guidelines for the interpretation of apocalyptic literature. Although these guidelines are general in nature, they will prove to be useful in pointing interpreters toward sound conclusions and away from faulty ones. They may be summarized as follows. First, in working with apocalyptic texts interpreters should pay close attention to grammatical details found in the original language. Equally important are matters of historical, religious, and cultural backgrounds that may be taken for granted in the text but may not be obvious to the modern reader. A grammatical-historical approach provides a sound foundation upon which to build. Second, interpreters should give attention to issues of genre, since these issues illumine the function and use of ancient texts. The apocalypse represents a distinct genre, one that differs in important ways from other genres of ancient literature. Sound exegesis must be sensitive to the requirements posed by this genre. Third, interpreters should attempt to isolate the explanatory clues that are often embedded in apocalyptic texts. These clues provide a general framework for the interpretation of texts. Difficult passages can often be understood in the light of these contextual clues. Fourth,

---

4. Hal Lindsey, for example, indulged in such speculation in his popular volume entitled *The Late Great Planet Earth*. Writing in 1970, Lindsey suggested that Jesus would likely return no later than 1988. His implied syllogism went something like this: (1) Jesus indicated that the generation alive at the rebirth of Israel (i.e., the "budding of the fig tree") would live to see his return (cf. Matt 24:34); (2) the modern rebirth of the nation of Israel occurred with the Balfour Declaration in 1948; (3) a generation in the Bible is about forty years. From these coordinates Lindsey hinted that Christ's return would likely be no later than 1988. See Hal Lindsey, with C. C. Carlson, *The Late Great Planet Earth* (Grand Rapids: Zondervan, 1970), 53–54; cf. 62.

interpreters should focus on macrostructure of apocalyptic texts and avoid getting bogged down in microscopic details that the author may not have loaded with significance. It is possible to fail to see the forest due to preoccupation with the trees. Fifth, interpreters should avoid reading into figurative language more than was intended by the author. Figurative language often exaggerates, frequently embellishes, and sometimes replaces the topic intended with a related item. Failure to grasp how such language works almost always leads to misinterpretation of these texts. Sixth, interpreters should respect the silence of the text and not try to wrestle from these ancient texts conclusions that are unfounded. Sound exegetes will not knowingly go beyond the parameters of the text.

This chapter has also considered four pitfalls that frequently confront interpreters of apocalyptic texts. While these are not the only pitfalls into which an interpreter can stumble, they are some of the more common ones encountered in the study of this literature. First, there is the pitfall of opting for ignorance by choosing to avoid apocalyptic literature. The difficulties inherent in this literature should not become an excuse for not reading and studying it. Apocalyptic literature is not so esoteric as to be incomprehensible. Second, there is the pitfall of misplaced certainty with regard to the interpretation of these texts. It is best to admit the limits of our knowledge and avoid dogmatism. Humility is always a becoming virtue for would-be interpreters. Third, there is the pitfall of manipulation of details. Interpreters should avoid the temptation to exploit texts, particularly with a goal to forcing them into preconceived interpretive schemes. Fourth, there is the pitfall of mining apocalyptic literature for artificial or fanciful timetables of historical and/or end-time events. Speculative linkage of ancient apocalyptic descriptions to contemporary political events is risky and without foundation.

5

PROCLAIMING APOCALYPTIC LITERATURE

When Gordon Fee was asked to write an essay dealing with the proclamation of New Testament apocalyptic literature, he anticipated the ambivalence of some in his audience by announcing his topic in a rather surprising way. Knowing that some readers might question the practicality of any attempt to proclaim apocalyptic texts to modern audiences, Fee punctuated his topic with a question mark that was no doubt intended to tease: "Preaching Apocalyptic?" The remainder of the title was even more provocative. As if to concede the impossibility of the task he was about to discuss, Fee exclaimed in his subtitle, "You've Got to Be Kidding!"[1]

Many probably share the sentiment Fee had in mind, wondering whether apocalyptic literature properly belongs in the modern pulpit. There are good reasons for such reluctance. The proclamation of apocalyptic literature has often been characterized by approaches that are off-putting to many people. Some preachers deal with such texts in mind-numbing detail that inadvertently obscures the larger message of the biblical text. Others use apocalyptic texts as springboards for sensational messages that dogmatically speculate on the eschatological significance of events described in the morning newspaper. Still others ride idiosyncratic hobby horses, expounding strange interpretations of biblical texts that find little or no support in the history of biblical

---

1. Gordon D. Fee, "Preaching Apocalyptic? You've Got to Be Kidding!" *Calvin Theological Journal* 41 (2006): 7–16.

exegesis. No wonder some ministers face apocalyptic literature with a certain dread or reluctance, wondering whether a sane approach to the proclamation of such texts is anywhere to be found.

The thesis of this chapter is that biblical apocalyptic literature should have a welcome place in public proclamation of the message of the Bible. In many ways apocalyptic themes lie at the very heart of the Christian message. In a unique way apocalyptic literature brings together themes of divine sovereignty, human failure, and eschatological hope. Fresh and clear proclamation of these truths is needed in each generation. Rather than avoiding biblical writings such as Daniel and Revelation, preachers should instead take up the proclamation of these texts with enthusiasm and confidence. Without question, the proclamation of apocalyptic literature presents unique difficulties that must be thought through and handled appropriately. But to some degree this is the case with the proclamation of any ancient text, regardless of its genre. The difficulties inherent in understanding apocalyptic literature need not be an impediment to public proclamation of these texts. On the contrary, the private study of apocalyptic texts and their public proclamation belong together. It is possible to preach effectively from apocalyptic literature.

ANCIENT TEXTS, MODERN CONTEXTS, AND FINDING A BRIDGE

Those who seek to proclaim biblical truth are faced with a tension that must be resolved in order for proclamation to be effective. This tension has to do with bringing together two worlds that are very different. On the one hand, the biblical text is situated in a cultural, religious, and historical setting that is largely foreign to modern audiences. When speaking to their own generation, biblical writers could take for granted a general familiarity with the historical, religious, and cultural settings of their day. In most cases, these settings required no explanation for people who were conducting their daily lives in the awareness of such things. Ancient Israelites, for example, lived in the constant shadow of political and military threats from Egypt, Assyria, Babylon, or Persia. Initiatives taken by these foreign powers often threatened their very way of life and existence. When biblical writers alluded to such matters, they could expect that their readers would readily understand these allusions to contemporary events. Ancient Israelites were also intimately familiar with the realities of a pastoral and agrarian economy. They immediately grasped illustrations and analogies that were based on the experiences of farmers, merchants, Bedouin, fishers, and shepherds. The Old Testament is replete with allusions to common experiences that formed part of the fabric of daily life in the ancient Near East. Readers of the

Hebrew Bible intuitively understood these things and quickly related to practices familiar to them from everyday life. Ancient Israelites also had familiarity with many of the religious practices found throughout the neighboring Canaanite cultures. Popular Israelite worship sometimes even incorporated features of pagan religion. Consequently, such religious practices required little explanation for those who were confronted with these religious beliefs on a regular basis.

On the other hand, the modern preacher of the biblical message speaks to an audience that is removed by many centuries from the historical, religious, and cultural settings of the Old Testament. Most modern audiences have very little familiarity with many of the things taken for granted in the Old Testament. Political and historical allusions that were obvious to ancient readers demand explanation for modern readers if they are to be understood. Aspects of cultural setting that could be assumed by the biblical writers require exposition for modern readers who live in a very different culture. Features of ancient religious practice that were clear to the ancient audience must be explicated for modern readers who lack familiarity with such matters. Consequently, biblical writings have for many modern readers an unfamiliar and distant feel.

What is worse, parts of Old Testament literature may seem to be completely irrelevant to some modern readers. Their life settings are vastly different from those of Old Testament communities of faith. Those who proclaim the ancient text to modern audiences are speaking into a context that is in many ways very different from that of its original audience. These two worlds are sometimes poles apart from one another. Unless the implications of that fact are carefully thought through, those who seek to proclaim biblical truth are likely to encounter audiences with limited patience for ancient texts that may seem to be unconnected to modern life.

What is needed is a homiletical bridge for spanning this gulf. How do we get from ancient text to modern context in a way that is both practical and helpful to a contemporary audience, while at the same time remaining faithful and accurate with regard to the message of the ancient text? Effective proclamation requires a bridge that can take us from the ancient text to the modern context. In what follows we will consider some ways in which this transition can be successfully made, particularly with regard to proclamation of the apocalyptic literature of the Old Testament.

A PRACTICAL STRATEGY

In some ways the study of apocalyptic literature is no different from the study of other genres of the Old Testament. Many of the same exegetical and hermeneutical principles that govern the interpretation of non-apocalyptic portions of the Old Testament apply equally to the interpretation of apocalyptic literature. However, due to the distinctiveness of apocalyptic literature, there are also certain procedures that come into greater play in dealing with this literature. The following guidelines offer practical suggestions for preparing for the proclamation of apocalyptic literature. These guidelines are illustrative and not exhaustive; other things could be incorporated as well, if space permitted. We will focus on seven basic steps in this process.

Getting Familiar with the Text

It stands to reason that accurate proclamation of an ancient text requires on the part of the preacher a thorough familiarity with the text. To attempt to explain a text that one does not himself understand reasonably well can only lead to confusion. Close familiarity with the text is therefore essential. While in interpersonal relationships familiarity sometimes breeds contempt, in Bible study it is more likely to generate insight and understanding. Before presuming to proclaim the text to others, expositors must first seek to understand the text as accurately as possible. This does not mean that they must grasp all details of the text equally well before setting out to proclaim its message. If that were the case, no one would qualify for the task of proclamation. But it does mean that through careful reading and analysis preachers should become confident about the main message of the text and its proper relevance to the needs of their audience. This is an attainable goal for those who acquire some basic exegetical skills and who engage in serious study of the biblical literature.

At the outset of working on an apocalyptic text one should establish a regimen of repeatedly reading through the text. In the case of a book such as Daniel, there is no reason why the entire book could not be read in a single sitting on repeated occasions. Obviously, the more one reads the text, the more familiar one becomes with it. Things that went unnoticed in early readings will suddenly strike a reader with fresh import in later readings. If one were to read the book of Daniel three times a week for a period of ten weeks, he would find that in the thirtieth reading of the book certain things would stand out that went completely unnoticed in earlier readings. Repetition is the key. Since it is not possible for the mind to remain alert to a plethora of things at the same time, it is best to read with one or two things specifically in mind. Each time the text is read, one can watch for new features. Here are a few suggestions that may help to guide such readings.

What are the main units of the text and their subdivisions? In working on a text, one should always try to get the macrostructure in mind. The details can then be related to this larger picture. The two main divisions of the book of Daniel are rather obvious. The first six chapters consist of stories that portray key events in the life of Daniel or his colleagues. These events revolve around scenes that take place first in the Babylonian royal court and later, after the fall of Babylon, in the Persian court.[2] The first of these six stories is set in the final years of the Israelite monarchy, when Daniel and many other Israelites were taken captive to Babylon. The final story is set in the period following the defeat of Babylon by Persia and subsequent Persian domination of the political landscape of the ancient Near East. These six chapters of the book of Daniel thus span a period of time from about 605 B.C. to about 536 B.C.

The second half of the book of Daniel also consists of six chapters. However, these six chapters comprise only four divisions. Chapters 10–12 are actually a single unit, although the chapter divisions might seem to suggest otherwise. The first two of these four units present two separate visions received by Daniel, recounted in chapters 7 and 8. Chapter 9 contains a lengthy prayer offered by Daniel, followed by the famous prophecy concerning the so-called seventy weeks. Chapters 10–12 portray selected historical and political events of the sixth through second centuries B.C., culminating in an announcement of resurrection.

The events described in Daniel 7–12 are not chronologically successive to the events described in chapters 1–6. Instead, chapters 7–12 are interspersed with the events of the earlier chapters. Chapter 7 is situated in the first year of Belshazzar (Dan. 7:1); its events therefore take place prior to the events of chapter 5, which is situated in the final days of Belshazzar's reign. The events of chapter 8 take place in the third year of Belshazzar's reign (Dan. 8:1); they therefore follow the events of chapter 7 but precede the events of chapter 5. Chapter 9 is situated in the first year of Darius (Dan. 9:1); its events therefore approximately coincide with the events of chapter 6. Chapters 10–12 take place in the third year of Cyrus (Dan. 10:1), whose conquest of Babylon is mentioned in Daniel 5:30. Keeping in mind that the book does not follow a strictly chronological sequence is helpful for recalling the topical relationship of the chapters.

With the main divisions of the book in mind, one can then analyze each of the individual units in order to find the substructure. Creating an outline of each unit in the text, with main points and subpoints properly distributed, enables one to decide how much text to include in the public proclamation of the text. Each message should present a well-chosen selection of text whose logical relationship to the larger whole of the book is clear and coherent.

---

2. From a form-critical standpoint, many scholars classify the stories found in Daniel 1–6 as *court tales* or *court legends*. See John J. Collins, *Daniel, with an Introduction to Apocalyptic Literature*, Forms of the Old Testament Literature, ed. Rolf Knierim and Gene M. Tucker, vol. 20 (Grand Rapids: Eerdmans, 1984).

One should keep in mind that the traditional chapter divisions are not always a reliable guide for finding the proper divisions of the text. For example, in English translations of the book of Daniel, Nebuchadnezzar's acknowledgment of the Most High God appears as vv. 1–3 of chapter 4. However, in the traditional Hebrew text this confession appears as vv. 31–33 of chapter 3. Does Nebuchadnezzar's tribute to the Israelite deity form the climax of the fiery-furnace incident of chapter 3, or is it an anticipation of Nebuchadnezzar's restoration from insanity, which is the topic of chapter 4? How one understands this issue will affect both the exegesis of the passage and the demarcation of text selected for proclamation. Likewise, is Daniel 11:1 the beginning of a new section, in which case the "him" in this verse refers to Darius the Mede? Or is this verse the concluding comment of chapter 10, in which case the referent of "him" is Michael the archangel? Where one locates disjunction in the text affects, in some measure, interpretation and therefore proclamation as well.

What is the relationship of the parts to the whole? When working on an ancient text, one should resist the temptation to become atomistic or myopic in approaching the text. Smaller units of text usually have a logical connection to other units and contribute to the larger purpose of the book as a whole. In the book of Daniel there is an inner logic that has guided the structure of the book. This is particularly evident in the relationship of chapters 2, 3, and 4 to chapters 5, 6, and 7. There is a chiastic arrangement of material whereby pairs of chapters correspond to one another in terms of their general theme. These three pairs of chapters illustrate three major themes of the book of Daniel.

First, chapters 2 and 7 both present a succession of four world empires, the last of which is replaced by a divinely initiated kingdom that will continue without end. Chapter 2 does so within the context of Nebuchadnezzar's puzzling dream of a statue in human form, and chapter 7 does so within the context of Daniel's vision of four animals coming up from the sea. In the former instance these empires are represented by metals of declining value, and in the latter instance they are represented by animals of increasing ferocity and strength. Second, chapters 3 and 6 both present a life-threatening situation in which those who refuse to compromise their stand for what is right are miraculously delivered and set free through divine intervention. Chapter 3 does so within the context of a fiery furnace into which Daniel's three friends were thrown as punishment for their refusal to participate in worship of the statue, and chapter 6 does so within the context of a den of lions into which Daniel was thrown as punishment for his refusal to abandon his practice of regular prayer. In the former instance Daniel's friends were delivered from intense flames, and in the latter instance Daniel was delivered from ravenous beasts. Third, chapters 4 and 5 both present the terrible consequences of human pride and hubris when judged by God. Chapter 4 does so within the context of Nebuchadnezzar's arrogance and subsequent period of insanity, and chapter 5 does so within the context of Belshazzar's arrogance and subsequent death at the hands of the Persians. In the former instance divine judgment is followed by reprieve and restoration, and in the latter instance divine judgment culminates in Belshazzar's death and the fall of his empire to the conquering Persians.

Throughout this structural arrangement, God's sovereignty over human authority and his control of human government are stressed. At the center of this structure, chapters 4 and 5 complement one another to underscore the futility of human power when confronted with the purposes of a sovereign God. Both Nebuchadnezzar (chapter 4) and Belshazzar (chapter 5), in different ways but with no less certainty, painfully learn that "the Most High is sovereign over the kingdoms on earth and gives them to anyone he wishes" (Dan. 4:32; cf. 5:21). The chiastic structure of the book contributes to the underscoring of its theological emphases.

Who are the leading characters in the story, and how are they presented? The authors of biblical texts no doubt had more information at their disposal than they chose to present in their writings. Only a relatively small portion of available information actually made its way into the biblical text. These writers were selective, choosing to include or omit details on the basis of how well those details contributed to the theological purposes they had in mind in writing the accounts. The biblical stories are not full-blown biographical accounts, but episodic stories that make a theological point, sometimes directly but more often indirectly. In proclaiming these narratives, students of the text should try to get inside the biblical characters so as to understand why they are presented as they are. What lessons do the authors of these texts want us to draw from their characterization of the key players?

In the book of Daniel the characters of Nebuchadnezzar, Belshazzar, and Darius are presented as individuals of exceptional political power and military might who nonetheless appear as weak, uncertain, and vacillating at certain key moments in their reigns. At times these characters appear pathetic and even comedic in their inability to cope with the servant of Yahweh, whose wisdom and insight give evidence of "insight and intelligence and wisdom like that of the gods" (Dan. 5:11). The characterization of these kings in the book of Daniel contributes quietly but effectively to the theme of God's sovereignty and absolute control over human events.

On the other hand, Daniel is characterized at times as vulnerable and subject to the demands of unreasonable authorities and the schemes of jealous associates, while at the same time facing difficult circumstances with a confident faith in Yahweh. When required to participate in dietary choices that violated his convictions, he relies on tact and winsome appeal in order to find an alternative path. When sentenced to death along with the court officials who are unable to explain the king's dream, he humbly appeals to Yahweh for insight beyond the reach of his natural abilities. Against all human odds he prevails, overcoming formidable opposition. When unable to avoid jealous conspiracy that leads to his being cast into the den of lions, he prays for divine intervention. His unwavering faith leads to his deliverance, while in an ironic reversal of fortunes his accusers experience the very destruction intended for Daniel. The characterization of Daniel's life illustrates the providence and power of Yahweh, who enables his faithful servants to fulfill their mission and accomplish their calling. The way in which the characters of the book are presented contributes to the theological message of the book.

What key words or ideas appear repeatedly? Repeated reading of a biblical book will often surface vocabulary and themes that are favored by the author. When certain words and their cognates repeatedly appear in a book such as Daniel, their repetition hints at certain points of emphasis that should be noticed. By identifying these words or ideas and reflecting on their meaning and significance we gain insight into the author's purpose.

In the book of Daniel one frequently encounters the notion that, in contrast to fleeting human empires, the kingdom of God is an eternal dominion that will have no end. When explaining Nebuchadnezzar's dream to the king, Daniel describes a time when the Lord will inaugurate this kingdom:

> [T]he God of heaven will set up a kingdom that will never be destroyed, nor will it be left to another people (Dan. 2:44).

Even a pagan observer may be led to acknowledge this fact. Following his temporary period of insanity, Nebuchadnezzar acknowledges the ongoing nature of this divine kingdom:

> His dominion is an eternal dominion; his kingdom endures from generation to generation (Dan. 4:3, 34).

Later, following Daniel's miraculous deliverance from the lions, Darius the Mede confesses that the kingdom of Daniel's God is a lasting kingdom that will endure forever:

> For he is the living God and he endures forever; his kingdom will not be destroyed, his dominion will never end (Dan. 6:26).

Daniel himself repeatedly proclaims the enduring nature of this kingdom. Speaking of one said to be "like a son of man" who comes with the clouds of heaven, Daniel says:

> His dominion is an everlasting dominion that will not
> pass away, and his kingdom is one that will never be
> destroyed (Dan. 7:14; cf. 7:18).

The angel who explains to Daniel the meaning of his vision of the four beasts emerging from the sea comments on this kingdom. He says, "His kingdom will be an everlasting kingdom, and all rulers will worship and obey him" (Dan. 7:27).

What is the purpose of this repetition of vocabulary and theme on the part of various participants in the story? It serves to underscore a key emphasis of the book of Daniel. Human empires, no matter how great and powerful they might become, are only temporary and ephemeral in nature. Without exception they are subject to decline, decay, and eventual failure. By contrast, the kingdom of God in its final manifestation is permanent and not subject to such decline or change. Any proclamation of the book of Daniel that does not at some juncture make this point has missed a key element of the book.

In a similar way, the book of Daniel stresses the notion that all human power and rule are completely subject to the will of God, who is sovereign over all human governments. The angelic watchers who announce God's imminent judgment on Nebuchadnezzar explain the purpose of the divine verdict in terms that make this point clear. They exclaim:

> The decision is announced by messengers, the holy
> ones declare the verdict, so that the living may know
> that the Most High is sovereign over the kingdoms on
> earth and gives them to anyone he wishes and sets over
> them the lowliest of people (Dan. 4:17).

Clarifying the nature of his punishment and its duration, the angelic watchers issue to Nebuchadnezzar the following warning:

> You will be driven away from people and will live with
> the wild animals; you will eat grass like the ox and be
> drenched with the dew of heaven. Seven times will pass
> by for you until you acknowledge that the Most High
> is sovereign over all kingdoms on earth and gives them
> to anyone he wishes (Dan. 4:25)

Later Nebuchadnezzar acknowledges Yahweh's sovereignty, confessing that no one can thwart God's purposes or call him to account for his actions. He concedes:

> All the peoples of the earth are regarded as nothing. He

does as he pleases with the powers of heaven and the peoples of the earth. No one can hold back his hand or say to him: "What have you done?" (Dan. 4:35).

Daniel later reminds king Belshazzar of the significance of Nebuchadnezzar's humbling that had occurred many years previously:

> He was driven away from people and given the mind of an animal; he lived with the wild donkeys and ate grass like the ox; and his body was drenched with the dew of heaven, until he acknowledged that the Most High God is sovereign over the kingdoms of men and sets over them anyone he wishes (Dan. 5:21).

It seems clear that a cardinal element of the book of Daniel is the notion that all human kings and earthly kingdoms are destined to rise and fall in keeping with the will of the sovereign Lord, in spite of any and all appearances to the contrary. This is a major point that should be emphasized in contemporary proclamation of the book of Daniel.

What theological concepts are either stated or implied? Biblical authors frequently choose to express theological ideas implicitly rather than explicitly. These theological constructs often lie just beneath the surface of the text, where they present their theology in ways other than in propositional statements. One must therefore extrapolate the theology that is implied but not directly stated in these texts and isolate it from the narrative in which it is embedded.

One way to approach this matter is to ask the following questions as one reads the text. First, what does this text teach about God in terms of his character and his actions? Caution is needed here in determining whose point of view is being described by a given biblical text. It is possible that characters in the story may assume or attribute to God things that are not really correct. For example, when the queen mother commends Daniel to king Belshazzar, she says that he "has the spirit of the holy gods in him" (Dan. 5:11). Her point of view is that of a polytheist who acknowledges the existence of multiple deities. She is correct in her belief that Daniel is uniquely qualified to help the king understand divine revelation, but her theological framework is not shared by the narrator. A more reliable guide is the narrator's point of view.

Second, what does this text teach about human beings in terms of their nature and actions? Texts may implicitly invite theological reflection on certain events or discourses without providing a direct commentary on these events or discourses. When the narrator comments on the significance of an event, he often provides a theological assessment of that event. For example, the narrator explains Daniel's deliverance from the den of lions as the result of his trust in God (Dan. 6:23). This is a theological interpretation that would not necessarily be obvious to those who observed that Daniel had survived this experience.

Third, what does this text teach about God's interaction with humanity and his goals for human history? These ideas will provide further insight into the overarching theology of the book. Out of these areas a biblical theology will begin to emerge that expresses an author's theological point of view. Repeatedly, the book of Daniel stresses God's sovereignty over human leaders, governments, plans, and intentions. Proclamation of apocalyptic texts should capture these major theological themes and make them a focus in the presentation.

What did the author expect of his audience? Often in biblical writings the purpose of the writer and the intended response on the part of his readership are implied but not directly stated. In such cases the reader must infer the intended result that the writer has in mind and then act upon it. In reading the biblical writings it is always helpful to ask the question, "So what?" In other words, what is it that the author wanted his readers to conclude on the basis of what he told them in a given text? And what action did the writer want his audience to take in light of what he told them? If readers are to be compliant to the author's purposes, what response should they make to the text? To fail to grapple with questions of this sort is to fail to understand fully the thrust of the biblical text. Those who read a biblical text only to learn its factual content, failing to respond to its spiritual appeal, have not read the text in a proper way. As James exhorted his New Testament audience, "Do not merely listen to the word, and so deceive yourselves. Do what it says" (Jas. 1:22).

In order to proclaim accurately the message of an apocalyptic text one must be able to articulate clearly what the author expected of his original audience. Why did the ancient author write what he wrote? Formulating the intention of the writer is often the result of painstaking analysis of the text. But once this has been properly done, those who proclaim the text can re-express the author's intended outcome and contextualize it to the needs of a modern audience. While the specific needs and circumstances of the modern audience may differ significantly from those of the ancient audience, the theological message of the text is timeless. That message remains the same for all audiences. It is that message that should be the focus of modern proclamation.

Resolving the Main Difficulties

Repeated reading of apocalyptic texts will surface various uncertainties with regard to the precise meaning of the text. Depending on the particular biblical text under consideration, these difficulties may be of various sorts. For example, when the manuscript and/or versional witnesses are in conflict with regard to the wording of the text, it may be necessary to make decisions with regard to the precise wording of the text. From a logical standpoint, determination of the precise wording of the text is in fact the first step of exegetical method. One cannot properly expound a text until first he or she knows what it says. This requires making decisions regarding which reading among textual variants is the preferred reading. It also requires setting aside later accretions to the text that are not part of its original wording. This may call for more expertise in text criticism than most expositors have, in which case one can usually find help in the commentary literature. Reading the text in more than one modern version is often helpful in this regard as well. In doing so one will notice significant differences in text-form that warrant further investigation. The point to be emphasized here is that all exegesis and interpretation should be based on the most accurate form of the biblical text available.

Another type of difficulty expositors encounter involves grammatical uncertainty in the original language. Accurate interpretation often depends on determining the precise significance of a particular form or syntactical construction in the Hebrew or Aramaic text. If the grammar or syntax of a passage is unclear to expositors, to some degree their understanding of the text will be obscured. It is therefore vital to resolve such difficulties in order to clarify the meaning of the text. The expositor may need to spend time in a good reference grammar in order to sort out the grammatical options and decide which one best fits a particular construction before moving on to other tasks. All exegesis and interpretation should take into account the grammatical structures utilized in the original language of the text.

Sometimes key words warrant special attention in order to discover their particular nuance in the original language. For example, one often encounters the word "kingdom" (מלכותא) in the book of Daniel. But what exactly is meant by this term? Does the Aramaic word מלכותא necessarily refer to a visible empire with the external trappings of royal authority? Or may it refer to the reign of a sovereign, whether that reign is perceivable on the basis of external manifestations or not? In a case like this, a focused word study making use of concordance, lexicon, and theological dictionaries can enliven the proclamation of a biblical text.

The use of figurative language often presents interpretational difficulties. This is particularly the case with apocalyptic literature, which has a preference for figurative language. It is important that interpreters of apocalyptic texts develop facility in recognizing the various categories of figurative language and understanding how such language works to convey meaning. The significance of common figures of speech—such as simile, metaphor, metonymy, hypocatastasis, and synecdoche—should be clear to expositors of these texts. For figures of speech that occur less frequently, one can consult as necessary the descriptive tools that are available.[3] Interpreters must be able to transform figurative language into corresponding literal expressions in order to clarify the meaning. Until this transformation of language takes place, the text will likely remain enigmatic and puzzling.

A common problem in the exegesis of apocalyptic texts has to do with resolving conflicting options in the interpretation of particular phrases, verses, chapters, or even larger units. Expositors often disagree in significant ways about the meaning of these texts. The history of exegesis shows that apocalyptic literature has often been at the root of major differences of opinion on the part of biblical interpreters. In preparing for proclamation of these texts one will need to think through the pros and cons of various interpretive options and decide which are to be preferred and why. Reading representative works written from a variety of theological viewpoints is often helpful in this regard. A healthy dose of humility and a willingness to be corrected can go a long way in helping interpreters avoid the plethora of wrongheaded interpretations that lack credibility or validation.

There are many other types of difficulties that one encounters in the study of texts. Resolving such problems, especially when they involve major difficulties that affect one's understanding of the text to a significant degree, is an important step in the exegetical process as one prepares for proclamation of the text.

Clarifying the Structure

After establishing the proper boundaries of a section of text, one can prepare an exegetical outline that shows the development of thought in the passage. This serves to clarify the author's organization of his thoughts and his intended meaning. Having identified perhaps two or three main points in the **pericope**, one is ready to divide each of these sections into their constituent subdivisions. Further sub-levels of organization in the structure can often be identified as well, to whatever level of outline seems beneficial for the purposes of proclamation.

Daniel 7 provides an illustration of how this might work. The following analysis of this chapter lays out the relationship of the parts to the whole. At this stage in the outline, no attempt is made to relate the content of the passage to the modern setting that one encounters

---

3. Especially useful in this regard is the old work by E. W. Bullinger, which classifies and illustrates several hundred figures of speech. See E. W. Bullinger, *Figures of Speech Used in the Bible, Explained and Illustrated* (London: Eyre & Spottiswoode, 1898; reprint, Grand Rapids: Baker, 1968).

in proclamation of the text. That important step will come later. The
focus at this stage is on attempting to account for the content of the
chapter and the relationship of the parts to the whole.

Exegetical Outline of Daniel 7

I. In a dream, Daniel watches as a heavenly court passes sentence on
    the final and most dreadful of four human kingdoms, thus clearing
    the way for the advent of an everlasting kingdom (vv. 1–4).
    A. Daniel writes a summary of a dream which he had during the
        first year of the reign of Belshazzar king of Babylon (v. 1).
    B. In his vision Daniel sees a succession of four dreadful animals
        arise from the sea, the fourth of which is especially terrifying
        (vv. 2–8).
        1. Daniel sees the four winds of heaven stirring up the great
            sea (v. 2).
        2. Daniel sees four animals, each with unusual characteristics,
            emerge from the sea (vv. 3–8).
    C. A heavenly court exacts judgment on the final beast, while one
        like a son of man receives an everlasting kingdom (vv. 9–14).
        1. One called the Ancient of Days, clothed in white, sits on a
            radiant throne (v. 9).
        2. An innumerable company attends to the Ancient of Days as
            books are opened for judgment proceedings (v. 10).
        3. The animal speaking boastful things is destroyed and its
            body is burned (v. 11).
        4. The lives of the other animals are spared for a short time,
            although their dominion is removed from them (v. 12).
        5. One like a son of man, coming with clouds, is presented to
            the Ancient of Days (v. 13).
        6. He receives an everlasting kingdom in which all people
            serve him (v. 14).
II. An interpreter, in response to Daniel's request for an explanation,
    clarifies the significance of his vision (vv. 15–27).
    A. Daniel, overcome with distress over the vision, seeks to deter-
        mine the meaning of his vision (vv. 15–16).
        1. Daniel's reaction to the vision is one of great distress (v. 15).
        2. Daniel, having asked one of those standing nearby for an
            explanation, is provided with the interpretation of the vi-
            sion (v. 16).
    B. Daniel learns the significance of the four animals in his vision
        and of the kingdom which will follow them (vv. 17–18).
        1. The four animals represent four human kings (v. 17).
        2. God's holy ones will receive an everlasting kingdom (v. 18).

   C. Daniel seeks to know the meaning of the details associated with the fourth animal and the holy ones (vv. 19–21).
1. Daniel seeks clarification with regard to the significance of the destructive fourth animal and of its horns, especially the boastful little horn (vv. 19–20).
2. He watches the horn prevail in war against the holy ones (v. 21).
3. The holy ones are vindicated and receive the kingdom from the Ancient of Days (v. 22).
   D. Daniel learns the significance of details associated with the fourth animal and the holy ones (vv. 23–27).
1. The interpreter informs Daniel that the fourth animal represents a fourth kingdom that will bring wholesale destruction upon the earth (v. 23).
2. The ten horns represent ten coming kings; the little horn represents a king who will subdue three other kings (v. 24).
3. The little horn will oppose God and his holy ones; for a time the holy ones will be delivered into his hand (v. 25).
4. His dominion will be brought to an end by action on the heavenly court (v. 26).
5. Universal dominion will be given to the holy ones (v. 27).
   E. Daniel, deeply troubled by the vision and its interpretation, continues to meditate on the vision (v. 28).

Such an outline enables one to identify at a glance the main elements of the chapter and the relationship of the smaller units to the overall flow of thought that is developed in the chapter. By keeping this larger structure in mind, one can avoid becoming overly atomistic with regard to the interpretation of particular verses. Instead, it is possible to see the parts in relation to the larger whole that the chapter represents. Of course, this is only one of twelve chapters of the book of Daniel. Eventually each of the twelve chapters of Daniel should be analyzed in this way, and each chapter should then be situated in its proper relationship to the book as a whole.

Summarizing the Main Point(s)

Once an exegetical outline of the passage has been determined, one is ready to summarize the main idea of the pericope. It is preferable to do this in a single sentence that captures the main elements of the unit and accurately summarizes their content. This is best done as a straightforward statement that interprets any figurative language that may be present in the biblical text. If the exegetical outline has been properly done, the summary of main point for the passage is simply a matter of incorporating the key elements found in the main points of the outline. The content of Daniel 7 may be summarized by the following statement:

> *In a dream Daniel learns of four successive world empires, portrayed as dreadful animals with peculiar characteristics, which will eventually be superseded by an everlasting heavenly kingdom.*

This statement can now help guide the development of an expositional outline for the chapter. By allowing the exegetical outline to form the basis of a homiletical outline the expositor seeks to maintain faithfulness to the biblical text, while at the same time adapting its content and message to a contemporary setting. The main point of the sermon should correspond to the main point of the passage.

Framing the Presentation

With the exegetical outline as a template, one is ready to move to a homiletical outline that will guide the public proclamation of the biblical text. The main points of the exegetical outline can now be expressed in terms of a more general theological statement that is both true to the biblical message and relevant to a modern life setting. In extrapolating the more general theological truths from the exegetical outline, the expositor will drop most of the specific and limiting references that appear in the text, such as allusions to Daniel and his particular circumstances. Instead, the expositor will express the significance of the text in more general terms that make clear the wider application of meaning. A homiletical outline of Daniel 7 might look something like what follows here.

Homiletical Outline of Daniel 7

I.   Human history is moving toward a divinely determined goal (vv. 1–4).
   A. Some portions of this divine plan have been revealed to God's servants (v. 1).
   B. Some portions of this plan may seem alarming and even dangerous (vv. 2–8).
   C. Evil and human resistance will be overcome by divine intervention, which will bring about a righteous kingdom (vv. 9–14).
II. The divinely determined goal of human history is understandable only to the extent that God chooses to disclose it (vv. 15–27).
   A. Insight into divine purposes is not possible through human reflection alone (vv. 15–16).

B. Only through divine disclosure can one grasp the goal of history (vv. 17–18).

C. The righteous may experience suffering, but they will be vindicated in due time (vv. 19–21).

D. Resistance to God's purposes will be overcome (vv. 23–27).

E. Divine disclosure of coming events does not answer all our questions (v. 28).

With these generalized points in mind, for purposes of application one can restate the main point of the passage in the following way:

Believers should be encouraged by the realization that history is moving toward a divinely determined goal that will bring the kingdoms of this world to an end and result in the establishment of a messianic kingdom that will never cease.

This statement and the homiletical outline on which it is based can now serve to guide the proclamation of this text. The resulting message will be soundly based on the specifics of the biblical text, while at the same time emphasizing the general truth that is expressed by the passage.

Listening to Other Interpreters

Sound biblical interpretation is both an individual effort and a corporate endeavor. On the one hand, individual interpreters are obliged to approach the task of exegesis seriously, with a willingness to work hard at allowing the text to speak for itself. The goal is to determine as accurately as possible the meaning of the text without placing our own interpretive grids over the text and thereby forcing the text to yield predetermined conclusions. In its most basic sense, exegesis is nothing more than drawing forth from the text those things that are actually there but that may have gone unnoticed. Its opposite is eisegesis, which is reading into the text things that are not actually there. Interpreters must hone and develop their willingness to go where the text takes them, as opposed to pressing the text into service for their own ends and purposes. They must listen to the text, disassociating themselves from all external influences that would have the unintended effect of muzzling and silencing the text. Proper biblical interpretation brings with it a high level of personal commitment, effort, responsibility, and accountability.

On the other hand, biblical interpretation is a collective enterprise that works best in community rather than in isolation. Interpreters should always avail themselves of the opportunity to learn from what other expositors have observed in their study of the text. In preparing for proclamation of the biblical text, an important step involves reading at least some of the available expository and commentary literature. From a logical standpoint, this is best done toward the end of the process of preparation rather than at its beginning. Otherwise, one runs the risk of being unduly influenced by the secondary literature before he or she has developed a personal familiarity with the text. In reality, however, the interpretive process is cyclical rather than linear in nature. It has been likened to a spiral in which the interpreter is constantly moving through the various stages of exegesis and revisiting them in light of new discoveries in the text. While it is possible to compartmentalize the steps of exegesis in a logical sequence for purposes of instruction and learning, in actual practice there is considerable overlap in these steps. Throughout the process of study of a biblical passage it is advantageous to consult reliable sources that can shed light on the meaning of the text.

The point to be made here is that preparation for proclamation of a biblical text should always include some reading in the commentary and exegetical literature that is relevant to the passage under consideration. In this way expositors become aware of insights that they may have overlooked in prior study of the passage. They may also become aware of flaws in their own thinking that require reevaluation, which may in turn lead to revision of earlier conclusions. All of this will have a beneficial effect on the process of preparing for proclamation.

Bridging to Application

One of the goals of public proclamation of biblical texts is to help audiences understand the application of biblical texts to their modern life setting. Most listeners want to know what difference a biblical text should make in their personal lives. What should they think, or what should they do, or how should they live, in light of what they hear through the proclamation of a biblical text? Most lay people have limited interest in studying a book like Daniel unless they are convinced that it has something to say to them. It is not enough to know what the book of Daniel has to say on this or that point within the context of the ancient Near East. The question that believers are most interested in resolving as a result of biblical proclamation is: How should we then live? (cf. Ezek. 33:10).[4] If proclamation is made with such questions in mind, the sermon will avoid becoming a disconnected collection of irrelevant comments on an ancient writing. Instead, it will allow the ancient biblical text to speak clearly to the modern context.

The message of Daniel 7 operates at two main levels. First, this text reminds us that no matter how powerful, influential, wealthy, or strong

---

4. Cf. Francis A. Schaeffer, *How Should We Then Live? The Rise and Decline of Western Thought and Culture* (Old Tappan, NJ: F. H. Revell, 1976).

a nation and its leaders might become, they are subject to the changing tides of history. Nations and their leaders rise; nations and their leaders fall. Regardless of how charismatic its leaders or how vast its natural resources, nations—like individuals—appear for a limited time and then, sometimes suddenly, pass away. What has proven true for all past empires will also prove true of all present ones. History is ever changing and constantly moving in new directions. Though these changes may seem to be random events lacking cohesion and purpose, the book of Daniel affirms that they are actually part of a divinely determined system that is moving to a grand finale. Second, this text reminds readers that nothing can ultimately interfere with God's purposes. In spite of fierce opposition and bleak circumstances that may seem to be insurmountable, a new day will dawn. A divine breakthrough in human history is coming. It will bring an end to human history as it is presently conceived and will usher in a new age of messianic fulfillment. The biblical message is, in that sense, an apocalyptic message. The coming divine kingdom announced by Daniel, by other Old Testament writers, and by the New Testament authors as well, will bring an end to human history as we know it. That coming kingdom will know no end.

CONCLUSION

Is it possible to proclaim in a relevant way the message of apocalyptic texts within the setting of modern contexts? The answer is "yes." Apocalyptic literature is an essential part of biblical revelation and as such deserves a prominent place in proclamation of the Christian message. However, the one who sets out on such a course must give careful thought to the way in which proclamation can be most effective for modern audiences. The purpose of apocalyptic literature is not to provide esoteric clues that enable one to calculate when the end of the age will occur. Preoccupation with such interests is not helpful. The purpose of apocalyptic literature has to do with extending eschatological hope to believers, particularly those experiencing persecution and rejection. This literature is about coming to grips with the sovereignty of God in the midst of a pagan society filled with hubris and pride. Through apocalyptic literature, one gains a renewed sense of the greatness and majesty of God, who is unaffected by the changing tides of human events. Unlike the transitory and crumbling edifices that are the result of human effort, his kingdom shall never pass away. Through apocalyptic literature, readers develop an awareness of the feebleness of even the mightiest of human rulers, who often rise quickly to power and just as quickly fade into shadowy insignificance. Through this literature readers gain an appreciation of the grand plan of an eternal sovereign who deigns to involve himself with the lowliest of human beings.

These are truths that spoke powerfully millennia ago to believing communities whose faith was sorely tried and tested. These truths speak with equal effectiveness to believing communities in our modern world who are faced with similar trials and difficulties. The proclamation of apocalyptic literature offers hope for an ultimate solution to the human predicament that lies outside this life. This hope finds its fulfillment in a promised future that exceeds all present expectations.

6

SAMPLE TEXTS FROM
APOCALYPTIC LITERATURE

IN THIS FINAL CHAPTER WE WILL APPLY PREVIOUSLY discussed principles to two examples of Old Testament literature containing apocalyptic motifs. The first of these passages comes from Daniel 8:1–27; the second is found in the book of Joel, especially Joel 2:28–32. These passages have been selected in order to illustrate two different stages in the use of apocalyptic themes and language in the Old Testament.

Although the two accounts have certain similarities, they differ significantly in the degree to which they reflect an apocalyptic emphasis. In the book of Joel, the apocalyptic emphasis is embedded within a more general prophetic message similar to Old Testament prophetic literature found elsewhere. Joel reflects an incipient apocalypticism that finds expression within a larger framework of national disaster and communal lament dealing with prior historical circumstances. The book of Daniel, on the other hand, takes the apocalyptic emphasis to another level. It reflects a full-blown apocalypticism that moves well beyond the common features of Old Testament prophecy. While the book of Joel is illustrative of a transition from traditional Israelite prophecy to an emerging apocalypticism, Daniel 8 is illustrative of a fully developed apocalypticism. On a continuum, the book of Joel thus stands somewhere between classical Israelite prophecy and the genre known as apocalypse. The book of Daniel stands at the end of this continuum so far as canonical books are concerned; the second half of this book is a full-featured apocalypse.

A RAM, A GOAT, AND THE WORD OF THE LORD
(DANIEL 8:1–27)

Daniel 8 presents an apocalyptic vision received by Daniel in a vision during the third year of the reign of Belshazzar (ca. 551 B.C.). Through the angel Gabriel, Daniel also receives an interpretation of the main features of this vision. The chapter makes extensive use of animal symbolism to describe divinely determined events relative to human history. Daniel's vision concerns events that pertain to the ancient empires of Persia and Greece, as well as developments related to the immediate successors of Alexander the Great. Identification of the historical referents in the vision is rather clear in light of the interpretation provided by the biblical text itself. This interpretation receives corroboration and further specificity from extrabiblical historical records. The historical fulfillment of the events of chapter eight spans several centuries, taking place from the sixth to second centuries B.C.

Most modern readers (or listeners) will initially find this chapter puzzling; to some it may even seem bizarre. Its apocalyptic features will seem unfamiliar and unclear to those who are inexperienced with this genre of literature. The task of public proclamation of such a text must therefore overcome greater obstacles than is the case with most other biblical writings. How should one approach Daniel 8 with the task of proclamation in mind?

Getting Familiar with the Text

The first step is to become as familiar as possible with the biblical text that has been selected for proclamation. No matter how much expositors may have read or studied the book of Daniel previously, they should commit a significant block of preparation time to renewing familiarity with the book of Daniel in general and chapter 8 in particular. This means reading and rereading the passage at hand; it means studying and restudying the biblical text. This should be done in several different formats.

First, the expositor should work through the biblical text in its original language. Depending on one's facility with the Hebrew language, this may be a rather laborious process. Such is particularly the case the first time one works through an unfamiliar passage in the Hebrew Bible. But the effort expended in drawing close to the text will be richly repaid in exegetical insight and understanding. There will be new Hebrew vocabulary words to learn and unfamiliar Hebrew verbs to parse, as well as new syntactical patterns and linguistic features that may seem rather different from what one has encountered elsewhere in the Hebrew Bible. A good computer program for Bible study such as BibleWorks, Logos, or Accordance is essential for efficient electronic searching of texts and convenient access to a variety of electronic resources. A standard Hebrew dictionary, such as *HALOT*, should be kept close at hand, as well as a good summary of Hebrew syntax, such as the works by Arnold and Choi or Waltke and O'Connor.[1] One might also find useful a reader's edition of the Hebrew Bible that provides relevant vocabulary and parsing help at the bottom of each page of the biblical text.[2]

After the initial spade work has been done in working through the Hebrew text of this passage, each rereading of the text becomes increasingly more manageable and profitable. Those engaged in regular proclamation of the Old Testament should keep in mind that there is no substitute for sustained study of the Hebrew text. Luther's advice to ministers is very much to the point: "Keep hard at the languages, for language is the sheath in which the sword of the Spirit rests."

Second, it will be helpful to read through the passage in a variety of translations, either in English or whatever modern language one is most comfortable with. Watching for specific points of interest will lend focus to the study. In the first place, one will want to get in mind the flow of thought in the passage. The general structure of Daniel 8 is fairly obvious. There are two main divisions. The first half of the chapter (vv. 1–14) describes Daniel's vision of a ram and a goat engaged in furious conflict and the consequences of that violent confrontation. Various horns that appear on the goat are also described. One of these, the so-called "little horn," receives greater attention than the other horns (vv. 9–12; cf. vv. 23–25). It is clear from the personification utilized in these descriptions that we are dealing with a figurative account of various human conflicts that are described in startling terms. The descriptions found in this chapter intend to arrest the attention of readers and provoke their curiosity about the meaning of the figurative language that is employed. The second half of the chapter (vv. 15–27) provides a key to the interpretation of the vision that confirms the reader's initial suspicion that much of the language is highly symbolic and figurative. Since the general interpretation of much of this figurative language is provided in the biblical text itself, we can be confident about its intended meaning.

The apocalyptic vision of chapter eight concerns a military conflict between Persia and Greece and related historical events of the follow-

---

1. Bill T. Arnold and John H. Choi, *A Guide to Biblical Hebrew Syntax* (Cambridge: Cambridge University Press, 2003); Bruce K. Waltke and M. O'Connor, *An Introduction to Biblical Hebrew Syntax* (Winona Lake, IN: Eisenbrauns, 1990).

2. *Biblia Hebraica Stuttgartensia: A Reader's Edition*, ed. Karl Elliger, Wilhelm Randolph, and Adrian Schenker, lexical and grammatical apparatus by Donald R. Vance, George Athas, Yael Avrahami (Peabody, MA: Henrickson, 2014).

ing centuries. The text makes this quite clear. According to verse 20, "The two-horned ram that you saw represents the kings of Media and Persia." Other elements in the interpretation are also provided, clarifying the identity of the characters and the time-period that is involved. According to verse 21, the shaggy goat represents the king of Greece. The large horn between the eyes of the goat stands for a king of Greece. The four horns that appear after the first horn was broken off represent four weaker kingdoms that will emerge after the death of the earlier king. These key interpretive elements are set forth in verses 21–22:

> The shaggy goat is the king of Greece, and the large horn between his eyes is the first king. The four horns that replaced the one that was broken off represent four kingdoms that will emerge from his nation but will not have the same power.

The so-called little horn described in some detail in this chapter represents a fierce king who will arise in the latter stages of this divided kingdom. His rise and fall are depicted in verses 23–25:

> In the latter part of their reign, when rebels have become completely wicked, a fierce-looking king, a master of intrigue, will arise. He will become very strong, but not by his own power. He will cause astounding devastation and will succeed in whatever he does. He will destroy those who are mighty, the holy people. He will cause deceit to prosper, and he will consider himself superior. When they feel secure, he will destroy many and take his stand against the Prince of princes. Yet he will be destroyed, but not by human power.

While the kings represented by these horns are not specifically named in the book of Daniel, we are able with confidence to establish their identity by correlating extant historical records with the corresponding biblical descriptions. It is clear that the general tenor of the passage has to do with the surprising military victory of Greece (i.e., "the goat") over Persia (i.e., "the ram"), the subsequent death of the renowned Greek leader Alexander the Great (i.e., "the large horn"), the division of his kingdom following his death to his four main successors (i.e., "the four horns"), known in the historical records as the **Diadochoi**, and the subsequent rise in the second century of a Seleucid ruler known as Antiochus IV Epiphanes (i.e., "the little horn"). A central focus of this chapter has to do with the intersection of these events with the destiny of the Jewish people, who are referred to as "the holy people" (עַם קְדֹשִׁים, v. 24) and who are led by "the Prince of princes" (שַׂר שָׂרִים, v. 25), a reference to the God of this people. The main concern of the chapter is the Persian and Greek conflict in the fourth century and the profound impact on the Jewish people of the historical events that followed this conflict.

A second area of interest has to do with characterization of key figures in the text. What sort of information does the text present with regard to these key figures, and what is the significance of that information in terms of how we understand the text? A prominent personality in this chapter is the so-called "little horn," which is a reference to the Seleucid ruler Antiochus Epiphanes. His characterization in this chapter is entirely negative, in spite of the fact that he is portrayed as incredibly influential and powerful. A plethora of expressions calls attention to the danger he poses for Daniel's people. He is referred to as "a fierce-looking king" (v. 23), "a master of intrigue" (v. 23), one enabled by a power not entirely his own (v. 24), one responsible for incredible devastation (v. 24), one highly successful in accomplishing his devious goals (v. 24), one causing painful damage to the Jewish people (v. 25), a facilitator of deceitful dealings (v. 25), one adamantly opposed to the Israelite deity (v. 25), and one subject to certain destruction by God (v. 25). This profile portrays a powerful human leader who violently opposes the people of God and threatens their way of life and indeed their very existence. However, his destructive influence is said to continue only for a limited time. Due to intervention by the God of Israel, his opposition to the people of God will ultimately fail (cf. v. 25).[3]

The theology of Daniel 8 reflects two distinct elements. First, the chapter assumes that God is in control of human history, even when that history negatively impacts the people of God in profound ways. According to this text, events yet future to Daniel's time have already been determined in detail by God. History is not the random accumulation of time and events that occur apart from a divine purpose. Rather, history unfolds according to a divine plan, whether with regard to individual lives or with regard to national events. As is the case with many apocalyptic works, the theology of Daniel 8 is deterministic in the way it portrays future events. Second, the theology of Daniel 8 involves a highly developed angelology. In this chapter angels are key participants in divine communication with human beings. Illumination of the meaning of the vision comes to Daniel through angelic participation and mediation. The angelic participant Gabriel is mentioned by name, while other angelic participants are present but remain nameless.

---

3. This chapter of the book of Daniel did not escape the attention of the Jewish historian Josephus. After summarizing Daniel 8, Josephus says, "And these misfortunes our nation did in fact come to experience under Antiochus Epiphanes, just as Daniel many years before saw and wrote that they would happen." See Josephus, *Ant.* 10.276.

It is noteworthy that the only two angels named in the Old Testament, Gabriel and Michael, both appear in the book of Daniel. The angelology of this book is more developed than is the case for most other books of the Old Testament.

According to verse 13, a conversation takes place between two "holy ones" (קָדוֹשׁ) regarding the length of time that would be required for the fulfillment of the vision. When Daniel tries in vain to understand the meaning of the vision he has just seen, "one who looked like a man" (כְּמַרְאֵה גָבֶר) appeared before him, instructing Gabriel to explain to Daniel the meaning of the vision (vv. 15–16). After explaining the vision, Gabriel instructs Daniel to "seal up the vision, for it concerns the distant future" (v. 26). This sort of angelic mediation of divine revelation and angelic instruction to the human recipient of a vision or dream is characteristic of much of apocalyptic literature, which like the book of Daniel tends to have a complex and elaborate angelology.

In reading through the biblical text in the initial stages of investigation the expositor will also want to ascertain the purpose of the author. Why is the reader of the book of Daniel presented with this information, and what did the author expect his readers to conclude or do on the basis of this presentation? What is the general theological truth that the recorded events point to or illustrate?

It appears that the **implied reader** of Daniel 8 is expected to draw consolation from the description of this vision, realizing that there is a divinely intended plan and purpose to history. The original Jewish audience was expected to see God at work in mysterious ways in the unfolding of this history, bringing about his intended purposes even as evil seemed to have the upper hand over good. Subsequent readers could be expected to draw a similar conclusion. If God worked in such unusual ways through the events of Persian, Greek, and Seleucid history, rescuing his people from unprecedented violence and adversity, surely he could be expected to do so in their day as well. The believing community was therefore expected to draw hope, comfort, and assurance from this chapter, concluding that God would also work in their behalf for the fulfillment of his purposes whenever they confronted similar experiences of difficulty, confusion, and uncertainty. This theme should guide contemporary exposition of this passage.

Resolving the Main Difficulties

Before going very far in the study of Daniel 8, interpreters will need to resolve several types of difficulties in the chapter. The first of these has to do with the condition of the received Hebrew text that has come down to us. The available textual evidence indicates that there are places in this chapter where the Hebrew text requires emendation due to damage sustained in the process of transmission. In the critical apparatus of *BHS* the editor calls attention to forty-two textual issues for this chapter. This is not an exhaustive presentation of textual variants for this chapter; other variants found in Hebrew manuscripts and ancient versions could be mentioned as well. But in the opinion of the *BHS* editor, these are the ones that are most likely to be of interest to translators and exegetes. Some of these variants turn out to be rather inconsequential, involving minor details of Masoretic vocalization that do not affect the meaning of the text. Others are conjectural emendations, lacking sufficient external and/or internal evidence to warrant changing the wording of the text. Only a few of the variants mentioned in *BHS* for this chapter are significant for expositors of the text. But these should be given careful attention.

First, in verse 20 the Masoretic text has the plural expression "the *kings* of Media and Persia" (מלכי מדי ופרס). However, several versional witnesses have the singular expression "the *king*" of Media and Persia. These witnesses include the Old Greek, Theodotion, Syriac Peshitta, and Latin Vulgate. The difference in an unvocalized Hebrew text is a single letter, namely a final *yod* on the word for "king" (מלכי vs. מלך). However, the difference significantly affects interpretation of this text. Does the ram represent a succession of kings of Media and Persia, or does it represent only a single king? The wide-ranging scope of the chapter suggests that a plurality of kings is intended here. This lends credence to the possibility that a *yod* was overlooked by these versional witnesses (or by the scribe of their Hebrew ***Vorlage***) than that a *yod* was added by our extant Hebrew witnesses. It seems best, therefore, to retain the plural reading of the Masoretic text.

Second, in verse 22 the Masoretic text has the phrase "from *a* nation" (מגוי), referring to the origin of the four kingdoms that will replace the king of Greece. However, the Old Greek, Theodotion, and Latin Vulgate attest to a Hebrew text that had "from *his* nation" (מגויו). This reading implies the presence of a final *waw* on the expression מגוי that is absent in the Masoretic text. It seems likely that the Masoretic text has suffered here from **haplography**, whereby the *yod-waw* sequence of letters was written simply as *yod*. Due to the similarity of these two letters in the ancient script, confusion of *waw* and *yod* is in fact one of the most common of all scribal mistakes. It seems best to emend the Masoretic text to read "from *his* nation" rather than "from *a* nation." From the context it is clear that the origin of these four kingdoms is specific rather than indefinite. In this instance the reading of the Old Greek, Theodotion, and Latin Vulgate is to be preferred over that of the Masoretic text.

Third, in verse 23 the Masoretic text has "the *transgressors*" (הפשעים), referring to a time "when *the transgressors* have reached their full measure" (RSV; cf. ASV, KJV, NKJV, NASB, NIV, ESV). However, the Old Greek, Theodotion, Latin Vulgate, and Syriac Peshitta have instead "(their) *transgressions*" (cf. NET, NRSV, NJB, NLT, Tanak). This is a matter of proper vocalization of the Hebrew word in question; the consonants can be read either way. It is more likely that the text should be read as referring to *transgressions* (rather than *transgressors*) reaching their full measure, since this expression is used elsewhere in the Old Testament (cf. Gen. 15:16). It seems best to emend the vocalization of the Masoretic text in verse 23 to read "transgressions," in keeping with the evidence of the ancient versions. In the remainder of this chapter, the Masoretic text may be accepted without change.

The second type of difficulty encountered in Daniel 8 has to do with interpretation of the text. The biggest single problem of interpretation in this chapter concerns the meaning of the reference to "2,300 evenings and mornings" (v. 14; cf. v. 26). This enigmatic expression seems to refer to a precisely defined period of time. But it is not immediately clear what specific starting and ending points are in view here. This reference has led to considerable speculation and even eschatological date-setting on the part of some interpreters.[4] However, in light of the context the verse is best understood as pointing to certain historical events of the second century B.C. rather than to eschatological events. At issue is a crucial period of time during which the Jerusalem temple was subject to profane actions on the part of Antiochus Epiphanes. But exactly what period of time is referenced by this phrase, and what is the significance of this period of time? Some interpreters take the phrase to mean the equivalent of 1,150 days. In this view the 2,300 evening and morning sacrifices (התמיד) were offered during half as many days, since two sacrifices (i.e., one in the morning and one in the evening) were offered each day. However, in light of similar language ("evening and morning") used for the days of the creative week in Genesis 1, it seems more likely that each "evening and morning" refers to one day in a period of time consisting of a total of 2,300 days.

Even so, the conclusion of this period of time is easier to establish than its beginning. Extrabiblical historical records enable us to be rather precise with regard to the conclusion of this period of time. Following atrocious profanations that included the offering of a pig on the sacred altar, the Jerusalem temple was reconsecrated on December 25, 165 B.C. This event is likely to be the concluding date of Daniel's 2,300 days. However, we do not know of a singular event that occurred 2,300

---

4. For a detailed account of the modern history of interpretation of this text, see Samuel Nuñez, *The Vision of Daniel 8: Interpretations from 1700 to 1800*, Andrews University Seminary Doctoral Dissertation Series, vol. 14 (Berrien Springs, MI: Andrews University Press, 1987). In spite of its title, this volume covers the history of interpretation of Daniel 8 from 1700 to 1900.

days prior to that rededication to which this reference might point. For that reason, the expression remains rather puzzling to most interpreters. Still, it seems best to understand this period of time as finding fulfillment in the latter years of the reign of Antiochus Epiphanes, rather than pointing to some distant eschatological event. The earliest audiences of the book of Daniel probably found the correlation easier to grasp than would later audiences distantly removed from those events.

Some interpreters take a very different view with regard to the 2,300 evenings and mornings of Daniel 8. Understanding the phrase to be a cryptic reference to years rather than days, they suggest that this verse provides a timetable for calculating the end of the world as we know it. By taking the commencement of this period to be the decree of Artaxerxes in 457 B.C., and by taking the time period to be 2,300 years rather than days, some interpreters concluded that Christ's return to reconsecrate the temple would occur in A.D. 1844.[5] During the first part of the nineteenth century this interpretation was very influential in the United States, leading many to abandon the normal activities of life and gather to wait for Christ's return at the expected time. When the expected events did not materialize, devotees of this interpretation were shattered and disillusioned. The experience came to be known as "the Great Disappointment."

Such views were based on a flawed understanding of the meaning of Daniel's reference to 2,300 "evenings and mornings." A biblical text that is best understood as referring to a crucial time of profane action taken against the Jewish temple in Jerusalem by a second-century autocrat became instead a prooftext for a novel understanding of the timing of the return of Christ.

Clarifying the Structure

We may now turn attention to the boundaries and structure of this pericope. Two things stand out. First, the boundaries of the pericope are clearly indicated by the traditional chapter division. The pericope begins in verse 1 and concludes in verse 27. Its delimitation is not disputed. Second, the structure of the chapter is not particularly difficult. This structure can be displayed by an exegetical outline that shows the relationship of the various parts of the chapter to one another. Such an outline might look something like the following.

---

5. On the basis of Daniel 8:14, William Miller (1782–1849) expected the return of Christ in 1843. His follower Samuel S. Snow revised Miller's date to October 22, 1844. For a similar view see Jacques B. Doukhan, *Daniel: The Vision of the End*, rev. ed. (Berrien Springs, MI: Andrews University Press, 1989), especially 23–44. For an analysis of Miller's life, views, and influence, see David L. Rowe, *God's Strange Work: William Miller and the End of the World*, Library of Religious Biography, ed. Mark A. Noll, Nathan O. Hatch, and Allen C. Guelo (Grand Rapids: Eerdmans, 2008).

Exegetical Outline of Daniel 8

I.   Daniel sees a vision of a ram, helpless to stand before a destructive goat on which there appears a vicious little horn that wreaks havoc upon the heavenly host and the sanctuary for a period of time (vv. 1–14).
  A. Daniel has a vision in which he appears in Shushan at the Ulai canal (vv. 1–2).
    1. In the third year of the reign of king Belshazzar another vision appears to Daniel (v. 1).
    2. In his vision Daniel appears in Shushan the citadel at the Ulai canal (v. 2).
  B. In his vision, Daniel watches a male goat with a large horn as it overpowers a two-horned ram, only to have its own large horn broken and four other horns to appear (vv. 3–8).
    1. Daniel sees a ram appear with two horns, the longer of which came up last (v. 3).
    2. Daniel sees the ram pushing westward and northward and southward, completely unrestrained, doing as he pleased and increasing in power (v. 4).
    3. Daniel sees a male goat with a conspicuous horn between its eyes coming swiftly from the west (v. 5).
    4. Enraged, the goat charges at the ram (v. 6).
    5. Daniel sees the goat strike the ram and break his two horns, leaving him a helpless and unaided victim of the goat's destructive power (v. 7).
    6. When the goat becomes increasingly great, its large horn is broken and four other horns emerge (v. 8).
  C. A small horn appears, increasing in size and wreaking havoc upon sacred things (vv. 9–12).
    1. A small horn emerges from the others and increases in size toward the south, the east, and the west (v. 9).
    2. The horn continues to increase, throwing down and trampling some of the stars of heaven (v. 10).
    3. The horn removes the daily sacrifice and casts down the place of the sanctuary (v. 11).
    4. Due to rebellion the host and the daily sacrifice are given over to the horn, while it continues to prosper in disregard for truth (v. 12).
  D. A holy one indicates that after a specific time the sanctuary will be restored (vv. 13–14).
    1. Another holy one asks the one speaking to Daniel how long it will take for the vision to be fulfilled (v. 13).
    2. He is told that the sanctuary will be restored after 2,300 evenings and mornings (v. 14).

II. When the angel Gabriel explains to Daniel the meaning of his vision, Daniel is left astounded and perplexed (vv. 15–27).
    A. The angel Gabriel is sent to provide Daniel with the meaning of the vision (vv. 15–18).
        1. As Daniel reflects upon the meaning of the vision, one with a human likeness appears (v. 15).
        2. Gabriel is instructed to explain the meaning of the vision to Daniel (v. 16).
        3. Gabriel tells a frightened Daniel that the vision pertains to "the time of the end" (v. 17).
        4. Daniel slips into a trance, from which Gabriel draws him back (v. 18).
    B. Angel Gabriel explains the details of the vision (vv. 19–26).
        1. Gabriel again indicates that the vision pertains to "the time of the end" (v. 19).
        2. Gabriel explains the significance of the ram and of the goat (vv. 20–21).
            a. The ram with two horns represents Media and Persia (v. 20).
            b. The male goat represents Greece, and the large horn represents its first king (v. 21).
        3. Gabriel explains the significance of the horns (vv. 22–25).
            a. The four horns represent four subsequent but weaker kingdoms, which emerge from the same nation (v. 22).
            b. In their latter stage a king will arise by intrigue (v. 23).
            c. His might will be great and his influence destructive (v. 24).
            d. His destructive influence will be brought to an end apart from human agency (v. 25).
        4. Gabriel instructs Daniel to preserve the vision because of its future relevance (v. 26).
    C. After a period of illness induced by the vision Daniel resumes his activity, although still perplexed by the vision (v. 27).

The advantage of developing an analytical outline of this sort is apparent. The expositor can see at a glance the organizational structure of the pericope and use this as a basis for formulating an expositional outline that can guide the proclamation of the passage. In that way one allows the text to guide the exposition, rather than forcing the text into an artificial and arbitrary grid that may obscure rather than clarify its message.

Summarizing the Main Point(s)

On the basis of the structural outline of Daniel 8 we can summarize the general content of the chapter. If the outline is accurate, to a large extent formulation of the main point of the pericope will amount to a synthesis of the main points of the outline. For this chapter the following statement serves this purpose:

> *An angel explains to Daniel the significance of a vision in which Daniel sees a powerful goat overpowering a two-horned ram and a little horn causing even greater destruction.*

This statement summarizes the content of the chapter in very broad terms. Later we will convert this exegetical statement to a more general theological statement that will guide the proclamation of this passage.

Framing the Presentation

We are now ready to frame our presentation in theological and homiletical terms, using the exegetical outline as a template for this purpose. We will follow the general outline of the author's message in this chapter, but we will shape it and adapt it to fit our modern context. Rather than retaining the specific details regarding persons and events as found in the exegetical outline, it will be helpful to expand these details into corresponding timeless truths. Such an outline might look something like what follows here.

Homiletical Outline of Daniel 8

I. History is unfolding in a way that God has determined, even in those instances when it appears that the viability of God's people is threatened (vv. 1–14).
    A. God has chosen to disclose to the writers of the biblical texts glimpses of coming events (vv. 1–2).
    B. God is mysteriously at work in the progress of human history (vv. 3–8).
    C. As history unfolds, the welfare of God's people is sometimes threatened by hostile forces (vv. 9–12).
    D. Evil may prosper for a season, but God intervenes in due time (vv. 13–14).
II. God's revelation provides insight into life's circumstances, even though it does not answer all our questions (vv. 15–27).
    A. God has provided a means for understanding his revelation (vv. 15–18).
    B. His revelation offers guidance for understanding the events taking place around us (vv. 19–26).
    C. His revelation is at times perplexing and awe-inspiring (v. 27).

This outline calls attention to the main points that will be the focus of proclamation of this biblical text. In keeping with the main points of this homiletical outline, which is based on the corresponding exegetical outline presented earlier in this chapter, we may now state the applicational message of our text:

> *Believers should find hope and encouragement in God's sovereign working in history to accomplish his purposes, even though they may not fully understand all the implications of that plan.*

While this statement is based on the exegetical main idea, that idea has been reexpressed in more general and applicational terms. The exegetical outline and summary statement described previously have now morphed into timeless truths in order to show the relevance of the biblical text to a contemporary audience, while at the same time remaining anchored to the content and purpose of the biblical text.

Listening to Other Interpreters

Since biblical interpretation is best done as a collaborative rather than independent effort, it is important for expositors to be aware of the contributions of other serious students of the text. Reading widely in the secondary literature (i.e., commentaries and specialized essays that treat the passage in question) helps expositors in at least two ways. First, such reading often provides valuable insights into the meaning of the text that one may have overlooked in earlier research. These insights can contribute a richness and precision to one's presentation that otherwise might be forfeited. Second, such reading in the secondary literature serves as a potential corrective to erroneous conclusions that the expositor may have previously drawn. By learning from expositions found in the commentary literature expositors have the opportunity to submit their own views to critical evaluation and make adjustments in their thinking prior to public presentation. This process can save one from needless mistakes and potential inaccuracies.

Unlike some portions of the Old Testament, the book of Daniel is fairly well served with helpful commentaries. Some of these works are strongly exegetical and technical in nature. Others are more expositional and practical in their approach. They all have certain strengths as well as certain weaknesses. Which commentary one will find most useful depends in part on the type of help one seeks. Expositors should make use of various types of commentaries in order to glean critical, exegetical, linguistic, expositional, and applicational help as needed.

The following commentaries are selected with various types of information in mind. The selections are limited to treatments of the book of Daniel in English. In addition to commentaries, there is also a large body of essays and journal articles dealing with various aspects of Daniel scholarship. We will not attempt to deal with that literature here.[6]

Archer, Gleason L., Jr. "Daniel." In *The Expositor's Bible Commentary*, edited by Frank E. Gaebelein et al., vol. 7, 1–157. Grand Rapids: Zondervan, 1985. A brief but helpful exposition of the book of Daniel from a conservative, premillennial perspective.

Baldwin, Joyce G. *Daniel: An Introduction and Commentary.* Tyndale Old Testament Commentaries, ed. D. J. Wiseman. Downers Grove, IL: InterVarsity Press, 1978. One of the best expositions of the book of Daniel from a generally conservative viewpoint. Baldwin's explanations are typically brief but incisive and helpful.

Charles, R. H. *A Critical and Exegetical Commentary on the Book of Daniel, with Introduction, Indexes, and a New English Translation.* Oxford: Clarendon Press, 1929. Reprint, Eugene, OR: Wipf and Stock, 2006. An older critical work by a well-known specialist in apocalyptic literature. Its strengths lie in the areas of text criticism, language, and familiarity with a broad range of apocalyptic literature.

Collins, John J. *Daniel: A Commentary on the Book of Daniel.* Hermeneia, ed. Frank Moore Cross. Minneapolis: Fortress, 1993. The best and most up-to-date critical commentary on the book of Daniel. It is especially strong on text-critical and form-critical matters, as well as historical backgrounds that inform the study of Daniel.

Goldingay, John E. *Daniel.* Word Biblical Commentary, eds. David A. Hubbard and Glenn W. Barker, vol. 30. Dallas: Word, 1989. An exegetical commentary on the book of Daniel by an evangelical Old Testament scholar. This work pays attention to literary form and historical backgrounds. It interacts with an impressive array of secondary literature on Daniel.

---

6. See, for example, Henry O. Thompson, *The Book of Daniel: An Annotated Bibliography*, Books of the Bible, ed. Henry O. Thompson, vol. 1, Garland Reference Library of the Humanities, vol. 1310 (New York and London: Garland, 1993).

Hartman, Louis F., and Alexander A. Di Lella. *The Book of Daniel.* Anchor Bible, ed. William Foxwell Albright and David Noel Freedman, vol. 23. Garden City, NY: Doubleday, 1978. A critical commentary on the book of Daniel written by two Roman Catholic scholars. It gives attention to text-critical and linguistic issues.

Hill, Andrew. "Daniel." In *The Expositor's Bible Commentary.* Rev. ed. Edited by Tremper Longman III and David E. Garland, vol. 8, 19–212. Grand Rapids: Zondervan, 2008. A brief but helpful treatment of the book of Daniel by a conservative Old Testament scholar. Hill takes an early date for Daniel, concluding that this book "was composed in the Babylonian **Diaspora** by Daniel, or more likely by associates who outlived him, sometime after 536 BC . . . and before 515 BC" (p. 25).

Longman, Tremper, III. *Daniel.* NIV Application Commentary, ed. Terry Muck. Grand Rapids: Zondervan, 1999. A brief exposition of the book of Daniel that seeks to point out applications to modern life and culture. This is a big-picture work that focuses more on major themes and theological ideas and less on technical details. It is especially useful for those preaching from the book of Daniel.

Lucas, Ernest. *Daniel.* Apollos Old Testament Commentary, eds. David W. Baker and Gordon J. Wenham, vol. 20. Downers Grove, IL: InterVarsity, 2002. A conservative study of the book of Daniel. Each unit of the commentary proper is divided into four sections. First, notes treat significant issues of textual criticism, grammar, and semantics. Second, a section on form and structure highlights major concerns of genre, organization, unity, and word usage. Third, a section labeled "comment" examines matters of historical, cultural, and religious backgrounds. Fourth, a section entitled "explanation" stresses major theological issues, with some consideration of contemporary implications.

Miller, Stephen R. *Daniel.* New American Commentary, ed. E. Ray Clendenen, vol. 18. Nashville: Broadman & Holman, 1994. A helpful exposition of the book of Daniel from a conservative, premillennial point of view.

Montgomery, James A. *A Critical and Exegetical Commentary on the Book of Daniel.* International Critical Commentary, ed. S. R.

Driver, A. Plummer, and C. A. Briggs. Edinburgh: T. & T. Clark, 1927. For many decades this critical work was without peer in its treatment of textual, linguistic, and historical matters for the book of Daniel. Although now out-of-date, it is still useful for technical and critical matters. But for a readable and uncluttered exposition, one must look elsewhere.

Newsom, Carol A., with Brennan W. Breed. *Daniel: A Commentary*. Old Testament Library. Louisville: Westminster John Knox, 2014. This unique commentary has two distinct parts. Newsom's commentary on Daniel provides a great deal of exegetical and historical detail, while Breed's treatment of reception history provides a thorough summary of the use of Daniel in literature, music, and art from ancient to modern times.

Pace, Sharon. *Daniel*. Smyth & Helwys Bible Commentary, ed. R. Scott Nash, vol. 17. Macon, GA: Smyth & Helwys, 2008. An exposition of the book of Daniel from a moderately critical perspective. This book is well illustrated, user-friendly, and makes frequent connections to modern life.

Young, Edward J. *The Prophecy of Daniel: A Commentary*. Grand Rapids: Eerdmans, 1949. An older treatment of the book of Daniel from a conservative amillennial perspective.

Bridging to Application

Apocalyptic literature in general, both biblical and extrabiblical, holds out hope and encouragement for those who have reason to wonder about justice and equity in the world, particularly as these issues affect the believing community. Apocalyptic communities often see the world as being hopelessly on a path of opposition to what is right and deserving of divine retribution. In such a context is there room for hope and encouragement? For apocalyptic writers, the answer is "yes." Hope comes from the realization that, in spite of evil forces that are at work in the world, God is also at work in bringing his purposes to fruition. Encouragement derives from the realization that the suffering of the righteous and their affliction do not go unnoticed by God. In due time God will interrupt the normal flow of history and bring his kingdom into full realization. The ungodly will be punished, and the righteous will be vindicated. In dark days when it might appear that evil has the upper hand and the righteous are downtrodden and oppressed, apocalyptic texts point to a future in which history will come to its intended end and the kingdom of God will prosper without hindrance or detraction. Right will ultimately prevail. This is a common theme in apocalyptic literature.

Daniel 8 is an example of such an apocalyptic hope. To a community undergoing persecution and adversity for their faith this chapter holds out hope and encouragement, based on a theological understanding of what is happening in the world. Application of the content of the chapter to a modern setting should focus on two important truths. First, God is sovereign. He is working in and through human history to accomplish his purposes. Empires come and go. Charismatic leaders rise and fall. Nations flourish for a time and then experience decay and decline. Eventually they disappear altogether. No human empire is exempt from this process of decay and eventual collapse. Yet God is at work, unhindered by human successes and failures of the past, the present, or the future. He determines what has happened in the past, what is presently happening, and what yet will happen in the future. He is in control of human history, and he has a plan that is moving unfailingly toward its intended goals. Second, the ultimate hope of believers is not in this life but in the next. Suffering and persecution may be their lot for a time, but their hope is in the approaching kingdom of God. Evil is present in the world, but God is greater than any threat or danger that evil can pose. The message of Daniel 8 is one of divine sovereignty and eschatological hope. These themes provide guidance for the public proclamation of this intriguing chapter.

LESSONS FROM LOCUSTS
(JOEL 2:28–32)

Sometimes Old Testament accounts of historical events contain pronouncements of surprising proportions that seem to transcend their original context. Such a scenario occurs in Joel 2:28–32.[7] Here a detailed poetic description of a locust plague becomes the basis for describing future events that are typologically related to the locust and famine disaster described in the book of Joel. Moving from type to antitype, Joel describes the day of the Lord as follows:

> And afterward, I will pour out my Spirit on all people.
> Your sons and daughters will prophesy, your old men will
> dream dreams, your young men will see visions. Even on
> my servants, both men and women, I will pour out my

---

7. For convenience, I follow here the chapter and verse divisions of the English text of the book of Joel, which is consistent with earlier translations such as the Latin Vulgate. Since the sixteenth century, the printed Hebrew text has followed a slightly different division, whereby Joel 2:28–32 is presented as Joel 3:1–5 in the Hebrew text, and chapter 3 is presented as chapter 4 in the Hebrew text.

> Spirit in those days. I will show wonders in the heavens and on the earth, blood and fire and billows of smoke. The sun will be turned to darkness and the moon to blood before the coming of the great and dreadful day of the LORD. And everyone who calls on the name of the LORD will be saved; for on Mount Zion and in Jerusalem there will be deliverance, as the LORD has said, among the survivors whom the LORD calls.

Several things in this passage suggest the presence of incipient apocalyptic motifs. First, there is a transformational element that points to democratization of spiritual gifts regardless of gender, age, or social standing. Joel associates this event with an approaching time known as the day of the Lord. Second, there is an emphasis on unusual displays of cosmic phenomena that portend special divine activity. Third, there is an element of divine intervention and deliverance for a people who are identified with the Lord through individual faith. Fourth, there is a sense of vindication for the righteous, with implied punishment for the unrighteous. Such themes, elsewhere developed more fully in full-blown apocalyptic texts, are common features of Jewish apocalyptic literature.

Getting Familiar with the Text

In order to grasp the grand prophecies found in Joel 2:28–32, it is helpful to have a sense of the argument of the book of Joel as a whole. The apocalyptic message of this prophet is situated in a set of historical events that, according to the prophet, anticipate even greater events of the future. The key historical event on which Joel focuses has to do with a series of unparalleled locust invasions that had left the agrarian economy of Judah in a state of disaster.[8] To make matters even worse, these locust invasions were accompanied by conditions of severe drought. As a result, human, animal, and plant life alike were reduced to conditions of deprivation and abject misery. The book of Joel describes in detail these difficult times, and sees them as harbingers of even more alarming things to come.

Following a brief superscription that identifies the author of the book, Joel describes a locust plague of unprecedented proportions that will form part of the collective memory of his readers for many generations to come (1:2–4). Successive swarms of locusts have consumed everything edible, leaving nothing for drunkards to drink

---

8. In 1915 Palestine experienced a severe locust invasion that had dire consequences for the local economy. John Whiting was present at the time and able to provide a detailed account of this plague, along with photographs. See John D. Whiting, "Jerusalem's Locust Plague," *National Geographic Magazine* 27.6 (December 1915): 511–50.

(1:5), for priests to sacrifice (1:9–10), nor for farmers to harvest (1:11–12). Not only have locusts consumed the leafy vegetation but they have even stripped off the bark of branches, leaving the pithy core exposed (1:7).[9]

The prophet therefore calls for a communal lament, summoning all the people to appeal to the Lord for mercy (1:13–20). The devastation is graphically described in military terms, likening the scene to the carnage of war. In figurative language the locusts are referred to as a "nation" and a "mighty army"; they are likened to large ravenous beasts that leave destruction in their wake (1:6). At the same time, there is a failure with regard to rainfall, with the result that the landscape appears as though a fire has burned through the land (1:19–20). The locust army is hyperbolically described as a mighty army methodically marching through the countryside, leaving only destruction in its path (2:1–9). This army moves at the Lord's command; it is in fact "his army" (2:11).

Joel's locusts prefigure an eschatological scene called "the day of the Lord" (2:1–2, 11). The proper response to these alarming events is one of repentance and appeal to the Lord for mercy rather than judgment (2:12–17). When his people become the scorn of neighboring nations who observe their plight and question the presence of their God, the divine reputation inevitably suffers as well (2:17).

Joel 2:18 marks a turning point in the book. The Lord responds favorably to the pleas of his people and brings deliverance from the economic destruction that had visited the land (2:18–27). The locusts are again identified as the Lord's great army sent by the Lord himself (2:25). But now, the Lord promises to repay his people for the years the locusts have taken (2:25–26). The Lord will be vindicated, and the people will never again have cause for shame (2:27).

At this point the prophet looks ahead to a time of unprecedented divine activity. A new day will dawn, in which bestowal of the Spirit will show no regard for distinctions based on age, gender, or station in life (2:28–29). There will be wonders in the heavens and on earth; cosmic signs will underscore this divine activity (2:30–31). The Lord will bring deliverance to those who trust in him (2:32). Here the language takes on apocalyptic tones, and the description transcends the events of Joel's day.

The final chapter of the book describes a scene of divine recompense for the enemies of Judah. Joel reverses Isaiah's description of a time of peace and tranquility in which swords and spears will be transformed

---

9. The significance of Joel's use of four words for locusts in Joel 1:4 is not entirely clear. Do these words refer to successive stages of locust life-cycle? Or do they refer to successive waves of locust invasion? Or are they more-or-less synonymous terms, chosen to emphasize the enormity of the threat? They are probably near-synonyms, chosen to underscore the severity of the plague.

into farming instruments (Isa. 2:4). Here ploughshares are turned into swords and pruning hooks into spears, as the Lord readies for judgment in the Valley of Jehoshaphat (3:2, 10–13). Again Joel's language is apocalyptic in nature. Cosmic signs are said to accompany these activities (3:15). Judah, on the other hand, is promised protection, vindication, and times of unprecedented prosperity (3:17–21).

Several things stand out from this overview of the book of Joel. First, much of the book stands squarely within the normative prophetic tradition. It is concerned with a natural calamity that threatened the norms of individual and communal life in Israel. It uses standard prophetic motifs and literary genres to describe these concerns. Second, at times the language breaks forth into heightened descriptions of eschatological significance. The prophet's language takes on an apocalyptic tone, vividly describing an imminent and decisive irruption of divine activity. Third, there is no clear boundary between these disparate units. At times familiar prophetic motifs are interlaced with vivid apocalyptic language. While as a whole the book of Joel is not apocalyptic in nature, portions of the book adopt an apocalyptic tone and make use of apocalyptic imagery.

Resolving the Main Difficulties

Several issues of interpretation confront the student of the book of Joel. First, it is very difficult to ascertain the date of the book. Some scholars date this book as early as the ninth century. This conclusion is based partly on an argument from silence, namely the absence of any mention of a king and the fact that the implied leaders seem to be elders and priests (e.g., 1:2, 13; 2:16). It also draws on the canonical position of Joel early in the Book of the Twelve, which some view as indicative of an early date. However, these and other arguments for a ninth-century date are inconclusive. A later date is more probable. The fact that the book assumes the operation of the Jerusalem temple (e.g., 1:9, 13–16; 2:15–17) seems to rule out an exilic date, since the Temple was destroyed in 586 and its rebuilding was not complete until 515 B.C.[10] Many scholars prefer a postexilic date for Joel, which fits the internal evidence of the book reasonably well.

A second problem is the interpretation of Joel 2. It seems clear that the first chapter of Joel describes a locust invasion of surprising proportions. Does chapter two also have this locust invasion in mind, or is a

---

10. The possibility of an exilic date cannot be completely ruled out, however. Assis has tried to make a case for thinking that the book of Joel is best understood as originating in the exilic period, sometime between 587 and 538 B.C. See Elie Assis, "The Date and Meaning of the Book of Joel," *Vetus Testamentum* 61 (2011): 163–83.

different scenario in view? Some interpreters think that the locusts of
Joel 1 prefigure a historical human invasion of Judah, perhaps of the
Babylonians, which is thought to be the focus of Joel 2. Others see
Joel 2 as portraying an apocalyptic invasion of locust-like creatures portrayed in highly figurative language. The exegetical evidence seems to
favor thinking that the referent of chapters one and two is the same.
In that case, both chapters refer to a locust invasion accompanied by
severe drought. Since there is in the text no clear indication of change
in subject, it seems likely that chapter two continues the description of
the locusts of chapter one.

A third issue concerns the temporal implications of Joel 2:18, which
is a major turning point in the argument of the book. The Hebrew
text here is best understood as describing a recent past event when it
says, "Then the LORD was jealous for his land and took pity on his
people." Some translations instead treat these verbs as future (e.g., KJV,
NKJV, NASB, NIV, NLT). But they are preterites with *wāw* consecu-
tive (ויחמל, ויקנא), indicating that at the time of writing the prophet
already saw evidences of the Lord's renewed favor with his people (cf.
ASV, NAB, NET, NJB, NRSV, TNIV). The people had properly re-
sponded to Joel's earlier appeal, and the Lord had begun the needed
work of renewal, prosperity, and blessing.

Clarifying the Structure

Expositors of Joel 2:28–32 will want to situate this passage within
the larger context of the book as a whole. If the message of an individual pericope is to be properly understood it is important to see it
in proper relation to the overall message of the book. The following
outline may be useful for seeing the relationship of Joel 2:28–32 to
the rest of the book.

Exegetical Outline of the Book of Joel

Superscription (1:1).

I.   A locust plague, accompanied by severe famine, devastates the land
     of Israel (1:2–20).
     A. The enormity of the problem (1:2–4).
         1. It is without precedent (1:2–3).
         2. It has resulted in total devastation of crops (1:4).
     B. The consequences for the society (1:5–12).
         1. The people are without wine (1:5–7).
         2. The priests are without sacrifices (1:8–10).
         3. The farmers are without crops (1:11–12).

    C. A call for lament (1:13–20).
       1. The priests are to call a sacred assembly (1:13–15)
       2. The devastation of the land requires divine intervention (1:16–20)
II. The locust invasion prefigures the day of the Lord (2:1–27).
    A. Fearful consequences of the day of the Lord (2:1–11).
       1. The people tremble in fear (2:1–2).
       2. Nothing escapes destruction (2:3–11).
    B. A call for repentance (2:12–17).
       1. Genuine repentance may be met with the Lord's gracious response (2:12–14).
       2. Every element of society must appeal to the Lord for mercy (2:15–17).
    C. The Lord's gracious response to his people (2:18–27).
       1. The economy will be restored (2:18–26)
       2. God's presence with his people will be obvious to all (2:27)
III. The day of the Lord has consequences (2:28–3:21).
    A. The day of the Lord brings blessings (2:28–32).
       1. Bestowal of the Spirit (2:28–29).
       2. Provision of cosmic signs (2:30–31).
       3. Deliverance for those who turn to the Lord (2:32).
    B. The day of the Lord brings vindication (3:1–21).
       1. Judgment against Israel's enemies (3:1–16).
       2. Prosperity for the people of Israel (3:17–21).

With this overview of the prophet's message in mind we are ready to consider the main point of the book as a whole, as well as the main message of the pericope found in Joel 2:28–32 in particular. Grasping the central message of Joel will bring clarity to the proclamation of each individual section.

Summarizing the Main Point(s)

If the exegetical outline presented above is accurate, the main point of the book of Joel can be deduced by articulating the main points of this outline. Such a summary statement might look something like this:

> *A devastating locust plague typifies the coming day of the Lord, which will bring great blessing for God's people and judgment for his enemies.*

Embedded within this larger argument, there is the particular message of the pericope found in Joel 2:28–32. This message can be summarized in this way:

The approaching day of the Lord will bring a bestowal of the Spirit without regard for normal distinctions. The coming of the Spirit will be accompanied by cosmic portents and will bring spiritual deliverance for those who turn to the Lord.

In light of the apostolic interpretation of Joel 2:28–32 found in Acts 2:17–21, Christian proclamation of Joel's message will focus on the events of the day of Pentecost following the death and resurrection of Jesus. As Peter points out, those events mark the initial fulfillment of Joel's prophecy, although this initial fulfillment allows for a later eschatological fulfillment as well.

Framing the Presentation

Proclaiming the message of Joel involves communicating the meaning of the text in its original setting, and relating that message to general theological truths and points of practical application for a contemporary audience. The following outline is based on the exegetical outline presented above, but it has been adapted to express a more timeless theological message with contemporary relevance. The proclamation of this text could be accomplished in a single message that treats all the book of Joel, or it could be adapted to a series of several messages.

Homiletical Outline of the Book of Joel

I. God sometimes uses natural disaster to call attention to spiritual truth (1:1–20).
    A. Life sometimes presents difficulties of unusual proportions (1:2–4).
    B. The consequences of such problems can be severe (1:5–12).
    C. The proper response is one of turning to the Lord for help (1:13–20).
II. Present difficulties are relatively minor when compared to divine judgment (2:1–27).
    A. The day of the Lord will be a fearful experience for many (2:1–11).
    B. Repentance and turning to the Lord are the path to his favor (2:12–17).
    C. The Lord's grace is abundant to his people (2:18–27).
III. The day of the Lord means different things to different people (2:28–3:21).
    A. The day of the Lord brings blessings to the believing community (2:28–32).
        1. Bestowal of the Spirit without distinction (2:28–29).
        2. Provision of cosmic signs (2:30–31).
        3. Deliverance for those who turn to the Lord (2:32).

B. The day of the Lord brings vindication of the Lord's promises
(3:1–21).
1. Judgment for the Lord's enemies (3:1–16).
2. Provision and blessing for his people (3:17–21).

The following summary statement is based on the outline presented above, and provides focus for a message of proclamation based on this Old Testament passage:

> *God sometimes uses unusual difficulties of life to call attention to human accountability in the light of approaching divine judgment and blessing to come.*

Listening to Other Interpreters

Expositors of the book of Joel will want to consider the insights and observations of other students of Joel's prophecy as a check-and-balance against their own exegetical and interpretive work. Exposition is best undertaken with competent conversation partners, either in person or through published works. The following resources are especially useful for study of the book of Joel. In addition to these works, the standard commentaries on the book of Acts will also be helpful for considering Peter's use of Joel's prophecy in Acts 2:17–21.

Allen, Leslie C. *The Books of Joel, Obadiah, Jonah and Micah.* New International Commentary on the Old Testament, ed. R. K. Harrison. Grand Rapids: Eerdmans, 1976. A helpful exposition of four of the Minor Prophets, this commentary is based on the Hebrew text but written in a lively style with attention to historical backgrounds and theological significance.

Coggins, R. J. *Joel and Amos.* New Century Bible. Sheffield: Sheffield Academic Press, 2000. A brief exposition of Joel and Amos.

Crenshaw, James L. *Joel: A New Translation with Introduction and Commentary.* Anchor Bible, ed. William Foxwell Albright and David Noel Freedman, 24C. New York: Doubleday, 1995. A good critical commentary, with an emphasis on historical and grammatical details as well as the overall message of the book of Joel.

Dillard, Raymond Bryan. "Joel." In *The Minor Prophets: An Exegetical and Expository* Commentary, ed. Thomas Edward McComiskey. 1:239–313. Grand Rapids: Baker, 1992. A

two-level commentary on Joel. One section provides technical grammatical and historical information; the other section
provides a more general exposition of the book.

Finley, Thomas J. *Joel, Amos, Obadiah*. Wycliffe Exegetical
Commentary, ed. Kenneth Barker. Chicago: Moody, 1990.
Helpful exegetical comments based on the Hebrew text of
three of the Minor Prophets, with attention to the argument
of the book and its theological significance.

Hubbard, David Allan. *Joel and Amos: An Introduction and
Commentary*. Tyndale Old Testament Commentaries, ed.
D. J. Wiseman. Downers Grove, IL: InterVarsity, 1989. A
brief, conservative exposition of Joel and Amos.

Stuart, Douglas. *Hosea–Jonah*. Word Biblical Commentary, ed.
David A. Hubbard and Glenn W. Barker, vol. 31. Waco, TX:
Word, 1987. A helpful exposition of five of the Minor Prophets,
with some attention to issues of text, genre, and theology.

Watts, John D. W. *The Books of Joel, Obadiah, Jonah, Nahum,
Habakkuk and Zephaniah*. Cambridge Bible Commentary.
Cambridge: Cambridge University Press, 1975. A brief ex-
position of six of the Minor Prophets.

Wolff, Hans Walter. *Joel and Amos: A Commentary on the Books
of the Prophets Joel and Amos*. Trans. Waldemar Janzen, et al.
Hermeneia. Philadelphia: Fortress, 1977. A good treatment of
Joel and Amos, with emphasis on historical backgrounds and
grammatical analysis.

Bridging to Application

As noted above, Christian understanding of Joel 2:28–32 takes its
lead from the New Testament use of this passage. The prophecy of
Joel plays a prominent role in the apostolic preaching as recorded in
the book of Acts. The major pericope where this may be seen in Acts
2:17–21, where Peter quotes Joel 2:28–32 in his sermon on the day of
Pentecost. The quotation from Joel is introduced with a claim that the
outpouring of the Spirit on the day of Pentecost was predicted by the
prophet Joel. Peter clearly says, "This is what was spoken by the prophet
Joel" (Acts 2:16). According to Peter, the Pentecostal outpouring of the
Spirit on all sorts of people, accompanied by unusual signs and salvific
consequences, corresponds to the events described in Joel 2:28–32.

Christian preaching of Joel's message must take seriously the equative language of "this is that" used by the apostle Peter. According to him, the fulfillment of Joel's prophecy has Christological and pneumatological significance in that it finds its initial fulfillment in events shortly after the death and resurrection of Jesus at the coming of the Spirit at Pentecost. Furthermore, according to Romans 10:13, this Old Testament passage also has salvific significance. Quoting Joel, the Apostle Paul says, "'Everyone who calls on the name of the Lord will be saved'." Joel's apocalyptic language, describing divine activity accompanied by cosmic wonders and signs, thus underscores the significance of these momentous times for the birth of the New Testament church.

APPENDIX

ANTECEDENTS OF
APOCALYPTIC LITERATURE

THE DISTINCTIVENESS OF JEWISH apocalyptic literature has long caused scholars to puzzle over how exactly this literature developed into a unique genre that has no precise antecedents in earlier literary genres used in the ancient Near East. The roots of Jewish apocalyptic literature are less than obvious, and scholars disagree with regard to how this literature evolved from its cultural and religious antecedents into such a new and widely adopted genre in late Judaism and early Christianity. There is in modern scholarship no consensus with regard to how such questions should be answered. However, various proposals have been made in an attempt to bring clarity to modern understanding of the origins of apocalyptic literature. In each case, these theories have certain strengths that commend their point of view. At the same time, they each have certain weaknesses that limit their ability to present a coherent and holistic picture of how apocalypticism developed in ancient Israel. The roots of apocalyptic literature are too complex and variegated to permit a facile solution.

A methodological issue bedevils the search for the roots of apocalypticism at the outset. On what basis can one hope to establish the origins of

Jewish apocalyptic literature? Does the existence of literary, thematic, or theological parallels found in certain ancient Near Eastern texts necessarily establish causation in the relationship of those texts? In other words, if one finds in text A certain similarities to a later text B, does that necessarily mean that text A has directly influenced text B, or perhaps even that it is the primary source of text B? The answer must be "no." It is at least theoretically possible that two texts have arrived at similarities independently, or perhaps that they are both indebted to a common source but not necessarily to each other. It is also sometimes difficult to determine which of two texts is the earlier, or to establish how much earlier certain ideas are than the relatively late texts in which they are found. To assume that similarity of content or similarity of form necessarily indicates direct influence or an immediate source for ancient texts is an unwarranted assumption. Some proposals that scholars have offered regarding the origins of apocalyptic literature have not escaped this logical fallacy.

In considering the antecedents of Jewish apocalyptic literature it will be helpful to be aware of the main options that scholars have proposed in the past. The following proposals are often encountered in discussion of the origins of apocalyptic thought. Each of these theories has certain strengths that commend it as well as certain weaknesses that limit its ability to account for all the data.

Canaanite Mythology

Certain themes found in Jewish apocalyptic texts correspond to motifs found at least in seminal form in much earlier Israelite belief. On the basis of these similarities it may be possible to trace the trajectory of these themes backward from their prominence in apocalyptic literature to earlier stages in the religious life of ancient Israel. In some cases such motifs may ultimately go back to ideas either borrowed from, or to some degree influenced by, Israel's neighboring cultures. Old Canaanite mythology is such an area, one that has often been explored in the search for apocalyptic origins. Especially helpful in this regard are the Ugaritic texts found in 1929 at the modern site of Ras Shamra in Syria. Even before the modern discovery of these texts, the Old Testament form critic Hermann Gunkel had explored possible connections between apocalyptic literature and ancient Near Eastern myth.[1] Other scholars have done so since Gunkel's time.

Frank Moore Cross pointed to several traits or patterns in apocalyptic literature that, in his opinion, ultimately derive from epic themes that

---

1. Hermann Gunkel, *Creation and Chaos in the Primeval Era and the Eschaton: A Religio-historical Study of Genesis 1 and Revelation 12*, trans. K. William Whitney Jr. (Göttingen: Vandenhoeck & Ruprecht, 1895; Grand Rapids: Eerdmans, 2006).

ancient Israel incorporated and transformed for its own use.[2] Key to this process were the catastrophic times of the late exilic and early postexilic period. It was at that time, according to Cross, that earlier prophetic traditions were reformulated in a manner that set the stage for their later incorporation and expansion in apocalyptic literature. Cross singles out three areas in particular: First, there was what he calls a "democratizing and eschatologizing" of certain themes and forms found in classical prophecy; second, there was an emerging doctrine of two distinct ages, the old and the new, which treated historical events in a typological manner; third, there was a reemphasis on myths of creation as a way of stressing transcendental significance for history.[3] Cross traces the immediate origins of Jewish apocalypticism to the sixth century B.C., at which time a new synthesis of themes produced a proto-apocalyptic understanding of history. According to him, this transfiguration of old epic themes that appear in late exilic and early postexilic literature led to the development of Jewish apocalypticism, which adapted and further developed these motifs in new and distinct ways. According to Cross, the eschatological transformation of creation myths can already be seen in certain passages of the book of Isaiah (e.g., Isa. 51:9–11; 25:6–8; 65:17–25). This transformation was further developed by the apocalyptic writers.

Clifford also concludes that the roots of apocalypticism lie in ancient Near Eastern myth.[4] He appeals to several lines of evidence. First, there are various genres shared by apocalyptic literature and ancient Near Eastern myth, such as the ancient combat myth, prophecies given after the fact, and the dream vision. Second, there are recurrent elements found in both apocalyptic literature and ancient Near Eastern myth, such as the divine assembly reacting to a significant threat, fearsome monsters representing cosmic enemies, heavenly beings, esoteric knowledge, and the wise man who reveals divine knowledge. Third, there are topics found in both apocalyptic literature and myth, such as the nature of evil and the new creation. Clifford regards these similarities as sufficiently numerous and prominent to justify the conclusion that apocalyptic literature of the intertestamental period drew from and made use of these earlier religious traditions. A number of modern scholars adopt a similar approach.[5]

---

2. Frank Moore Cross, "A Note on the Study of Apocalyptic Origins," in *Canaanite Myth and Hebrew Epic: Essays in the History of the Religion of Israel* (Cambridge, MA: Harvard University Press, 1973), 343–46.

3. Ibid., 346.

4. Richard J. Clifford, "The Roots of Apocalypticism in Near Eastern Myth," in *The Continuum History of Apocalypticism*, ed. Bernard J. McGinn, John J. Collins, and Stephen J. Stein (New York and London: Continuum, 2003), 3–38.

5. Cook, for example, has attempted to work out the details of alleged mythological imagery in Ezekiel 31 and Daniel 4. See Stephen L. Cook, "Mythological Discourse in Ezekiel and Daniel and the Rise of Apocalypticism in Israel," in *Knowing the End from the Beginning:*

It is clear that apocalypticism did not suddenly develop during the postexilic period out of a total vacuum of historical or religious influences. Rather, it was indebted to earlier religious thought as found both within and outside of Israel. On the other hand, it should not be assumed that there is no distinction between biblical and nonbiblical writings in terms of the ways in which they utilized mythology. Biblical writers did on occasion incorporate mythological elements into their own writings. But this was usually done in a polemical way, in order to show the deficiency of these views in the forms in which they appeared in pagan cultures. Old Testament writers utilized mythopoeic imagery as a way of distinguishing Israelite belief from that of Israel's neighbors. But the literary parallels between Jewish apocalyptic literature and Canaanite mythology do not necessarily mean that this mythology is uniquely the source of Jewish apocalyptic literature.

Akkadian Prophecy

In recent decades there has been a good deal of interest in the genre of prophecy and/or apocalypticism as found in certain Akkadian texts. Some scholars have suggested that the presence of this genre in East Semitic literature may hold a key for understanding the origins of apocalyptic literature found in Hebrew Bible. Hallo has made a case for thinking that certain Akkadian texts dating to the Neo-Assyrian period or earlier should be viewed as apocalyptic in nature.[6] According to him four cuneiform texts in particular, previously regarded as prophecies in terms of their genre, have features similar to those found in biblical apocalyptic texts, most notably the book of Daniel. He points out that the Akkadian texts in question are pseudonymous, they reflect a deterministic and cyclical understanding of history, and they engage in *ex eventu* prophecy—features that are often associated with later Jewish apocalyptic literature. He prefers to designate these texts as Akkadian apocalypses rather than calling them Akkadian prophecies, as earlier scholars tended to do. If Hallo is correct in his assessment, these texts may indicate that the roots of Second Temple Jewish apocalyptic lit-

---

The Prophetic, the Apocalyptic and Their Relationships, ed. Lester L. Grabbe and Robert D. Haak, Journal for the Study of the Pseudepigrapha: Supplement Series, vol. 46 (London and New York: Continuum, 2003), 85–106. In Cook's view, "Apocalypticism and mythology are inextricably interconnected" (p. 85). See also Daniel C. Olson, "Jeremiah 4.5–31 and Apocalyptic Myth," *Journal for the Study of the Old Testament* 73 (1997): 81–107; and D. S. Russell, "Interpreting Scripture: Myth and Remythologizing," *Expository Times* 104 (1992): 356–59.

6. See W. W. Hallo, "Akkadian Apocalypses," *Israel Exploration Journal* 16 (1966): 231–42; idem, "The Expansion of Cuneiform Literature," *Proceedings of the American Academy of Jewish Research* 46–47 (1979–1980): 307–22.

erature are to be found at least partly in East Semitic literary developments. Such apocalyptic features may have been adopted and elaborated by later Israelite religious culture of the intertestamental period, when apocalyptic thinking flourished and apocalyptic literature proliferated.[7]

The following example of such a text is taken from what Grayson and Lambert label as Text A.[8] It predicts the rise of certain Assyrian kings whose reign is summarized as either "good" or "bad," and it describes various events that will occur during their reigns.

> [A prince will arise] and rule for eighteen years.
> The land will rest secure, fare well,
> (and its) people will enjoy prosperity.
> The gods will obtain good things for the land,
> favourable winds [will blow].
> The . . . and the furrow will yield abundant crops.
> Sakkan (the god of beasts) and Nisaba (the god of grain) will . . . in the land.
> There will be rain and floods.
> The *people* of the land will enjoy themselves.
> But that prince will be put to the sword in a revolution.
> A prince will arise and rule for thirteen years.
> There will be an Elamite attack on Akkad
> And the *booty* of Akkad will be carried off.
> The shrines of the great gods will be destroyed.
> Akkad will *suffer* a defeat.
> There will be confusion, disturbance and disorder in the land.
> The nobility will lose prestige.
> Another man who is unknown will arise,
> seize the throne as king and put his grandees to the sword.
> He will fill the wadis of Ṭuplijaš, the open country and hills, with half the extensive army of Akkad (i.e., they will die in battle there).
> The people will suffer need (and) hardship.
> A prince will arise but his days will be short and he will not be master of the land.
> A prince [will arise] and rule for three years. . . .

---

7. Longman identifies what he regards as a growing acceptance of Hallo's conclusions over the past several decades, especially with regard to the alleged apocalyptic features found in the Uruk and Dynastic prophecies of these texts. Longman discusses the following five texts in this regard: the Marduk Prophecy, the Šulgi Prophecy, Text A, the Uruk Prophecy, and the Dynastic Prophecy. See Tremper Longman III, *Fictional Akkadian Autobiography: A Generic and Comparative Study* (Winona Lake, IN: Eisenbrauns, 1991), 168–171.

8. A. K. Grayson and W. G. Lambert, "Akkadian Prophecies," *Journal of Cuneiform Studies* 18 (1964): 13–14.

The predictions and warnings found in this text bear some similarity to things found in later apocalyptic literature. However, it seems doubtful that Hallo's Akkadian texts should be regarded as fully apocalyptic in nature. Their prophecy has to do with anticipated historical events described *ex eventu* rather than an eschatological scenario of imminent divine intervention and upheaval. At best they may reflect an incipient form of apocalypticism, one that is not nearly as developed or pronounced as what characterizes Jewish literature during the Second Temple period.[9] These Akkadian texts seem to fit best into a genre of pseudo-prophetic literature, although one could argue that they exactly fit into the category of neither apocalyptic nor prophetic.[10] They can perhaps be viewed as standing toward one end of a continuum of prophetic-apocalyptic writings, with fully developed apocalyptic texts of the intertestamental period standing at the other end.

Mesopotamian Traditions

Kvanvig locates the roots of apocalyptic literature in early Mesopotamian traditions that according to him were used and reinterpreted by later apocalyptic writers.[11] In his view, the Enoch material goes back to Mesopotamian traditions concerning primeval time, while the Son of Man material of Daniel 7 goes back to Mesopotamian traditions concerning the underworld and visions. Israelite contact with Mesopotamian traditions was heightened during the experience of the Babylonian diaspora and was later amplified during the postexilic

---

9. Hunger and Kaufman, commenting on an Akkadian prophecy text dating to the time of Nebuchadnezzar, offer the following caution concerning the nature of such texts: "Although we cannot yet rightfully speak of these texts as forming a genre, there can be little doubt that more and more texts of a similar nature will turn up. Even from what we know already, however, clear and interesting parallels can be drawn with other literary types of the Ancient Near East; but not all of them, it must be emphasized, are with the apocalyptic literature. Nor are the similarities with the apocalyptic literature which can be detected strong enough to indicate any direct relationship at this point in time." See Hermann Hunger and Stephen A. Kaufman, "A New Akkadian Prophecy Text," *Journal of the American Oriental Society* 95 (1975): 375. See also Stephen A. Kaufman, "Prediction, Prophecy, and Apocalypse in the Light of New Akkadian Texts," in *Proceedings of the Sixth World Congress of Jewish Studies, 13–19 August 1973*, ed. Shinan Avigdor (Jerusalem: World Union of Jewish Studies, 1977), 1:221–28 .

10. See Martti Nissinen, "Neither Prophecies Nor Apocalypses: The Akkadian Literary Predictive Texts," in *Knowing the End From the Beginning: The Prophetic, the Apocalyptic, and Their Relationships*, ed. Lester L. Grabbe and Robert D. Haak, Journal for the Study of the Pseudepigrapha: Supplement Series, ed. Lester L. Grabbe and James H. Charlesworth, vol. 46 (London and New York: Continuum, 2013), 143.

11. Helge S. Kvanvig, *Roots of Apocalyptic: The Mesopotamian Background of the Enoch Figure and the Son of Man*, Wissenschaftliche Monographien zum Alten und Neuen Testament, ed. Ferdinand Hahn and Odil Hannes Steck, vol. 61 (Neukirchen-Vluyn: Neukirchener, 1988), 1–13, 603–13.

period, due to syncretistic tendencies prevalent in Palestine at that time. Kvanvig maintains that this Mesopotamian influence on apocalyptic literature is suggested by the visionary form of apocalyptic literature, its adaptation of transcendental imagery to depictions of history and eschatology, and its modified dualistic perception of reality.

Kvanvig's study is comprehensive in scope, but his conclusions are somewhat limited in application to study of apocalyptic literature. Even if one accepts his thesis regarding the background of the extrabiblical Enochian material and the Son of Man material of Daniel 7, a question remains regarding the extent to which these conclusions might apply to apocalyptic literature as a whole. Kvanvig himself acknowledges this methodological limitation.[12] Since the focus of his study is specifically the Enoch figure found in extrabiblical literature and the Son of Man figure found in Daniel 7, his conclusions regarding Mesopotamian origins should not be generalized to describe apocalyptic literature that does not emphasize these same themes. Consequently, this view is of limited help in determining apocalyptic origins.

Egyptian Apocalypticism

Some scholars have looked to Egypt for the roots of apocalyptic literature. That Egyptian influences might be found in ancient Hebrew literature would not be surprising in light of the contacts experienced between these two cultures over a long period of time.

In 1925 McCown marshaled evidence to show that Egyptian apocalyptic literature had influenced Hebrew prophetic and apocalyptic literature in various ways.[13] According to him, Egyptian texts such as the *Proverbs of Amenemope* and Ikhnaton's *Hymn to Aton* provide striking parallels to passages in the Psalms. Egyptian love poems resemble passages in the Song of Songs, and certain Egyptian wisdom texts call to mind the book of Job. McCown concluded that other Egyptian texts are "indirectly apocalyptic," such as the *Song of the Harper*, the *Admonition of Amenemhet*, the *Dialogue of the Man-weary-of-life with his Soul*, and the *Searchings of Heart of Khekheperresonbu*. More directly apocalyptic in nature, according to McCown, is the *Admonitions of Ipuwer*. He regards it as "the first Egyptian document to be recognized as an apocalyptic prophecy."[14] This text describes civil war throughout the land of Egypt,

---

12. Ibid., 603–604.
13. C. C. McCown, "Hebrew and Egyptian Apocalyptic Literature," *Harvard Theological Review* 18 (1925): 357–411. McCown acknowledged that he was not himself a specialist in Egyptology; to some extent he was apparently following up on suggestions made by the Egyptologist Eduard Meyer.
14. Ibid., 371.

accompanied by foreign invasion, the breakdown of societal structures, widespread war and unrest, and devastating famine—all of which led to despair and resignation on the part of the inhabitants of the land. McCown maintained that this Egyptian text and certain others similar to it, such as the *Vision of Neferrohu* and the later *Demotic Chronicle*, are archetypes of developments to be found in Old Testament literature. He concludes that texts such as Ipuwer's warnings influenced—not directly, but indirectly—the Old Testament prophets and apocalyptic writers, who adopted and expanded these motifs. According to McCown, these influences can be seen in the following areas: woe-and-weal eschatology, use of physical disasters and social disturbances, interest in social righteousness, and anticipation of a coming god-sent king.[15]

Two problems stand out with such an interpretation. First, the parallels that McCown identifies are features common to almost any literature that describes historical events of social or political upheaval, military conquest, and natural disaster. These parallels are too general to suggest that they require literary or intellectual dependence on the part of later writers who use similar language to describe similar events. Second, McCown uses the term *apocalyptic* in too broad a sense. For him, apocalyptic is defined "as a type of thinking and writing which criticizes present evils and promises future improvement, all under the guise of denunciations and predictions that are usually based upon supposedly supernatural visions and revelations."[16] But as McCown himself goes on to admit, under such a definition "all the canonical prophets and the pseudepigraphic apocalypses of the Hebrews are comprised in apocalyptic literature," and a wide array of Egyptian documents as well. Such a definition is too inclusive to be useful.

To classify the Egyptian texts in question as apocalyptic does not therefore seem to be a helpful strategy. Perhaps for that reason, as Bergman points out, "'apocalypticism' is really an *avis rara* among Egyptologists today."[17]

Wisdom Literature

A few scholars have argued that wisdom ideas and motifs are at the root of Jewish apocalyptic literature. There does seem to be some sort of relationship between wisdom themes and apocalyptic ideas. In the

15. Ibid., 405.

16. Ibid., 368.

17. Jan Bergman, "Introductory Remarks on Apocalypticism in Egypt," in *Apocalypticism in the Mediterranean World and the Near East: Proceedings of the International Colloquium on Apocalypticism, Uppsala, August 12–17, 1979*, ed. David Hellholm (Tübingen: J. C. B. Mohr [Paul Siebeck], 1983), 51.

book of Daniel there is an interest in motifs associated with **mantic** wisdom, which was a part of Babylonian religion. In the stories found in the first half of Daniel wise men and wisdom motifs play a prominent role in the royal Babylonian court. During the second century, in the tumultuous times of Seleucid control of Judah, it was wise men (Heb. *maśkîlîm*) who provided instruction and leadership for the Jewish people (Dan. 11:33, 35; cf. 12:3, 10). It is clear that the wisdom motif plays a prominent role in the book of Daniel.

Wisdom motifs also appear in some of the extrabiblical apocalyptic literature. Perhaps the best example of this is found in the *Similitudes of Enoch*, where wisdom is portrayed in a way reminiscent of Proverbs 8:

> Wisdom found no place where she could dwell, and her dwelling was in heaven. Wisdom went out in order to dwell among the sons of men, but did not find a dwelling; wisdom returned to her place and took her seat in the midst of the angels. And iniquity came out from her chambers; those whom she did not seek she found, and dwelt among them, like rain in the desert, and like dew on parched ground (*1 En.* 42).

It is therefore not surprising that some scholars have sought the origins of Jewish apocalypticism in the wisdom schools of the ancient Near East and in the wisdom literature associated with those schools. In the early twentieth century G. Hölscher concluded that wisdom was the source out of which apocalyptic thought developed. More recently, von Rad has maintained that wisdom rather than prophecy is "the real matrix from which apocalyptic literature originates."[18] According to von Rad apocalyptic does not derive from prophecy, since there is a "great gulf which separates apocalyptic literature from prophecy."[19] Instead, according to von Rad, wisdom and apocalyptic are very closely intertwined in Jewish apocalyptic literature.[20] To demonstrate this relationship von Rad appeals especially to wisdom texts that stress divine sovereignty in human events, a theme that also appears in apocalyptic texts. For example, Sirach's observation concerning God's involvement in the history of nations is not unlike certain observations found in the book of Daniel.[21] Sirach says:

---

18. Gerhard von Rad, "Daniel and Apocalyptic," in *Old Testament Theology*, vol. 2 (New York: Harper & Row, 1965), 306.

19. Ibid.

20. See "The Divine Determination of Times (Excursus)," in Gerhard von Rad, *Wisdom in Israel*, trans. J. D. Martin (London: SCM, 1972), 263–83.

21. According to Aitken, Ben Sira "occupies a position between the biblical writings and the

The government of the earth is in the hand of the Lord,
and over it he will raise up the right leader for the time.
Human success is in the hand of the LORD, and it is he
who confers honor upon the lawgiver. . . . Sovereignty
passes from nation to nation on account of injustice and
insolence and wealth (Sir. 10:4–5, 8, NRSV).

However, von Rad's thesis that wisdom is the root of apocalyptic literature has not commanded a great deal of acceptance among Old
Testament specialists.[22] His theory accounts better for similarities between wisdom and apocalyptic literature than it does for the significant
differences between them. Nonetheless, his observations have served
to call attention to the relationship between the two, a relationship
that was previously often overlooked.[23] Increasingly biblical scholars
have come to realize that there is not a sharp line that divides between
the categories of wisdom and apocalyptic.[24] The boundary lines between wisdom and apocalyptic literature are often imprecise, blurred,
indistinct, and permeable.[25] Wisdom literature sought to explain and

overtly apocalyptic Qumran texts." See James K. Aitken, "Apocalyptic, Revelation and Early
Jewish Wisdom Literature," in *New Heaven and New Earth: Prophecy and the Millennium: Essays
in Honour of Anthony Gelston*, ed. P. J. Harland and C. T. R. Hayward, Supplements to Vetus
Testamentum, vol. 77 (Leiden: Brill, 1999), 188. Perdue has also addressed the relationship of
wisdom and apocalyptic in Qohelet. See Leo G. Perdue, "Wisdom and Apocalyptic: The Case
of Qoheleth," in *Wisdom and Apocalypticism in the Dead Sea Scrolls and in the Biblical Tradition*, ed.
Florentino García Martínez, Bibliotheca ephemeridum theologicarum lovaniensium, vol. 168
(Leuven: Leuven University Press and Peeters, 2003), 231–58.

22. For critical evaluations of von Rad's view see especially the following contributions: Magne
Sæbø, "Old Testament Apocalyptic in Its Relation to Prophecy and Wisdom: The View of
Gerhard von Rad Reconsidered," in *In the Last Days: On Jewish and Christian Apocalyptic and
Its Period*, ed. Knud Jeppesen, Kirsten Nielsen, and Bent Rosendal (Aarhus: Aarhus University
Press, 1994), 78–91; James Edwin Howard, "A Critical Evaluation of the Thesis That the
Roots of Jewish Apocalyptic Are in Israelite Wisdom Rather than Prophecy" (Ph.D. diss.,
Baylor University, 1971); Jonathan Z. Smith, "Wisdom and Apocalyptic," in *Visionaries and
Their Apocalypses*, ed. Paul D. Hanson, Issues in Religion and Theology, ed. Douglas Knight
and Robert Morgan, vol. 2 (Philadelphia and London: Fortress and SPCK, 1983), 101–20.

23. There is merit to the suggestion that in terms of its origins Jewish apocalyptic literature
is indebted to both prophetic and wisdom sources. Rather than being a matter of either-
or, it may instead be a matter of both-and. See, for example, the synthesis suggested by
James VanderKam, "The Prophetic-Sapiential Origins of Apocalyptic Thought," in *From
Revelation to Canon: Studies in the Hebrew Bible and Second Temple Literature*, Supplements to the
Journal for the Study of Judaism, vol. 62 (Leiden: Brill, 2000), 163–76.

24. See, for example, George W. E. Nickelsburg, "Wisdom and Apocalypticism in Early Judaism:
Some Points for Discussion," in *Conflicted Boundaries in Wisdom and Apocalypticism*, ed. Benjamin
G. Wright III and Lawrence M. Wills, Society of Biblical Literature Symposium Series, ed.
Christopher R. Matthews, vol. 35 (Atlanta: Society of Biblical Literature, 2005), 17–37.

25. See the helpful exchange between Nickelsburg and Tanzer that touches on this point.
Sarah J. Tanzer, "Response to George Nickelsburg: 'Wisdom and Apocalypticism in Early

systematize the principles and laws that determined outcomes in individual and collective life, providing guidance for those who wished to avoid the plight of the foolish. Apocalyptic literature shows a similar interest in historical outcomes, although it does so in a more esoteric and more dramatic literary fashion than is the case with wisdom literature. Even the apocalyptic interest in time and hidden events of the future finds some parallel in wisdom literature, where one is expected to understand that everything has its own time and season.[26]

That apocalyptic literature has close associations with wisdom motifs, particularly the sort of wisdom associated with royal court interpretations of enigmatic messages or events, seems quite clear. It is, as Perdue points out, "one of the important wellsprings for apocalypticism."[27] In that sense, von Rad was correct to emphasize wisdom as contributing to the development of apocalyptic literature. However, he went too far in regarding wisdom as the matrix from which apocalyptic literature developed to the exclusion of prophetic literature. Wisdom literature by itself cannot account for the origins of apocalyptic literature. There are other elements present in this literature that are distinct from those found in ancient Near Eastern wisdom literature. While the biblical figure Daniel functioned in a Babylonian court where mantic wisdom was highly valued and relied upon by Babylonian kings, his activities and practices stand in bold relief to those of his counterparts in the royal court. The differences outweigh the similarities.[28]

Judaism'," in *Conflicted Boundaries in Wisdom and Apocalypticism*, ed. Benjamin G. Wright III and Lawrence M. Wills, Society of Biblical Literature Symposium Series, ed. Christopher R. Matthews, vol. 35 (Atlanta: Society of Biblical Literature, 2005), 39–49; and George W. E. Nickelsburg, "Response to Sarah Tanzer," in *Conflicted Boundaries in Wisdom and Apocalypticism*, 51–54.

26. Although he disagrees with von Rad's view that wisdom is the root of apocalyptic, De Vries has attempted to demonstrate what he calls an "ideological kinship" between wisdom and apocalyptic with regard to their concept of time and history. See Simon J. De Vries "Observations on Quantitative and Qualitative Time in Wisdom and Apocalyptic," in *Israelite Wisdom: Theological and Literary Essays in Honor of Samuel Terrien*, ed. John G. Gammie et al. (Missoula, MT: Scholars Press, for Union Theological Seminary, 1978), 263–76. Regarding von Rad's position De Vries says, "We are thus entirely ready to admit that Gerhard von Rad is justified in stressing the strong affinity of apocalyptic with wisdom. But he is surely wrong in deriving apocalyptic directly from wisdom" (p. 264).

27. Leo G. Perdue, "Continuing Streams: Apocalypticism and Wisdom," in *The Sword and the Stylus: An Introduction to Wisdom in the Age of Empires* (Grand Rapids and Cambridge: Eerdmans, 2008), 356–71.

28. The following observation of Bedenbender is apropos: "[I]t is completely inappropriate, according to the context of the text and according to all we know about mantic wisdom of the ancient Near East, to see Daniel (or Joseph for that matter) as a mantic sage. Daniel neither acts like mantic sages act, nor does he in the stories narrated in the Bible deal with problems that confronted mantic sages. The roots of the apocalypticism of Daniel are to be sought in biblical prophecy." See Andreas Bedenbender, "Seers as Mantic Sages in

Temple Theology

Hamerton-Kelly traces the origins of Jewish apocalypticism to Israelite attitudes with regard to the temple in Jerusalem.[29] According to him, during the early theocracy two very different attitudes toward the temple prevailed. According to one of these views, later represented especially by the prophet Ezekiel, a heavenly temple would be established on Mount Zion during the eschaton (cf. Ezek. 40–48). This temple was understood to be the result of divine initiative and activity. It signified an eschatological intervention into human events and the creation of new realities that lacked the imperfections of the former order. According to the other view regarding the temple, represented especially by the Priestly material of the Pentateuch (the so-called P material), an earthly temple would be established on Mount Zion through human effort and priestly activity. It would be built to correspond in detail to a heavenly model, according to instructions found in various portions of the Pentateuch (e.g., Exod. 25:9, 40; 26:30; 27:8b).

According to Hamerton-Kelly, these two views of the temple co-existed among Israelites with a certain amount of tension, with the result that their advocates sometimes had very different agendas with regard to religious decisions and choices. When the prophets Haggai and Zechariah confronted the postexilic Restoration community with the urgent need to rebuild the temple, they were opposed by a group of their contemporaries who insisted that the rebuilding of the temple was something not to be undertaken apart from divine initiative. For them, the time to rebuild the temple was not yet right (cf. Hag. 1:2). Proponents of these two views struggled with one another to gain the confidence of the people.

Consequently, there were different attitudes toward the Jerusalem temple and toward those who controlled the temple. In apocalyptic literature the attitude toward the current status of the temple tends to reflect a negative assessment. Disillusioned by what they viewed as religious decline and apostasy at work in the Jerusalem temple, apocalyptic thinkers and writers identified more with Ezekiel's eschatological temple-message than with the temple-understanding of the P material of the Pentateuch. Ezekiel's eschatological temple thus

Jewish Apocalyptic (Daniel and Enoch)," in *Scribes, Sages, and Seers: The Sage in the Eastern Mediterranean World*, ed. Leo G. Perdue, Forschungen zur Religion und Literatur des Alten und Neuen Testaments, ed. Matthias Köckert, Dietrich-Alex Koch, Christopher Tuckett, and Steven McKenzie, vol. 219 (Göttingen: Vandenhoeck & Ruprecht, 2008), 263.

29. R. G. Hamerton-Kelly, "The Temple and the Origins of Jewish Apocalyptic," *Vetus Testamentum* 20 (1970): 1–15.

provided for apocalyptic writers a springboard from which to elaborate and develop their own eschatological speculations. Apocalyptic literature, according to this view, "arose in circles estranged from the theocracy by the temple—as well as by eschatology."[30]

Hamerton-Kelly rightly identified an issue that contributed to the rise of apocalyptic thought in the postexilic period. His analysis underscores the potential role of temple theology in the development of Jewish apocalyptic thought. However, this interpretation focuses too exclusively on temple theology as a source of Jewish apocalyptic thought.

Hellenistic Syncretism

Certain ideas and themes that appear in apocalyptic literature are similar to those that appear in extrabiblical literature of Hellenistic origin. According to Betz, Hellenism is the most likely source of Jewish apocalyptic thought. He thinks that Jewish apocalyptic writings are partly the result of syncretistic adaptations of ideas already found in Hellenistic literature of the day. Apart from such an approach to the question of origins, Betz thinks that it is unlikely that one can reach a proper grasp of apocalyptic literature.[31]

As a parade example of Hellenistic influence at work in apocalyptic literature, Betz probes the background of the vision of the bowls described in the book of Revelation. In that passage, an angel warns that since followers of the Beast are guilty of shedding the blood of saints and prophets, they themselves will be forced to drink water that has been changed to blood. Of particular interest is the following verse:

> The third angel poured out his bowl on the rivers and springs of water, and they became blood. Then I heard the angel in charge of the waters say: "You are just in these judgments, O Holy One, you who are and who

---

30. Ibid., 15.

31. Hans Dieter Betz, "On the Problem of the Religio-Historical Understanding of Apocalypticism," *Apocalypticism*, 155. On the relationship of apocalypticism to Hellenistic influences see also the following contributions: Hans Dieter Betz, "The Problem of Apocalyptic Genre in Greek and Hellenistic Literature: The Case of the Oracle of Trophonius," in *Apocalypticism in the Mediterranean World and the Near East: Proceedings of the International Colloquium on Apocalypticism, Uppsala, August 12–17, 1979*, ed. David Hellholm (Tübingen: J. C. B. Mohr [Paul Siebeck], 1983), 577–97; John J. Collins, "The Genre Apocalypse in Hellenistic Judaism," *Apocalypticism in the Mediterranean World and the Near East*, 531–48; John J. Collins, *Seers, Sybils and Sages in Hellenistic-Roman Judaism*, Supplements to the Journal for the Study of Judaism, ed. John J. Collins, vol. 54 (Leiden: Brill, 1997); and J. Gwyn Griffiths, "Apocalyptic in the Hellenistic Era," *Apocalypticism in the Mediterranean World and the Near East*, 273–93.

were; for they have shed the blood of your holy people and your prophets, and you have given them blood to drink as they deserve" (Rev. 16:4–6).

Betz argues that the clearest parallel to this idea is found in an Egyptian–Hellenistic document entitled *Kore Kosmu*, which describes a revelation given by the goddess Isis to her son Horus. According to this text, the four elements of the world register their complaints about the pollutions caused by mankind. In the complaint of the Water, the righteous judge Osiris is sent to provide purification from the pollution caused by those who misused the water of nature to wash blood from themselves. Betz regards this text as embodying older material of Egyptian origin that has been combined with elements of Greek philosophy and mythology, while also showing Gnostic influences as well. The angelic doxology of Revelation 16:4, according to Betz, derives from this old tradition. In that sense the biblical text in question is the result of **syncretism** of Hellenistic motifs and apocalyptic interests.

This view faces the same problem that confronts several other explanations of the origins of Jewish apocalyptic thought. On the one hand, there are similarities between apocalyptic texts and certain non-apocalyptic literature deriving from the Hellenistic period. Pseudepigraphy and determinism, for example, are among those features shared by many apocalyptic texts and texts coming from the Hellenistic milieu.[32] This is not surprising, since apocalyptic thought was not insulated from the culture in which it grew and developed. Identifying these similarities will sometimes be helpful in the exegesis of particular apocalyptic texts. On the other hand, such similarities should not be overemphasized, as though they hold the key to understanding apocalypticism in a holistic way. They do not. While Hellenism was a contributor to Jewish apocalyptic literature, it cannot by itself account for the origins of apocalypticism.

Persian Religion

Some theological ideas stressed in apocalyptic texts also find expression in certain Iranian texts. This is particularly true with regard to a dualistic understanding of history that sorts things into categories of good

---

32. See John J. Collins, "Jewish Apocalyptic against Its Hellenistic Near Eastern Environment," in *Essays in Honor of George Ernest Wright*, ed. Edward F. Campbell and Robert G. Boling (Missoula, MT: Scholars Press, 1976), 33. Collins goes so far as to say that "Most of the features by which apocalyptic is usually distinguished from prophecy—periodization, expectation of the end of the world, after-life, esoteric symbolism, dualism etc.—are found throughout the Hellenistic world and must be considered representative of the *Zeitgeist* of late antiquity."

and evil or light and darkness. Such dualism occurs frequently in apocalyptic literature; it also appears in Zoroastrian literature. Is this correspondence a coincidence, or is a cause-and-effect relationship involved
in these similarities? And if a causal relationship is involved, which of the
two entities influenced the other? The establishment of chronological
priority is crucial to answering this question in a convincing way.

That there might be Persian influence at work in cultural, political, or
religious backgrounds to Old Testament literature should not in itself be
surprising. The book of Esther, for example, has for its context a Persian
court setting. With the fall of Babylon in 539 B.C. Persia became the
dominant superpower. As a result, Persian influence became pervasive
in the ancient Near East from about the sixth to the fourth centuries.
Judah (or Yehud, as it was known in Aramaic) remained under control of
Achaemenid Persia for more than two centuries, until finally the Persians
were defeated by the armies of Alexander the Great. During this time
Israelite society was impacted in many ways by Persian influence, not
only in terms of political and social life but probably in religious aspects as
well. Consequently, it would not be surprising to find evidences of intellectual and religious contact in the literature of this period.

The possibility of Persian influence on certain biblical motifs is an idea
that has been around for a long time. Some participants in the history-
of-religions movement of the early twentieth century, such as Richard
Reitzenstein and Wilhelm Bousset, claimed that Iranian influence is
evident in certain ideas and motifs found in the Hebrew Bible. Some
recent scholars have also concluded that Jewish apocalypticism was influenced by Persian religion, especially by Zoroastrianism. In their understanding, the growth of apocalypticism in ancient Israel was related
to the impact of Persian dualism, which apocalyptic writers adopted
and further developed within their own religious frameworks. Hanson
even complains of scholarship's "infatuation with Zoroastrianism" to
the neglect of more profitable lines of research in connection with studies of apocalyptic literature.[33]

García Martínez has argued for probable Iranian influence on certain
ideas found in the Dead Sea Scrolls.[34] He singles out the dualism of the

---

33. Paul D. Hanson, "Prolegomena to the Study of Jewish Apocalyptic," in *Magnalia Dei:
    The Mighty Acts of God: Essays on the Bible and Archaeology in Memory of G. Ernest Wright*,
    ed. Frank Moore Cross, Werner E. Lemke, and Patrick D. Miller (Garden City, NY:
    Doubleday, 1976), 400.

34. See Florentino García Martínez, "Iranian Influences in Qumran?," in *Apocalyptic and
    Eschatological Heritage: The Middle East and Celtic Realms*, ed. Martin McNamara (Dublin
    and Portland, OR: Four Courts, 2003), 37–49. See also Florentino García Martínez,
    "Apocalypticism in the Dead Sea Scrolls," in *The Continuum History of Apocalypticism*,
    ed. Bernard J. McGinn, John J. Collins, and Stephen J. Stein (New York and London:
    Continuum, 2003), 89–111.

Tractate of the Two Spirits in the *Rule of the Community* and various phrases used of the final battle described in the *War Scroll*. He concludes that cross-fertilization from Iranian sources is the best explanation for such features in the Qumran texts.[35] In addition to dualism and eschatology, Persian ideas may also have influenced the angelology of Jewish apocalyptic texts.

Hultgård has called attention to features of Persian apocalyptic eschatology, some of which are attested in Zoroastrianism as early as the sixth century.[36] He does not suggest that the Judeo-Christian tradition directly borrowed such ideas from Persian apocalypticism. Rather, the influences were more indirect and subtle, the result of prolonged contact between two very different cultures. Among the Iranian ideas that Hultgård identifies as influencing the Judeo-Christian theological tradition are the following: the personification of evil (cf. Satan, Belial, the Devil); the development of dualistic notions of Good and Evil, especially in an eschatological context; a doctrine of two Spirits, as attested by the Qumran community; the doctrine of the resurrection of the dead. These distinctive ideas are found in ancient Persian texts and in Jewish apocalyptic texts. If Hultgård is correct, the origins of Jewish apocalypticism must be sought at least to some degree in Persian religion.

Significant for this discussion is the Persian apocalyptic text entitled *Zand ī Wahman Yasn*, also known as *Bahman Yasht*. According to Cereti, this text is "the most complete representative of the apocalyptic genre among Zoroastrian works belonging to late antiquity."[37]

35. García Martínez, "Iranian Influences in Qumran?," 38.

36. See Anders Hultgård, "Persian Apocalypticism," in *The Continuum History of Apocalypticism*, ed. Bernard J. McGinn, John J. Collins and Stephen J. Stein, 30–63 (New York and London: Continuum, 2003). See also Anders Hultgård, "Forms and Origins of Iranian Apocalypticism," in *Apocalypticism in the Mediterranean World and the Near East: Proceedings of the International Colloquium on Apocalypticism, Uppsala, August 12–17, 1979*, ed. David Hellholm (Tübingen: J. C. B. Mohr [Paul Siebeck], 1983), 387–411; Anders Hultgård, "*Bahman Yasht*: A Persian Apocalypse," in *Mysteries and Revelations: Apocalyptic Studies the Uppsala Colloquium*, ed. John J. Collins and James H. Charlesworth, Journal for the Study of the Pseudepigrapha: Supplement Series, ed. James H. Charlesworth, vol. 9 (Sheffield: Sheffield Academic Press, 1991), 114–34; Mary Boyce, "On the Antiquity of Zoroastrian Apocalyptic," *Bulletin of the School of Oriental and African Studies* 47 (1984): 57–75; Shaul Shaked, "Qumran and Iran: Further Considerations," *Israel Oriental Studies* 2 (1972): 433–46; David Winston, "The Iranian Component in the Bible, Apocrypha, and Qumran: A Review of the Evidence," *History of Religions* 5 (1966): 183–216.

37. Carlo G. Cereti, *The Zand ī Wahman Yasn: A Zoroastrian Apocalypse*, Serie orientale Roma, ed. Gherardo Gnoli, vol. 75 (Rome: Istituto italiano per il medio ed estremo oriente, 1995), 1. In addition to Cereti's edition of the Persian text with English translation of the *Bahman Yasht*, an edition of the Persian text with English translation is also available in the following work: Behramgore Tehmuras Anklesaria, *Zand-î Vohûman Yasn and Two Pahlavi Fragments with Text, Transliteration, and Translation in English* (Bombay: [Mrs. B. T. Anklesaria], 1957).

Bahman Yasht contains dream revelations concerning the periodization of either four or seven future epochs of history as represented by various metals (1:3–11; 3:15–4:65), a feature that calls to mind a similar scheme found in Daniel 2 and 7. *Bahman Yasht* also contains references to the resurrection of the dead and the final body (3:3; 4:67), to hell and paradise (3:15, 23, 27; 4:40, 67; 6:2; 7:26, 33), to a star falling from the sky as a sign at the birth of a certain leader (7:6), and to coming cosmic signs to be seen in the heavens (6:4). Although in its present form this text dates only to the ninth or tenth century A.D.,[38] it is usually regarded as an adaptation of earlier Avestan materials.[39] If so, it contains traditions that may actually date to a much earlier period, perhaps as early as the fourth century B.C. according to some Iranian scholars.

In light of this overlap of ideas and themes, *Bahman Yasht* is of interest for the study of Jewish apocalypticism. These similarities between Persian and Jewish texts, along with their differences as well, require explanation. The problem, however, with using this text in discussions of possible Persian influences on Jewish apocalypticism is its late date. Even if one grants that the traditions and beliefs described in *Bahman Yasht* are earlier than the ninth century, it is difficult to establish just how early these traditions may actually be. Extant manuscripts for this text are all late, coming from the thirteenth century or later. Although many Iranian scholars date the underlying Avestan text of *Bahman Yasht* to the late fourth century B.C., this view is conjectural and lacks documentary evidence. For this reason some scholars have strongly opposed the early dating of this core material.

While Hultgård is confident of "clear evidence of an ancient mythical and apocalyptic core in *Bahman Yasht*," the difficulty in determining exactly how early this core may actually be leads to caution about regarding such a core as contributing to the development of Jewish apocalypticism.[40] The question that must be asked is this: Which came first—the chicken or the egg? Was it Persian apocalypticism that influenced Jewish apocalyptic literature, or was it the other way around? The issue of dating with regard to the documentary evidence is crucial in this regard. Without clarification of this issue, it is not possible to demonstrate conclusively that Persian apocalypticism was the root of Jewish apocalyptic literature.

---

38. The earliest extant complete manuscript of the *Bahman Yasht* (i.e., K20) dates to the fourteenth century. See the discussion of the manuscript tradition in Cereti, *The Zand ī Wahman Yasn*, 2–7.

39. On the issue of dating for this text see Hultgård, "*Bahman Yasht*: A Persian Apocalypse," 118–20.

40. Hultgård, "*Bahman Yasht*: A Persian Apocalypse," 133.

Resistance to Imperial Rule

Not all scholars have accepted the view that Second Temple apocalyptic texts are largely eschatological in nature, or that their ideological concerns are mainly theological. Horsley maintains that Jewish apocalyptic texts have as their primary function resistance to imperial rule. He thinks that these documents were written by professional Judean intellectuals whose main job was to advise the priestly aristocracy who were in charge of the Jerusalem temple. When these priests succumbed to imperial pressures, and out of self-interests compromised their loyalty to Jewish traditions, some of the scribal intelligentsia chose a path of resistance to imperial rule.

Apocalyptic texts are thus coded descriptions of divine sovereignty confronting Hellenistic or Roman imperial rule. They are ultimately statements of resistance to that rule. In that sense, apocalyptic literature has less to do with eschatology and more to do with responding to imperial pressures that threatened the *status quo* of traditional Jewish ways of life during the Hellenistic and Roman periods. As Horsley puts it, "Far from looking for the end of the world, they were looking for the end of empire. And far from living under the shadow of an anticipated cosmic dissolution, they looked for the renewal of the earth on which a humane societal life could be renewed."[41]

Such an approach seems to be somewhat reductionistic in nature. While Horsley's exegesis often provides insight into the historical background that undergirds many Second Temple apocalyptic texts, it does not do justice to the otherworldly dimensions of much of this literature. Clearly these texts are rooted in historical contexts and to some degree are responding to those situations, as Horsley has demonstrated. But many of these texts are also forward-looking, anticipating a divine intervention that would originate outside of the immediate historical circumstances that concerned the apocalypticists. Horsley has rightly called attention to the one dimension, but he has not adequately accounted for the other.

Prophetic Literature

Many scholars identify the major source of influence on apocalyptic literature to be Old Testament prophetic literature. Whether Sweeney is

---

41. Richard A. Horsley, *Revolt of the Scribes: Resistance and Apocalyptic Origins* (Minneapolis, MN: Fortress, 2010), 207. See also Anathea E. Portier-Young, *Apocalypse against Empire: Theologies of Resistance in Early Judaism* (Grand Rapids: Eerdmans, 2011); idem, "Jewish Apocalyptic Literature as Resistance Literature," in *The Oxford Handbook of Apocalyptic Literature*, ed. John J. Collins (Oxford: Oxford University Press, 2014), 145–62.

correct to speak of a scholarly consensus to this effect is doubtful, since as we have seen in the preceding discussion there are many who emphasize influences other than prophecy in the development of apocalyptic literature.[42] However, many scholars favor the conclusion that prophecy is the main source of Jewish apocalyptic literature. Among them are Charles, Frost, Rowley, Blenkinsopp, Russell, Vawter, Hanson, and Ladd. [43] Such a conclusion does not exclude the possibility that other sources from the ancient Near East may have also had a role in this process. It is possible to allow for influence on Jewish apocalyptic literature from sources such as Persian, Hellenistic, and Egyptian, while at the same time viewing the Old Testament prophetic literature as the primary root of this literature.[44]

It seems best to view Jewish apocalyptic literature as standing in continuity with Old Testament prophetic literature rather than as being something altogether different from it. This literature derives much of its theological emphasis and literary style from late Old Testament prophecy, while at the same time taking it in new directions. It also drew from other sources as well. If apocalyptic literature had as its main root the prophetic literature, this might help to explain why attempts to distinguish rigidly between the two in terms of genre encounter such difficulty.[45]

---

42. See Marvin A. Sweeney, "The Priesthood and the Proto-Apocalyptic Reading of Prophetic and Pentateuchal Texts," in *Knowing the End from the Beginning: The Prophetic, the Apocalyptic and Their Relationships*, ed. Lester L. Grabbe and Robert D. Haak, Journal for the Study of the Pseudepigrapha, Supplement Series, ed. Lester L. Grabbe and James H. Charlesworth, vol. 46 (London and New York: Continuum, 2003), 167–78. Sweeney says, "Scholarly consensus correctly holds that apocalyptic literature developed initially from prophetic literature" (p. 167).

43. See R. H. Charles, "Apocalyptic Literature," in *A Dictionary of the Bible*, ed. James Hastings (New York: Charles Scribner's Sons, 1898), 109–10; Stanley Brice Frost, *Old Testament Apocalyptic: Its Origins and Growth* (London: Epworth, 1952), 83; H. H. Rowley, *The Relevance of Apocalyptic: A Study of Jewish and Christian Apocalypses from Daniel to the Revelation*, rev. ed. (Greenwood, SC: Attic Press, 1963), 15; Joseph Blenkinsopp, *Prophecy and Canon: A Contribution to the Study of Jewish Origins*, University of Notre Dame Center for the Study of Judaism and Christianity in Antiquity, vol. 3 (South Bend, IN and London: University of Notre Dame Press, 1977), 138; D. S. Russell, *The Method and Message of Jewish Apocalyptic, 200 BC–AD 100*, Old Testament Library, ed. Peter Ackroyd et al. (Philadelphia: Westminster, 1964), 88; Bruce Vawter, "Apocalyptic: Its Relation to Prophecy," *Catholic Biblical Quarterly* 22 (1960): 35–46; Paul D. Hanson, *Old Testament Apocalyptic*, Interpreting Biblical Texts, ed. Lloyd R. Bailey Sr. and Victor P. Furnish (Nashville: Abingdon, 1987), 33; George Eldon Ladd, "Why Not Prophetic-Apocalyptic?," *Journal of Biblical Literature* 76 (1957): 192–200; idem, "The Origin of Apocalyptic in Biblical Religion," *Evangelical Quarterly* 30 (1958): 140–46; idem, "The Place of Apocalyptic in Biblical Religion," *Evangelical Quarterly* 30 (1958): 75–85.

44. Davies, after calling attention to the existence of the apocalyptic genre not just in Israel but throughout the ancient Near East, confidently asserts: "Accounts of 'apocalyptic' which imply the absurd premise that apocalyptic derives essentially from Jewish prophecy (and such accounts have persisted with surprising vigor) indulge in blissful ignorance of the existence of such non-Jewish writings." See P. R. Davies, "Qumran and Apocalyptic or *obscurum per obscurius*," *Journal of Near Eastern Studies* 49 (1990): 129.

45. Longman makes a valid point when he says, "The solution to the impasse encountered by

The one may be but a form or subset of the other.[46] It is even possible to argue that there was no clear transition from prophecy to apocalyptic, since there is not a sharp line of distinction between the two.[47]

Both in terms of themes and in terms of style of writing, portions of the Old Testament prophetic literature anticipate what is found in certain later apocalyptic writings. It is reasonable to conclude that the prophetic literature is a significant source from which apocalyptic literature drew. It is a major root from which apocalyptic literature was nourished.

The implications of this conclusion have been creatively explored by Hanson, who maintains that the dawn of apocalyptic literature took place within an Israelite setting associated with late prophetic literature.[48] Hanson locates the social setting out of which apocalyptic arose in the early postexilic period. According to him, at this time two religious groups contended for leadership of the Restoration community that was faced with the task of interpreting the catastrophic events of the exile. One of these was a priestly group, which Hanson identifies as the Zadokites. The other was a visionary group whose eschatological views were moving away from the sort of eschatology found in the classical Hebrew prophets and more in the direction of an emerging

---

apocalyptic research is to understand 'apocalyptic' as a type of prophecy and not as a clearly defined, separate phenomenon. Thus, efforts should not be directed toward discovering a 'key,' or the essential characteristic(s), that differentiates apocalyptic from prophecy. Since apocalyptic is a type of prophecy, it is not susceptible to such an analysis." See Tremper Longman III, *Fictional Akkadian Autobiography: A Generic and Comparative Study* (Winona Lake, IN: Eisenbrauns, 1991), 174.

46. Grabbe, for example, adopts this approach: "It seems to me, though, that we are making a rod for our own backs by trying to make a clear distinction between prophecy/prophetic writings and apocalyptic/apocalypses. *The solution is to consider apocalyptic/apocalypses a subdivision of prophecy.*" See Grabbe, "Introduction and Overview," 22 [emphasis his]; cf. 37. Elsewhere Grabbe says, "Indeed, I would rather see apocalyptic as a sub-genre of prophecy than as a separate entity." See Grabbe, *Judaic Religion in the Second Temple Period: Belief and Practice from the Exile to Yavneh*, 235. Collins, however, has expressed reservations with Grabbe's approach on this matter, since in his view it leaves unresolved the question of the distinctiveness of apocalyptic literature. See John J. Collins, "Prophecy, Apocalypse and Eschatology: Reflections on the Proposals of Lester Grabbe," in *Knowing the End from the Beginning: The Prophetic, the Apocalyptic and Their Relationships*, ed. Lester L. Grabbe and Robert D. Haak, Journal for the Study of the Pseudepigrapha: Supplement Series, ed. Lester L. Grabbe and James H. Charlesworth, vol. 46 (London and New York: Continuum, 2003), 44–52, especially 50.

47. Hendel, for example, says, "On many levels, the words of the prophets are the wellspring of apocalyptic mysteries. The transition from prophecy to apocalyptic is a process that may never have happened (because they were never two contrasting things), but it also has never ceased." See Ronald Hendel, "Isaiah and the Transition from Prophecy to Apocalyptic," in *Birkat Shalom: Studies in the Bible, Ancient Near Eastern Literature, and Postbiblical Judaism Presented to Shalom M. Paul on the Occasion of His Seventieth Birthday*, ed. Chaim Cohen et al. (Winona Lake, IN: Eisenbrauns, 2008), 279.

48. Paul D. Hanson, "Old Testament Apocalyptic Reexamined," *Interpretation* 25 (1971): 456.

apocalypticism. The visionaries regarded the priestly group as illegitimate, in spite of Zadokite control of both the Temple cult and the high priesthood. They anticipated an eschatological victory accompanied by cataclysmic events and upheaval of unparalleled magnitude. These events would usher in divine judgment and would lead to establishment of a new social order. Over a period of several centuries the religious views of these visionaries, and their criticisms of the hierocratic party of the Zadokites, found increasing expression in Jewish apocalyptic literature. Hanson summarizes his understanding of the origins of Jewish apocalyptic literature in picturesque terms:

> Apocalyptic Eschatology was not born on Jewish soil of foreign parents. Both parents were natives. Somewhere in her training Persian magi or Egyptian wisemen may have fascinated her with their clever use of numbers and impressed her with their knowledge of the heavens; indeed she seems to have appropriated some of their learned teachings. But she used them to embellish a system of belief which was Jewish, for her birth occurred centuries before her contact with their learned secrets and calculations, and her early training was in the traditions of her own people. Though impossible to date with precision, her birth seems to have occurred in the latter half of the sixth century; by the close of the fifth century she had already come close to maturity.[49]

Hanson's synthesis demonstrates a strong connection between apocalyptic literature and Old Testament prophetic literature. He seems to be correct in identifying the dawn of apocalyptic with the late prophetic period and attributing this new development primarily to intellectual, political, and religious forces at work within rather than outside Israel. However, his synthesis has raised some methodological concerns. Two problems stand out in particular. First, his form-critical approach is conditioned by the social theories of Max Weber. Weber's understanding of societal development is a grid through which Hanson views the biblical text. His exegesis is significantly influenced by this grid. Second,

---

49. Hanson, *The Dawn of Apocalyptic*, 402. Hanson's *Dawn of Apocalyptic* has been very influential. For an appreciative but somewhat critical evaluation of Hanson's approach and conclusions, see Ferdinand Deist, "Prior to the Dawn of Apocalyptic," *Die Ou-Testamentiese Werkgemeenskap in Suid-Afrika* 25–26 (1982): 13–28. Carroll has also discussed Hanson's theory with both appreciation and criticism. See Robert P. Carroll, "Twilight of Prophecy or Dawn of Apocalyptic?" *Journal for the Study of the Old Testament* 14 (1979): 3–35.

he emends and rearranges prophetical texts when they pose a difficulty for anticipated outcomes relevant to his theory regarding the origins of apocalypticism. This raises a question of special pleading. Hanson's argument seems to be vulnerable to these criticisms.[50]

CONCLUSION

It seems best to adopt a multi-faceted approach with regard to the origins of Jewish apocalyptic literature. The main source contributing to the rise of this genre was Old Testament prophetic literature. Proto-apocalyptic portions of the Old Testament were, in germ-form, the beginnings of what later expanded into a genre with its own unique features. However, Old Testament prophecy was not the only contributor to this process. Other influences such as Wisdom literature, mythopoeic elements derived from Canaanite religion, and Persian dualism in all likelihood also influenced the trajectory of this literature. But it was Old Testament prophecy that wielded the greatest influence on the motifs that characterize Jewish apocalyptic literature.

---

50. Oswalt has called attention to the following objections to Hanson's theory as well: (1) an overemphasis on mythology as a source for apocalyptic literature; (2) an inappropriate application of the cosmic warrior motif to the exclusion of other explanations; (3) overconfidence in certain literary and sociological models which significantly influence the conclusions that are drawn; (4) assumption of textual dislocations in prophetic literature without due consideration of alternative explanations that may in fact be more likely; (5) too much reliance on hypothetical reconstructions of Old Testament history and social-setting. See John N. Oswalt, "Recent Studies in Old Testament Eschatology and Apocalyptic," *Journal of the Evangelical Theological Society* 24 (1981): 289–301.

GLOSSARY

angelology. The systematized teaching of a text, individual, or group with regard to the identity, function, activity, and nature of angels.

anthropomorphism. A figure of speech in which a limited or finite human attribute is attributed to deity in order to enliven a description or to facilitate comprehension of an otherwise difficult concept.

Antichrist. In biblical theology, an eschatological figure who embodies all that is antithetical to the divine will and who will lead humankind in a final rebellion against God that will result in catastrophic divine judgment; or in a more general sense, anyone who to a significant degree embodies characteristics of this eschatological figure.

apocalypse. "A genre of revelatory literature with a narrative framework, in which a revelation is mediated by an otherworldly being to a human recipient, disclosing a transcendent reality which is both temporal, insofar as it envisages eschatological salvation, and spatial, insofar as it involves another, supernatural world. [An apocalypse is] intended to interpret present, earthly circumstances in light of the supernatural world and of the future, and to influence both the understanding and the behavior of the audience by means of divine authority."

apocalyptic. Pertaining to or having the characteristics of an apocalypse.

apocalyptic discourse. The literary, ideological, and social features that characterize apocalyptic language.

apocalyptic eschatology. A form of eschatology characterized by a heightened use of figurative language, dreams, and visions to describe sudden divine intervention in human events so as to bring about judgment on the wicked and vindication of the righteous.

apocalyptic literature. Ancient literature that contains a significant proportion of those features that define an apocalypse, whether or not the writing in question itself fully qualifies as an apocalypse.

apocalypticism. Any worldview or outlook that is characterized by the theology, ideas, or expectations commonly associated with apocalypses.

apocalyptist. The author of an apocalyptic writing.

chiasm. A literary device whereby items are matched in the order of $a^1 + b^1 + b^2 + a^2$. The name is derived from the shape of the Greek letter *chi*.

Dead Sea Scrolls. [See Qumran literature.]

determinism. The belief that all of human history follows a fixed and unalterable course that has been determined in advance by God.

Diadochoi. The political successors of Alexander the Great who, after Alexander's death, ruled over major segments of his redistributed empire.

Diaspora. The scattering and resettlement of Jewish populations in parts of the world other than their ancient homeland.

diplomatic edition. A printed edition of an ancient text that adopts a particular manuscript as the basis of its text, often with a critical apparatus that indicates ancient evidence at variance with that text.

dittography. A scribal error that occurs when a letter or sequence of letters is written twice although it should have been written only once. The opposite of dittography is haplography.

dualism (or, ethical dualism). The belief that two diametrically opposing forces (e.g., light and darkness, good and evil) are constantly at work in the world, struggling with one another for control and ascendancy.

eschatology. The systematized teaching of a text, individual, or group with regard to personal afterlife or events related to the end of time.

eschaton. In biblical theology, the future consummation that will mark the end of history as we know it, introducing new and permanent realities of an altogether different sort.

***ex eventu* prophecy.** Alleged prediction of future events that was actually spoken or written after (rather than before) the events it describes.

external evidence. Evidence derived from ancient textual witnesses pertaining to the precise wording of a document such as the Hebrew Bible. Such witnesses may be Hebrew or Aramaic manuscripts, early translations of the Hebrew Bible into other languages, or citations of the Old Testament text found in early writers.

genre. Any type of writing that is characterized by unique literary form, distinct literary content, and specific literary function.

haplography. A scribal error that occurs when a letter or sequence of letters is written only once although it should have been written twice. The opposite of haplography is dittography.

Hellenization. The assimilation of Greek language, customs, and attitudes on the part of non-Greek peoples, particularly in the post-Alexandrian period of Greek influence throughout the Mediterranean world.

hyperbole. A figure of speech whereby a speaker or writer deliberately exaggerates for the sake of vividness or emphasis.

hypocatastasis. A figure of speech in which an unrelated item is substituted for a different item in order to make an implied comparison, leaving the intended item of the comparison to be grasped by the listener or reader.

immanent. Capable of being experienced or comprehended; lying within the boundaries of normal human experience.

implied reader. The reader presupposed by the author of a text.

internal evidence. Logical deductions regarding the precise wording of a document such as the Hebrew Bible based on such things as known types of scribal error, age of documents, and geographical distribution of documentary witnesses.

intertestamental. Belonging to the period of time between the completion of Old Testament literature and the beginning of New Testament literature, traditionally defined as roughly the fourth century B.C. till the first century A.D.

Maccabees. A family of Jewish revolutionaries and their associates in the second century B.C. who sought by violent means to overthrow Hellenistic influence in Palestine. The name derives from that of the movement's founder, Judas Maccabeus.

mantic. Pertaining to the practice of professional divination, especially in connection with attempts to discern the future through the interpretation of dreams, visions, omens, or ecstatic utterances.

Masoretic text. A fairly uniform type of text found in manuscripts and printed editions of the Hebrew Bible that derive from a group of Jewish scholars known as the Masoretes. These meticulous copyists lived during the second half of the first millennium A.D.

metaphor. A figure of speech that makes a comparison between two entities by stating that the one is in some sense the same as the other in order to enliven a description or to facilitate understanding of an otherwise difficult concept.

metonymy. A figure of speech in which an item is substituted for an item related to it in order to make an implied comparison, leaving the unstated main point of the comparison to be grasped by the listener or reader. The substitution may be of four major types: adjunct in place of subject, subject in place of adjunct, cause in place of effect, or effect in place of cause.

millennarian. Characterized by a belief in an eschatological millennium of divine rule on the earth, whether understood specifically of an age of a thousand years or more generally of an indeterminate period of time.

mythology. Ancient stories that describe alleged activities of the gods, especially as those activities affect the beliefs or worldview of human beings.

mythopoeic imagery. Poetic use and adaptation of mythological language for the purpose of graphically portraying certain theological ideas or polemically responding to elements of a competing religious ideology.

otherworldly journey. A divinely facilitated journey to the realms of heaven or hell, as described in certain apocalyptic texts.

pericope. A self-contained unit of text or passage of Scripture, with a beginning and end that can be clearly identified.

periodization. A portrayal of human history as predetermined by God and conceived of in terms of a specific number of successive periods of time that have a defined point of beginning and ending.

proto-apocalyptic. An incipient and limited display of apocalyptic features appearing in an ancient work that cannot itself be properly identified as an apocalypse in terms of genre.

pseudepigrapha. A collection of works whose authorship is falsely attributed to someone not actually responsible for the writing in question, usually a famous hero of the past. Pseudepigraphy usually serves the purpose of enhancing the perceived authority of a text.

Ptolemies. A dynasty of post-Alexandrian Greek rulers who mainly controlled Egypt and the regions to its south and who often vied with the Seleucids for control of Palestine during the fourth through second centuries B.C.

Qumran community. A sectarian and separatistic group of Jewish extremists who withdrew and settled on the northwest side of the Dead Sea at a site now known as Khirbet Qumran. Probably Essene in origin, the community lived at this site from the second century B.C. until its destruction by the Romans in A.D. 68.

Qumran literature. A collection of ancient Jewish writings hidden in caves by the Qumran community shortly before A.D. 70 and subsequently discovered in 1947 and the years immediately following. Also known as the Dead Sea Scrolls, this literature (written in Hebrew, Aramaic, and Greek) includes manuscripts of biblical writings, sectarian texts governing the behavior and beliefs of the members of this community, and certain other writings collected by the community.

reception history. A type of modern critical study that seeks to describe the early transmission and interpretation of ancient biblical or extrabiblical texts by communities that made use of those texts.

revelation. Otherwise inaccessible information that is disclosed by an otherworldly mediator to a human recipient who then makes this information available to a wider audience.

Second Temple period. A period of Jewish history marked by the rebuilding of the Solomonic Temple in 515 B.C. and its subsequent destruction by the Romans in A.D. 70.

seer. The human recipient of divine revelation that is conveyed through a dream or vision.

Seleucids. A dynasty of post-Alexandrian Greek rulers who mainly controlled Syria and the regions to its east, and who often vied with the Ptolemies for control of Palestine during the fourth through second centuries B.C.

simile. A figure of speech that presents a comparison between two entities, making use of words such as "like" or "as" to express the comparison.

Son of Man. An eschatological figure described in Daniel 7 who is associated with divine judgment and the establishment of a divine kingdom.

syncretism. An amalgam of intellectual or religious ideas formed by pulling together disparate elements from a variety of sources so as to create a new synthesis of beliefs.

synecdoche. A figure of speech in which a part of an entity stands for the whole or the whole stands a part.

testament. A genre of writing in which a famous individual of the past is portrayed as giving final instructions to his descendants from his deathbed, sometimes while also making predictions concerning the future.

transcendent. Not capable of being experienced or comprehended; lying beyond the boundaries of normal human experience.

vision. An allegedly divine impartation of information otherwise inaccessible to human beings whereby the human recipient has the impression of observing circumstances transpire before his eyes.

Vorlage (German, "that which lies before"). The source document from which a copy or translation is made. Ancient translators of the Old Testament usually, but not always, used a Hebrew *Vorlage*.

watcher. A term used especially in ancient Aramaic literature for angels, so called because of their perceived role as guardians or custodians appointed by God.

Wisdom literature. A collection of literature, biblical or extrabiblical, that is characterized by an interest in principles that offer guidance for practical living, or musings that probe the meaning and purpose of life.

zoomorphism. A figure of speech that uses physical attributes or behavior of an animal to describe human (or divine) attributes or behavior in order to enliven a description or to facilitate comprehension of an otherwise difficult concept.